Conversions

**New Directions In Narrative History**
*John Demos and Aaron Sachs, Series Editors*

The New Directions in Narrative History series includes original works of creative nonfiction across the many fields of history and related disciplines. Based on new research, the books in this series offer significant scholarly contributions while also embracing stylistic innovation as well as the classic techniques of storytelling. The works of the New Directions in Narrative History series, intended for the broadest general readership, speak to deeply human concerns about the past, present, and future of our world and its people.

# Conversions

Two Family Stories
from the Reformation and
Modern America

*Craig Harline*

Yale

UNIVERSITY PRESS

New Haven & London

Published with assistance from the
Louis Stern Memorial Fund.

Copyright © 2011 by Craig Harline.
All rights reserved.
This book may not be reproduced, in whole or in part, including
illustrations, in any form (beyond that copying permitted by Sections 107 and
108 of the U.S. Copyright Law and except by reviewers for the public press),
without written permission from the publishers.

Yale University Press books may be purchased in quantity for educational,
business, or promotional use. For information, please e-mail sales.press@yale.edu
(U.S. office) or sales@yaleup.co.uk (U.K. office).

Designed by Lindsey Voskowsky.
Set in Sabon type by IDS Infotech Ltd., Chandigarh, India.

Library of Congress Cataloging-in-Publication Data
Harline, Craig.
Conversions : two family stories from the Reformation and
modern America / Craig Harline.
p.   cm. — (New directions in narrative history)
Includes bibliographical references.
ISBN 978-0-300-19244-5
1. Rolandus, Jacob. 2. Catholic converts—Family relationships—Netherlands.
3. Mormon converts—Family relationships. 4. Mormon gays—Religious life. I. Title.
BX4668.R54H37 2011
248.2'40922—dc22
[B]   2011013199

A catalogue record for this book is available from the British Library.

This paper meets the requirements of ANSI/NISO Z39.48–1992 (Permanence of Paper).

He that loveth father or
mother more than me is not worthy of
me; and he that loveth son or daughter more
than me is not worthy of me.

—*Matthew* 10:37

The fact narrated must correspond
to something in me to be credible or intelligible. We,
as we read, must become Greeks, Romans, Turks, priest and
king, martyr and executioner; must fasten these images
to some reality in our secret experience, or
we shall learn nothing rightly.

—*Ralph Waldo Emerson, "History"*

# contents

# to the blesséd reader

With recent polls reporting that more than four in ten American adults have changed religions at least once, you may well be tempted to think of conversion as a casual, everyday sort of occurrence. But it was hardly so in the past, and is not necessarily so now, as you will see.

In the first place, conversion hasn't always been common in the western world—not at all. For seven long centuries, from 800 to 1520, the vast majority of western Europeans were born and buried Roman Catholic and had little chance or thought of becoming anything else (at least officially). Minority Jews and Muslims of Europe, unless forced to become Christian, typically stayed in their religions too.

In the second place, even when conversion has been common it has rarely been casual. Early conversions to Christianity in ancient Rome and medieval Europe, or conversions to and from the new churches of the Reformation after 1520, included conflicts so vicious that they tore asunder nations, societies, families, and friends. And this is to name only a few, famous, Christian examples.

This book is about conversion's most painful sort of tearing: that in families.

It starts with a story from the Reformation, to show how a family in that new age of religious choice might cope (or not) when some in the family chose one religion and some another. But it includes a story from the present as well, to show that the difficulties of conversion have hardly disappeared for families today, and that we moderns, who imagine ourselves far beyond the silly religious bickering of our fore-bears, are in fact wonderfully like them, and can therefore learn much from even the most obscure of them, if we would only look. For though our bickering may take on a few new forms, it is in spirit (and often in form too) much like theirs, and can just as easily lead us into the same terrible dilemma they knew: whether to choose our relationships or our convictions.

How to respond to such an awful choice? As an author from the Reformation itself might have put it: take heed, gentle reader, and see!

Quotations are in *italics,* as are, at first mention, unfamiliar foreign words. All translated quotations (usually from Dutch or Latin) are mine. Biblical quotations are from the King James version, favored here for its poetic quality, not its precision.

Place names are in the local form (such as Leuven), unless there is a well-known English form (such as Antwerp, Brussels, or The Hague).

# one

 May 24, 1654, a Sunday, near sunset.

The calm of late evening, in the unremarkable Dutch town of Boxtel.

A river winding through.

A single church tower in near-silhouette looming above a modest and jumbled skyline of brick, timber, plaster, and straw.

Canals and ponds shimmering all across the flat and soggy countryside.

A breeze pushing softly through leaves and mostly empty streets.

And, around nine, a young man walking alone near the church, toward the rectory, home of the preacher and his family.

But the tranquil scene is a ruse.

For night is coming, and night always means fear, even in towns, where torches are too few to reveal every scoundrel, and too dim to chase off every demon.

And the young man is carrying a message for the preacher's son that will shatter the preacher's heart, if the preacher hears it.

The knock at the rectory door stirs the family inside.

They have already locked up for the night, after all, but the preacher decides to open anyway when he realizes who is calling.

The young man at the door is no stranger, but a friend to both of the preacher's children and a member of the local nobility. He greets the preacher, then asks whether the daughter of the household, Maria, might be allowed on such a fine evening to stroll to the home of a mutual and highly respectable friend.

Despite the young nobleman's enviable breeding, and the worthy destination, the preacher says no. Is it the late hour? Or perhaps even the company, about which the preacher has more cause to worry than he knows?

The reason doesn't really matter, because the young nobleman isn't there to stroll at all; in fact he probably knew the answer to his question before asking it. Rather, he is there to whisper his message to the preacher's son, Jacob, who comes to the door to say hello while the slightly agitated preacher withdraws, rejoining his wife and (disappointed?) daughter in the background.

Privacy isn't complete, but it's enough for the young nobleman to convey his message *in two or three words*—enough for Jacob to know that the moment has arrived at last.

When the visitor leaves, the house is locked again, and Jacob goes back inside to his family, for the last time in his life.

Soon afterward, the family retires.

But how is Jacob to sleep, after what he has heard? Which was this: that a saddled horse, the getaway horse, would be waiting for him in a nearby field later that night.

It was the last and most difficult piece of the plan. Jacob had already arranged for the young nobleman and another friend to come by at 11 (when the last rays of May sunlight finally vanished), so that they can carry his heavy traveling bag to the field for him. This way he won't risk walking noisily down the stairs with it, or dropping it heavily to the ground from his bedroom window above the back garden, or being slowed by it as he climbs the back fence.

He now packs that bag quickly, making it a little heavier than necessary by stuffing in his father's Hebrew Bible and lexicon, reasoning that these would be useful in his studies. Then at 11, Jacob opens his bedroom window and sees the friends waiting in the garden below, as promised. He lowers the bag to them, and they take it to the field.

Perfect so far. One of the friends stays with the bag, keeping nervous watch. The other, the young nobleman, goes to fetch the horse.

Jacob remains in his room a while longer, giving his friend time to get the horse, his family time to fall more deeply into sleep, and himself time to sleep a little as well. But mostly he frets. Will he get enough of a head start? Will his parents realize too soon that he is gone and track him down before he reaches the border?

To calm himself, he prays, then tries to sleep, and dream.

He had been putting together his escape for three weeks now.

Ever since his secret conversion to the One Holy Catholic Roman and Apostolic Church. Ever since he decided that he could no longer pretend to be one thing on the outside while another inside. Ever since he realized that the good people of Boxtel, almost all of them Catholic, were being wrongfully deprived of their religion—their true religion— by his own father, leader of the tiny but state-sanctioned Reformed congregation here in town.

How long during those weeks of planning did it take Jacob to decide where to go?

Though he had plenty of relatives around the land, they professed the same Reformed religion as his parents and were unlikely to be sympathetic to his change of faith. He finally decided to leave the country altogether, and go south, to Antwerp, seventy miles away by land but an eternity by heaven, for Antwerp was gloriously Catholic, and there he could practice his new religion freely instead of secretly and thus work better to save his soul. Besides, he would not be among complete strangers there, for some of his friends in Boxtel had family and friends in Antwerp, who, it was promised, would help him when he arrived. And the big city's 50,000 people would provide him some badly needed anonymity.

Much simpler had been his decision of how to go: it had to be by horse, and by night, in order to stay ahead of pursuers.

But it was no simple matter for a young man without means, who wanted to leave his parents, to find a horse. Again local friends had been ready to help, starting with the young nobleman. Another friend had agreed to serve as guide on the unfamiliar road south and to bring back whatever horse Jacob managed to arrange. A third (the town's deposed Catholic pastor) had given Jacob 25 florins for expenses along the way. And a fourth—Jacob's best friend, another young nobleman named Christian Vlierden, who had headed south that very afternoon to war—had offered to meet Jacob the next morning near the border, at the home of yet another nobleman, where the travelers could refresh themselves and plan further.

There had been some close calls these past weeks, as might be expected with more and more friends learning of Jacob's plans and needs: which of them might let something slip? Just days before, the local sheriff had approached to ask about rumors that Jacob was thinking of going off to war with Vlierden: there was nothing to it, said an undoubtedly shaken Jacob. Stay at home and keep studying with your father, said the suspicious sheriff.

Today was nerve-wracking too, for while Jacob sat in church listening to his father's sermon, as he did every Sunday with his mother and sister, his mind was filled not with the mysteries of heaven but rather with the decidedly earthly matter of finding a horse. Just yesterday he thought he'd found one, but this morning had come word that it wasn't available after all. Yet he had to leave tonight, as he couldn't bear to stay another day. Besides, he had to meet young Vlierden at the border the next morning, or never.

The horse problem was solved only hours after the sermon, and thus only hours before the escape, when the first young nobleman came knocking at the Rolanduses' locked door and whispered in Jacob's ear. And it was solved, Jacob knew, by dubious means, which would complicate things for everyone.

Still, the appearance of a horse at the last possible moment must have seemed nothing less than a gift from heaven. He would ride it then.

Whatever sleep Jacob manages to find, whatever dreams cross his mind, he is at the window again at two, this time to leave forever.

He pushes it open and climbs through, quiet as a housecat, then scampers down into the garden.

Any sleepless neighbor looking out, any mischief-maker come to cast stones at the rectory's windows, would have paused, kept to the shadows, and held still. The preacher's home has been the gathering place, the pin cushion, for all the cursèd troubles of late, and any action there is sure to be worth watching.

Jacob moves across the back garden now, and climbs over the fence of his despised neighbor, the schoolmaster. Though his destination is the field where horse and bag are supposed to be waiting, he makes two stops along the way.

The first is at the home of the friend who'd promised to serve as guide—but this friend now quietly declares, through a cracked door or window, that he cannot go after all. Disappointment, but not disaster. Because the would-be guide assures Jacob that the friend waiting in the field will gladly go along instead.

The second stop is at the town's only convent, just around the corner, where in the darkness Jacob quietly, and sadly, bids farewell to two of the inhabitants.

And now the field at last! But here more disappointment: the horse still hasn't arrived, and the friend waiting with the bag says that he can't make the journey either, because he has a bad foot.

Jacob doesn't quit his plan, or see these obstacles as warning signs from God. More likely he sees the devil at work, trying to block his escape, just as the devil tried, through Pharaoh, to block the escape of the Children of Israel from Egypt. But the devil will have no more luck with Jacob than he had with Moses.

The sudden arrival of the young nobleman with the horse surely bolsters Jacob's resolve: he will go on alone, without a guide, bravely and perhaps foolhardily, like the legendary Roland figure on the Rolandus family crest—Roland who in the medieval epic waded hopelessly and heroically into battle against the infidels, not counting the cost.

After loading the bag onto the horse, and after hushed words about directions and where he should leave the animal, Jacob says goodbye and rides off. The young nobleman who *borrowed* the horse heads north for a few days, to lie low, until it's brought back. The other friend hurries home to rest, as he is the one, bad foot and all, who's been designated to do the bringing back.

Yes, anyone witnessing these scenes would have marveled, precisely because Jacob was the preacher's son: his unsettled, 21-year-old, minor (until 25), and only, son.

Certainly many in and around town (more than the preacher preferred) knew that things were not right between him and Jacob. But the generational struggle was old news by now, and rarely resulted in children—especially preachers' children—running away from home. That's why neighbors would have marveled that Jacob actually did so.

Some in town would rejoice when they heard the news later that day. Others, including even a few of the preacher's rivals, would grieve for the ruptured family.

And from the rectory itself, just as from Ramah in ancient Israel, there would be heard within hours *lamentation, and bitter weeping ... weeping for her children ... because they were not.*

Jacob's flight would help to make him *not*, for his devoutly Reformed family. He was leaving them, and their home, and their faith, to follow a religion they had rejected a century before, and had ever since regarded as the whore of Babylon, the kingdom of the devil, the fountain of all wickedness.

His family would never forgive him. And that is the heart of his story.

# two

[ July 1999, a weekday, after noon. ]

Setting the latest bundle of crumbling documents onto the immense brown table before me, I plop wearily into a chair, scoot forward, and helplessly watch a drop of sweat run down the left lens of my glasses.

The drop lingers for a moment at the bottom of the lens, then continues downward until landing with a tiny splash on the table, just missing the documents, thank goodness.

I remove my glasses and wipe them with part of my damp shirt, wipe the drop on the table with my damp hand, and wipe at my forehead with the back of my damp forearm, but not a damp thing gets dry.

It's hot and muggy in the archives in summer.

You'd think that an archive would be the coolest place around, even in air-conditioning-loathing Belgium, because everyone knows that heat and humidity damage documents.

In fact there is air-conditioning in some archives around Europe, including here at Belgium's national archive, but usually it blows only in the *depot*, where documents are stored, and rarely in the reading room, where documents are brought out temporarily to wilting researchers. Though healthy for documents, you see, air-conditioning is expensive, polluting, and most of all, according to northern Europeans I know, unhealthy for *homo sapiens*.

The natives in the reading room soldier on bravely and virtuously, buoyed by the thought that they are avoiding the sore throats and colds and horrible diseases sure to result from artificially chilled air. Foreigners have no choice but to soldier on as well, if lethargically and grumpily, with hair a little wet around the edges and forearms perpetually sticky, so that despite gallant efforts to hold elbows aloft in order to avoid touching fragile 400-year-old documents you still manage to drip a little sweat on them anyway, while they get a little of themselves on you as well—usually grains of sand that some scribe scattered across the once-fresh ink to help it dry but that now stick stubbornly to your skin.

Archives always post rules forbidding you to write on documents, or to bring a pen within a mile or so of the reading room (pencils and computers only). But they never post suggestions for how to stop sweating on everything, or what to do with leftover sand.

These trips to Europe are cooler when made in autumn or winter, but usually I'm teaching then. Besides, in winter the archives are crowded with local students who have just remembered that they'd better do some research for their senior thesis, and some archives are so cold that you have to keep your coat and gloves on while working, not to mention suffer the noise of the inevitable vintage radiator clunking so loudly in the background that you'd swear some goblin was whacking away in there with a crowbar to get the thing going.

And so I keep traveling to archives in summer, even when it's hot inside.

These aren't exactly Everest-like conditions, but they're unpleasant enough to make you wonder what else you might be doing with your time.

What keeps me and many other historians going back to archives, year after year, whatever the elements, is the hope of finding a fantastic new document.

Naturally one historian's *fantastic* can be another historian's yawner. For some, *fantastic* might mean discovering an old phone book, or a thrilling tax register filled with endless columns of figures.

For others, it could mean the tiniest new morsel about any over-studied historical celebrity (the ever-exploitable Leonardo da Vinci), or at least someone in that celebrity's inner circle (did you hear about Anne Boleyn's *sister?*).

And for still others (including me) a document is fantastic because it shouts out the drama of forgotten lives, revealing in astonishing detail people and ideas and assumptions and conditions that you've never imagined or heard of.

It's hard to find a document like that from the sixteenth or seventeenth century, even about the famous, and not just because many such documents were the victims of heat and fire and water and mice and rampaging clerks, but also because you have to sift through so many non-fantastic documents along the way. Even for the hopelessly unfashionable field of study that I prefer (religious life during the Reformation), far more documents have survived than anyone can hope to read, most of these documents are rather dull, many are barely legible, and almost all were written in languages not my own—and in older versions of those languages to boot.

No wonder that you come across fantastic documents (at least my sort) so rarely, and almost by accident. You're actually looking for something else. Or the archivist mistakenly brings you a document you didn't request. Or the archivist miraculously allows you to walk behind the forbidden door into the depot itself, the holy of holies, and pull out whatever you please.

Despite the hard going, you keep at it anyway, because you've found treasures before, and the memory of them makes you believe that somewhere inside the latest massive pile is another nugget, waiting just for you—not for you to see it first, of course, because just about every document from the Reformation has probably been seen already by someone else, but for you to see it with your particular eyes.

So far today, the documents have been, as usual, less than fantastic.

In fact it's been a superabundance of laws, charters, deeds, financial accounts, church decrees, and other official sorts of things, all about as lively as the straight-angled, sterile decor of the mostly brown reading room itself. Though useful, such documents have little flesh and blood, little drama, little story.

But all that changes as I undo the usual red ribbon that holds together the usual pile of faded tan papers, and take into my sweaty hands the not-so-usual sort of document I'm always looking for: the secret journal of Jacob Rolandus.

It wasn't even that hard to find—it wasn't squirreled away in some locked cabinet by an overprotective archivist, for instance—but was clearly described in the archive's easily accessible catalogue. The word *journal* was what grabbed me, as it would most any historian who studies far-off centuries, because ego documents (the rather clinical name for diaries and autobiographies) were rare before 1700. Certainly some disappoint, because they end up being grocery lists or account books rather than revealers of hearts. But you check anyway, just in case, even if you're working on something else, as I was.

At first glance Jacob's particular journal, from the year 1654, looks quite ordinary: it's smallish, bound in the familiar stiff yellowish calf-skin, and written in mostly legible Dutch. But then I start reading, and realize that the contents are hardly ordinary at all.

The author is not only recounting his desire to leave his family's Reformed religion and become Catholic, but doing so with breath-taking detail and passion. Within minutes there arrives that rare but exhilarating feeling of disbelief at what I've found.

I don't forget myself completely, like the ancient Greek mathematician Archimedes, who after a discovery he made supposedly ran naked into the street, excitedly waving his arms. Most archives, sticklers for quiet, would probably frown on that. But I do silently raise my hands in triumph.

Adding to the excitement is that parts of the journal are written in code. It takes a few hours to break the code, but I'm proud when I do so. Then I realize, sheepishly, that the key to the code had all the while been in plain sight on the journal's cover, set there by Jacob Rolandus himself—not in the tense days when he began his journal and was keeping it secret, but in the calm days years later, when he gave it to friends for safekeeping, so that they could make sense of his scribbles. The code followed a simple tic-tac-toe pattern, as below:

|       |       |       |
|-------|-------|-------|
| $abc$ | $def$ | $ghi$ |
| $klm$ | $nop$ | $qrs$ |
| $tuw$ | $xy$  | $z$   |

(No $j$ or $v$ was necessary in old Dutch, as $i$ and $u$ doubled for each.) A letter then took the form of the part of the figure where it fell. Thus:

$$b = \cdot\rfloor \quad k = \rceil$$

$$r = \lfloor\cdot \quad w = \cdot\cdot\rceil$$

And so on.

With the entire contents clear, the journal becomes even more riveting. Also riveting are the letters filed with it, composed by Jacob and his sister, Maria, who stayed in the family religion and was obviously against her brother's conversion to Catholicism. Although full of the usual and often tiresome debates that arose between any set of theological antagonists in the age of Reformation, these letters between siblings bleed with such affection and emotion that the old arguments suddenly seem vital again.

There's enough detail and drama here for a book, I am sure, and I decide that I would like to write it.

It's not merely the extraordinary detail that moves me to do so, nor the high drama, for many good stories and sets of documents have these. It's not even the chance to be one of the first to tell the story of the Rolandus family, nor the chance to add to the bigger and largely unknown story of which they were but a part (namely, how families of the Reformation handled conversion).

Rather, what moves me most to want to write this particular drama, what makes it so fantastic in my eyes, is a more emotional quality: something about this exotic seventeenth-century story feels terribly familiar, even personal—as if it's happening right now, as if I've got a stake in the outcome, as if I've heard it before.

And I suspect that anyone moved to read this story might feel much the same way.

# three

 Escape for thy life; look not behind thee, neither stay thou in all the plain.
—*Genesis* 19:17

Bouncing in tandem with the bag lashed down behind him, Jacob rode as rapidly as he dared through the darkness of early morning.

The long and flat terrain that sped his horse would also make Jacob stand out once it was light, around five. By then he wanted to be as far from home as possible, because he knew that his father, the preacher, would almost certainly come after him, and that his father, mother, and sister would be devastated at his flight.

This last wasn't something he had to think about, or articulate, or order neatly in his mind, but rather something he knew, all at once, in his bones.

He knew even more deeply in those bones the reason for his family's devastation. It wasn't merely that he had left them, though God knew that this was bad enough. Rather, it was that his leaving confirmed what until now they had simply feared: that he had become Catholic. And that he was thus rejecting the glittering Reformed legacy they all had inherited and which more than anything else gave the family its identity.

This needed less articulation than any of Jacob's swirling thoughts and emotions.

The family's Reformed tradition had begun more than a century before, when Jacob's paternal great-grandfather, Roeland Jacobsz

Uyttenhoven, left his Catholic faith for the new Reformed faith of John Calvin.

Born in Geneva in the 1530s, Calvin's Reformed religion was soon at the forefront of the rebellion against Catholicism that would one day be called the Protestant Reformation. By the 1550s Calvin's movement had spread far beyond Geneva, including to the Netherlands, where Roeland Uyttenhoven found it sometime around 1560.

Around the same date as his conversion, Roeland emigrated from the southern provinces of the Netherlands to the northern. Did he move for his new faith? (The great waves of Reformed converts to the north did not come until the next decades.) Perhaps for economic reasons? Or did he, to the contrary, perhaps suffer material loss by leaving, not to mention disdain and even alienation from Catholic relatives? Whatever the case, he stayed with his new religion.

Settling in the province of Holland, in the town of Delft (still more famous for its beer than its stoneware), Roeland and his wife had a son, whom they named Jacob Roelandsz Uyttenhoven. This son eventually dropped the Uyttenhoven, kept the Roelandsz, but Latinized it to Rolandus, so that he became simply Jacob Rolandus.

Here was the first Jacob Rolandus, Old Jacob, born in 1562. He was the grandfather of Young Jacob Rolandus, born in 1633, and now riding furiously south to escape his family's legacy.

Old Jacob not only gave the Rolandus family its name, but more than anyone else he made that name inseparable from the Reformed religion.

Mostly he did this as a distinguished preacher for 45 years, beginning in 1587 in western German lands where he worked among Reformed refugees, then back in his home town of Delft, and finally from 1603 until his death in 1632 in the largest Reformed community of all the Netherlands: Amsterdam.

Amsterdam was fussy about its Reformed preachers, who were expected to be among the city's brightest stars—as bright as the painter Rembrandt, or the poet Vondel, or the wealthy merchants who adorned the city's canals with their impressive homes and stores.

Old Jacob, though less fiery than some of his brethren, lived up to those high expectations, and even exceeded them, for in Amsterdam he became a full-fledged celebrity.

In fact Amsterdam became almost as much a part of the Rolandus identity as the Reformed religion. Not only Old Jacob's children considered themselves *Amsterdammers*, wherever they moved, but even his rebellious grandson, Young Catholic Jacob, who never actually lived in Amsterdam proper and was now riding as far away from it as possible, all his life signed his name *Jacob Rolandus of Amsterdam*, so that he might have been confused with his Reformed grandfather.

Young Jacob knew from an early age what had made his grandfather more famous than the average Reformed preacher.

It wasn't merely his regular position in the largest church of the land, but more especially his election as Assessor, or second in command, at the only national Reformed synod ever held in the Netherlands, at Dordt, in 1618 and 1619. There, for 154 sessions over a six-month period and before some 125 delegates from all of Protestant Europe, Old Jacob helped direct what turned out to be matters of life and death. And most especially the elder Jacob's fame resulted from his appointment, by the same national synod, as one of only six official translators for a new Dutch Bible.

True, the synod itself didn't have quite the lasting impact that many had hoped, and true, the work of translation took far longer than anyone had imagined and brought Old Jacob into enormous personal difficulties. But his contribution to both monuments was enough to immortalize the name Rolandus in the annals of the Reformed Church, and to put that name on the lips of the great all over Europe.

Young Jacob knew a final thing about Old Jacob besides his celebrity: he hadn't exactly liked Catholics. In fact he had the same attitude toward them that a woodsman had toward poachers.

To be a Reformed preacher wasn't merely to deliver weekly sermons, or to drive out contamination from among the flock, or even brilliantly to translate the Bible. It was also to combat and condemn rival churches—especially the Catholic Church, the largest rival of all in the Dutch Republic.

Reformed preachers would have preferred to have no religious rivals, period. They disliked the (in)famous tolerance of the Republic, with its abundance of religions, and would rather that there be one faith only: the Reformed. But preachers didn't get their wish. Only a minority of the Dutch belonged to the Reformed religion, and civic leaders, who knew well the old Dutch saying that *strict rulers don't rule long*, wanted nothing to do with the troubles that would surely follow any attempt to impose a religion on the populace. These leaders were willing to acknowledge the importance of the Reformed Church in the nation's birth, and therefore declared it the *public* church—yet that wasn't the same as the usual arrangement in Europe of an *official and exclusive* church. Public status simply meant that the Reformed alone were allowed to worship in public—but other-believers were allowed to stay, and to be fully Dutch, as long as they kept their heads down and worshiped in private.

The problem for Old Jacob and many of his brethren was that other-believers (especially Catholics, who made up about a third of the entire Dutch Republic) didn't keep their heads down enough. And Old Jacob spent as much time as anyone grousing about it to civil authorities. He and his fellow preachers considered Catholics nothing less than a *snake and an adder in the bosom of the land, a cancer and a plague, and a gangrene and cold fire which eats up the insides of the state and church;* it needed to be cut out.

Surely Old Jacob never could have imagined that one of his grandsons, especially one named after him, would ever become Catholic himself. In fact, after Old Jacob how could anyone named Rolandus ever be anything at all except Reformed?

Young Jacob knew that question, and its answer, all too well.

Every one of the eight children born to Old Jacob and his wife Maria stayed Reformed. Two of those children, Timothy and Daniel, even followed their father and became preachers themselves, then hoped that one or more of their sons might become preachers too.

In fact, just months after Old Jacob's death in June 1632, Timothy and Daniel each named their latest newborn Jacob, in honor of their famous father, perpetuating his name and nudging the infants along the path toward the ministry.

Thus it happened that by early 1633 two new Rolandus cousins came into the world, as if to refresh it: both were male, both were named Jacob, and both were intended to become Reformed preachers.

The plan almost worked.

Jacob son of Daniel went on to become such a preacher, just as hoped, and fathered still more preachers, magnificently perpetuating the family legacy.

Jacob son of Timothy went on to become, against all hope, a Catholic priest, and fathered no one, hopelessly devastating his family. He continued riding south, to the promised land.

# four

[ Of course people are interested only in themselves. . . .
The strange and foreign is not interesting—only the
deeply personal and familiar.
—*John Steinbeck* ]

That the Rolanduses' story was beginning to feel familiar, and personal, wasn't exactly surprising.

It happens all the time, and not only to historians (at any archive in the world at just about any hour of the day) but to readers as well (right in the comfort of their own living rooms). You might first be attracted to a story because it's something new and exotic, but even in the most exotic story you sense something familiar, and your special History muscle goes into action to find it—flattening time in your head, dragging the past forward, pushing the present back, until the story from five or fifteen centuries before looks a lot like a story that happened to you just last week, and seems just as vital and personal too.

The whole process reminds you again that the study of the past is not about the past but about life, including your particular life. In fact when a story from the past seems fantastic it's probably because that story is somehow about you as well.

The problem is, it's not always easy to see what some old story, especially a really old story, can possibly have to do with you, right now.

If a story is about, say, your ancestor, your religion, or your country, then its relevance may seem obvious enough. But a story about an obscure Dutch family that lived 350 years ago and 3,500 miles away and isn't related to you and doesn't speak your language or share your religion can seem as foreign as the moon.

Even when you sense the immediate relevance of such remote stories, as historians often do, you might be reluctant to explore it, because the task of showing how the past connects to the present is just so difficult. The past is strange, and other, and foreign. Sometimes it's even completely impenetrable, despite your best efforts to understand it. Other times you think you have it right, then it slips between your fingers and fools you (as a little Shakespearean English teaches you). If you can't ever be sure that you're right about the shadowy past, then how can you ever hope to compare it to the flesh-and-blood present? It's a lot safer, and simpler, to stick to the past alone, especially the small corner of the past you've chosen to study, rather than to discuss how that past might also be about you today.

This time, however, despite the perils, I wanted to understand thoroughly, and not merely sense vaguely, the connection I was sensing—between the Rolanduses and my own life and time. I wanted to do so not as some intellectual exercise, but because I was convinced by now that not only are we most interested in the past when we see what it has to do with us personally, we learn best from it too.

The trick to seeing your connection, of course, is to see through all the differences that can blur it. You don't ignore those differences: they are real, and wondrous, and give you an eye-opening glimpse into how other human beings have done things. Instead, you study these differences thoroughly, until you begin to see that many may not be so different after all: they just need to be looked at in new ways.

For example, to make the strange and foreign past familiar you can follow the example of medieval theologians, who used the concepts of *accident* and *essence* to see that different external forms may in their internal quality be much the same.

You can imitate translators, who render different words and expressions and contexts into something essentially the same even if not literally the same.

You can borrow from transposers, who rewrite music meant for one instrument or key for another, so that the new score sounds both different and the same.

But most apt for the Rolanduses' story, it seemed, might be to do some converting. Not as in religious conversion this time, but as in a conversion table.

Such a table sets an unfamiliar form next to an equivalent familiar form, to help you see that though they appear to be different they are in fact the same. This many meters equals this many yards. This many euros equals this many dollars. And so on for differing measures of shoe size, temperature, months, flow rates, distance, power, volume, weight, and more. All different, but all the same.

Maybe this would work for past and present too—a sort of historical equivalency. Find a present story that, when the differences are converted, roughly equates to a past story, in order to understand both more deeply than if you had merely studied each alone.

Of course no two stories will ever be completely equivalent, even after all the converting is done. But that isn't the goal. Rather, it's to bring the past story into the realm of the recognizable, the possible, the familiar, the intelligible. And it's to give the present story more depth than you realized it had.

Finding your connection to some past story requires more than your mind, however.

You have to use your gut too, and dig around in your private emotions and thoughts and *secret experience*—in the sorts of things you usually keep hidden from others, and even yourself, but that may hold the key to understanding.

Here you might try the method actor's technique of Affective Memory, daft as it may seem for a rational historian (especially one who can't act). This calls for an actor to search out emotions and experiences from her own life that will help her grasp similar emotions and experiences in the character she is playing. She may uncover an experience that is similar to one faced by the character, but most important is to find a similar intensity of emotion.

It's not child's play. The prophets of Affective Memory urge beginners to undertake this memory search only under the supervision of qualified guides, and they solemnly warn about the possibility of hyperventilation and anxiety. They also suggest searching memories that are at least seven years old, to reduce the already strong risk of *psychological trauma* that may result. Yet despite the risks, believers insist that the process is necessary, because it's primarily through an *honest and intense emotional response*, rather than merely through rational thought, that an actor best achieves understanding, and sameness, with her character.

And perhaps a historian, or a reader, with the past as well.

I decided to go ahead and try—to search out the specific memories that were causing the Rolanduses to resonate so strongly within me, in the hope that this might help me to understand both the Rolanduses and those memories more profoundly than otherwise.

It's the same process that any historian or reader must go through as well, in order to understand why any past story resonates with them.

Despite all the warnings to search among older memories only, the first memory up in my mind was recent, involving the parent-child conflict.

I remembered easily how challenging it sometimes was to be a grown but dependent child, like Jacob. But that memory was manageable, probably because it was a lot more than seven years old. Less manageable was the fresh memory of being the often inept parent of such a child. The experts were right: that memory was too painful. I needed something else.

Other possible candidates emerged from my long memories of conversion, of the religious sort. I wasn't a convert myself, but I had been around conversion my whole life.

Many of my ancestors were converts who emigrated from Europe to America for their new Mormon faith, and throughout my childhood I heard recounted in reverent tones the stories of how they gave up family and home and native land to do so. How better to show our gratitude, was the message to us, just as it had been to the Rolandus children and grandchildren learning about their Reformed forebears, than to stay true to that faith?

Thanks largely to those ancestors, I became a missionary myself as a young man, going back (as it were) to Europe for two years in order to find still more converts. There I saw firsthand the pressure that even the possibility of conversion could put on family relationships.

Moreover, before and after that time as a missionary I witnessed and read about hundreds of other conversions that invariably featured some element of familial stress. One of the most recent was a young student I met whose conversion prompted his heartbroken father, thousands of miles away, to send someone to take the boy's car, computer, phone, and everything but the clothes on his back, and to inform the boy (in case it wasn't clear) that he was cut off.

But the story that kept coming back to heart and mind with greatest force, perhaps because I learned the whole of it in such an unforgettable and improbable way just after finding the Rolanduses, involved two ancestors, named Carl and Mathilda, who for the sake of their new religion left their family in Sweden forever.

Surely here was my strongest connection of all.

# five

 She weepeth sore in the night, and her tears are on
her cheeks.
—*Lamentations* 1:2

At mid-morning, Jacob reached his first destination, a castle near the border, where his friend Christian Vlierden was waiting as promised, thanks be to God.

Did Jacob interrupt the happy reunion with the thought that by now his family back in Boxtel was surely wide awake and already reeling from the shock of his departure?

How long was it on that dread-inducing Monday morning, never to be banished from their hearts and nightmares and sobs, before they realized he was gone? Who went to see why he was late coming down for breakfast and prayer? Which unfortunate soul looked into his room and saw his empty bed? Did they all hope that he had simply gone out for an errand? Or did they notice immediately that many of his possessions were gone, along with the prized Bible and lexicon?

No one bothered to say. But certainly there was weeping and wailing and gnashing of teeth among all the Rolanduses left behind.

First came Catharina, who had given birth to Jacob.

Other than this fact, little is known of her. Her family name was Ruts, she married Timothy in 1626 at age 28, had two children with him, and left behind a single document in her own hand.

Such historical anonymity wasn't unusual for a preacher's wife, that new creature of the Protestant Reformation, whose husband was always the more public and better documented figure in the relationship. But during her lifetime a preacher's wife enjoyed a certain status in her community—more than the *concubine* of the old medieval pastor ever did. Precisely because of her status, the preacher's wife also had more pressure to be a model in all things.

If Catharina was anything like the sturdy Dutch woman sketched by foreign visitors, then she would have been strong and independent (though as a preacher's wife not overly so).

If she matched the fantasy woman immortalized by Dutch poets, then she would have possessed eyes like golden beams, a forehead like alabaster, cheeks that glowed like a dew-dropped rose in morning, skin white as snow, hair as golden as a grain field in summer, and flawless manners.

If she fit the model of responsible wife and mother advocated by moralists, then she would have been emotionally mature at marriage, shared the same religion, economic background, and social standing as her husband, and carefully fed and disciplined her children.

And if she resembled the preacher's wife and mother dreamed up by Protestant churchmen, then she would always have been friendly and helpful, modest and civil, restrained in drink and dress and speech, forbearing of her husband's weakness and faults and *never with his views disputeful,* and more successful than ordinary mothers at instilling religious and moral precepts in her children (not to mention always pleasing and delighting those children rather than crossing or threatening them).

But it was doubtful that Catharina, or any other mortal, ever lived up to such ideals. More likely was that she fit the modest model found in a self-help book from 1553 on housewifery, which concluded that being a wife and mother meant brief moments of joy and much unpleasantness.

The flight of Jacob only brought her more of the last. And not merely because her son was gone, but because his departure made heavier still the formidable burden of expectations already resting upon her shoulders: she, the preacher's wife, the foremost example in all things religious and virtuous, could not keep her own son at home or in the church.

And so when she wept it was surely not only at the loss of her son, but at the blow to her honor.

Next came Jacob's older sister Maria, who suffered too.

Like Jacob she was named after one of Timothy's parents, Grandmother Maria, wife of Old Jacob. But more than her brother Maria treasured the responsibility of perpetuating the family's religious heritage. That was why she had, since arriving in Boxtel, worried about her brother's friendships with those *light-minded* Vlierdens and their fellow Catholics. And look how right she had been!

To Maria, Jacob's flight was a fall from the truth, a descent into the worldly habits of his popish noble friends, not a conversion. What a *light thing* the Catholic religion was, believed Maria, and what better evidence than the behavior of those friends? They engaged in *ridiculous feasting* during Carnival, and then equally ridiculous fasting during Lent to make up for it—as if by eating no meat for a time they somehow pleased God!

And what of *that lighthearted dancing* Jacob had praised so highly to his sister, and his betting and playing cards *without end*, in unsavory places, even though Jacob knew that such things displeased their father? Not to mention powdering his hair and face, in the latest noble fashion, at every *sneaky opportunity*. This didn't *suit a preacher's son in the least, who ought to walk without giving offense and to bear in mind his father's position.* But then Jacob had always been inclined *to follow that worldly allure* and his own foolishness.

Finally there were *those other sins* Jacob had committed, which she didn't like to think about (or specify), but which caused their parents deeper sorrow than anything else Jacob had done—*a great sin before God*, was all she would say.

These were the real causes behind Jacob's spiritual blindness and flight, she thought.

Last but not least came Timothy, who may have felt that he suffered most of all, as his hopes for Jacob had always been greatest.

Timothy had been the first of Old Jacob's children to perpetuate the family tradition of preaching. He never said why he chose his vocation. Maybe he, like so many young men of the time, found it easiest simply to do as his father did, especially when that father was so successful. For there were not only royal dynasties and printing dynasties and banking dynasties at the time of Timothy's birth in 1594, but preaching dynasties as well, all around Protestant Europe.

But what giant shadows such fathers might cast, especially one like Old Jacob! And what a rough road to the ministry for anyone who set out upon it! Even a preacher's son had to feel some measure of personal calling to make it through.

Like his father, and many prospective Dutch preachers, Timothy had gone to the trouble of studying in faraway places, five long years, including in the Reformed centers of Geneva and Basel (in Switzerland), then also Heidelberg and Marburg (in German lands). When finished in 1619, he returned to Amsterdam with the intent of becoming a preacher there, which meant that he had to be accepted into the classis, the body of preachers and elders from in and around the city.

Over several grueling days before the classis (which included of course an anxious and proud Old Jacob), Timothy produced his educational certificates, endured questions about his personal habits and life, demonstrated the proficiency in Latin required of all preachers but as the son of the great translator showed off his Greek and Hebrew as well, delivered a short sermon on a scriptural verse, and especially, especially, proved his orthodoxy by answering correctly more than a hundred questions on Reformed theology.

Was the Law God gave to Moses of one nature? Why was the Law of Ceremonies now finished? How could you prove that a man, before his rebirth, was inclined to hate God? How could you prove that Christ was eternally God? Through what means did God instill faith in the elect? Were good works necessary for salvation? And so on through the latest Reformed concerns, the answers to which the classis considered matters of life and death, not to mention of everlasting salvation.

Timothy passed the exam, and was accepted into the classis. Months later, in 1620, a small community just outside Amsterdam, named

Ouderkerk, called him to be their preacher, or, in Dutch, their *dominee*. It was a respectable start for someone just past his 25th birthday. But no doubt both Timothy and Old Jacob hoped for something bigger in the future, preferably in Amsterdam itself.

It never came. There would be no brilliant career like his father's. Was Timothy not quite the preacher his father was? He certainly wasn't quite the linguist: though skilled in Hebrew, Greek, and Latin, the only official assignment he ever received in connection to holy writ was to check for typos in the new Dutch Bible—far less glorious than actually translating the thing.

Whatever the reasons, Timothy labored for the rest of his life (47 more years) in a variety of small and undistinguished communities, each farther and farther from Amsterdam, and each more difficult than the last, with his current wretched community in Boxtel the most difficult and distant of all.

Yes, Timothy suffered for his calling, and the family tradition. Still, he fulfilled his duties, preaching twice every Sunday, as required, even in the depressingly empty church where he labored now. And though his own hopes might have been dashed long before, he had always held out great hopes for his son, his only son, his bright son, who with the proper direction could not only perpetuate the family's preaching tradition further but do so in glorious fashion—maybe something in the way that Old Jacob had!

To that end, Timothy not only named his son after Old Jacob, but took him to be baptized in one of the churches where Old Jacob had preached, in Amsterdam proper, to reinforce the family's ties with that city and the boy's sense of his heritage. (The local church in Ouderkerk had apparently been good enough for Jacob's sister Maria, as her name wasn't recorded in the baptismal records of Amsterdam.)

Timothy had also seen personally to the education of Young Jacob, for he could teach the boy far more than could any of the pathetic schoolmasters in the towns where they had lived. As the years passed, and Young Jacob grew increasingly sour-faced about studying with his father, Timothy endured anyway, for the sake of his son, and the tradition. And maybe himself.

For make no mistake: Timothy was just as likely as Catharina to feel that Jacob's departure was a blow to his own honor and reputation and name.

Any parent's reputation might suffer from the censure that arose in neighbors' minds when they saw someone else's child straying. But the reputation of a Reformed preacher suffered especially, more than that of other parents—even more than that of a Catholic priest. While a priest might be valued for the numerous rituals he performed, even if his personal life and preaching skills were lacking, a Reformed preacher performed few rituals: his authority stemmed from his ability to preach and to live what he preached—and to see that his family lived it as well.

The awful thought of his escaped son helped Timothy to understand why the pagan father of the ancient Christian convert Perpetua pleaded with his daughter to renounce her new faith and come back to the family religion: not only would she escape execution if she did so, but her family would avoid ruin. *Do not abandon me to people's scorn*, pleaded that father. *Think of your brothers; think of your mother and your aunt; think of your child. . . . You will destroy all of us! None of us will ever be able to speak freely again*, he wailed.

And he wasn't even a preacher.

The most certain and tangible of all the unarticulated sentiments spinning around in the head of Timothy Rolandus on that fateful Monday morning, however, was this: Jacob was 21, and subject to his father's authority until 25, the age of majority.

This fatherly authority, and the responsibility accompanying it, made Timothy feel that it was up to him to save his impressionable son, who had obviously been led astray only because of so-called friends.

Wounded though Timothy was, he wasn't ready to give up yet. Neither were Catharina and Maria, who had not yet sunk into the awful gloom that would envelop them in years to come. They still had hopes that Jacob would return, and justifiably so: plenty of minor children around Europe briefly ran away for another religion, then came to their senses and returned to home and faith. Why wouldn't Jacob do the same? Especially if he had a little help from those who cared about him most.

Within hours, perhaps minutes, of the discovery, Timothy sent messages to some of his nearby relatives, telling them what had happened and asking whether anyone wished to go along to chase Jacob down and bring him home.

Then he set out to learn just exactly where Jacob might have gone. He had a good idea where to start.

# six

[
I had a vision, I don't know what else to call it.
]

I often heard the names Carl and Mathilda while growing up, but I came to know them in a meaningful way only after a cosmic alignment of events at the crowded new Immigrant Museum on Ellis Island in spring 2004.

Having already been in New York for several days with my family, I was weary of lines. So when my wife and daughter willingly joined another at the Immigrant Museum, this one leading to a bank of computer terminals where you could check whether any of your ancestors had passed through, I found a bench to rest, certain that there would be no fantastic discoveries here.

As my wife and daughter at last neared the front of the line, they couldn't help peeking over the shoulder of the woman just before them as she typed out a name. With each letter, their astonishment increased, for eventually this woman typed out my family name. My rare family name. Okay, without the *e* at the end. But still.

While my wife struck up a conversation, my daughter ran to tell me the news, bringing me at last to my feet. We soon learned that the woman, named Annika, was from Sweden, and in New York for only a few days. The name she had been typing was that of her long-lost great uncle, Carl Härlin. She was thinking that he might have gone to America around 1890, when the family lost track of him.

I said that my great-grandfather was named Carl Harline, that he had also immigrated from Sweden to America around 1890, and that he had altered the spelling of his last name but I couldn't remember how. Perhaps there was a connection.

My daughter called my parents to ask where our Carl was from. *Simtuna*, came the reply, a parish west of Stockholm. I repeated it to Annika, who nearly fainted. That's where she was from, and where her Carl had lived.

Now I nearly fainted. We must be cousins, we thought, related to the same Carl. We took group pictures, commented on the likeness between Annika and my father (perhaps not the most flattering comparison for a woman around 50, since my father was male and nearly 80), and promised to keep in touch.

More investigations over the next months revealed that Annika and I were not cousins after all, and thus any resemblance between her and my father was far-fetched thinking of the farthest kind. Instead there had been two Carls—both in the Swedish army, both with the same last name (thanks to the army), and both had lived (one after the next) in the same small house in Simtuna.

Still, even that coincidence was wondrous. And the wondrous meeting led to new friends, to the discovery of previously unknown relatives, and to Sweden itself, where I learned more than I ever dreamed I would about my great-grandfather Carl, and his wife, my great-grandmother Mathilda—who not only became real people for me now, but also happened to help me better understand the Rolandus family, and vice versa.

Carl Eriksson and Mathilda Petersson were born in 1859, in neighboring parishes west of Stockholm.

Their parents were all farmhands and maids, which meant that Carl and Mathilda too would almost certainly be farmhand and maid. As children they worked at home and attended the local Lutheran school, like almost all Swedish farm children.

Every year, the local Lutheran pastor visited his flock, to test all of them on their religious knowledge, and to counteract the pull of rival religious movements spreading around the countryside. The pastor even recorded a score for each person in his little book: Carl and Mathilda always received an *average* or *below average* score, just like their siblings and parents.

In their middle teens, Carl and Mathilda began their full-time working lives, on other people's farms, to ease the burden on their own parents. They received room and board in exchange for their labor.

The young single farmhands and maids moved around regularly from farm to farm, usually not far from their home parish, and in 1880 Carl and Mathilda found themselves working on the same farm, in the hamlet of Mälby, just east of Mathilda's parish church. The farm was simply designated in church records as Mälby number 3.

This was where they met. It was the same farm where Mathilda's parents had met 21 years earlier.

Around 1878, a couple of years before Carl arrived at Mälby 3, Mathilda had encountered Mormon missionaries for the first time.

Some of the new religions criss-crossing Sweden were especially unwelcome, with Mormons perhaps the least welcome of all—even less than Baptists—surely because of stories about polygamy. Mathilda was curious enough, however, that when she heard missionaries were in the area she decided to go listen to them.

One night after work she walked by moonlight to a meeting about a mile away, where she sang songs and believed what they preached. Yet when the missionaries asked whether she wanted to be baptized as a Mormon, 19-year-old Mathilda replied, *Not yet.* After they left, she saw no more missionaries for nine years.

In the meantime she continued her work at Mälby 3 and got to know Carl.

By June 1881 they knew each other very well, for in this month Mathilda became pregnant with Carl's child.

Chances were excellent that conception occurred on Midsummer, June 24, the longest day and party of the year, which people of all classes celebrated with pent-up enthusiasm throughout the sunlit night.

Chances were also excellent that by the time of conception Carl and Mathilda were already engaged. As had been the practice for centuries in rural Europe, pregnancy often followed closely after engagement, as if the couple were testing whether they could conceive. Once they did, then came marriage. Carl and Mathilda married in October 1881.

They had to leave Mälby 3, which had no place for married farmhands, and find a farm that did, or go find work at one of the new factories near a city.

There was one other choice: Carl could join the army. Like farmhands, soldiers got a small house in the country, and the usual acre or so of land for potatoes. Yet unlike farmhands they also got some cash and a little social status. They had to train, but only a few weeks a year, and Sweden had avoided war since 1814.

Thus the ambitious, or desperate, Carl chose the army. In his home parish of Simtuna, there were 33 houses set aside for soldiers, and one of those houses, in the hamlet called Björk, was then vacant. Carl was assigned that house, along with the rank of grenadier (even though at five feet eight inches he was under the six foot minimum for that rank). According to the army's custom, Carl also took the name of his house, which in this case was simply the same as the hamlet's: thus Carl Eriksson was now Carl Björk.

The couple's first child, a son, was born soon afterward, but died within a year. Four daughters followed over the next eight years.

In May 1887, Carl and Mathilda moved again, to a soldier's house in the hamlet of Härfsta, also in the parish of Simtuna but closer to both of their parents. This soldier's house was called Härlin, and Carl Björk was suddenly Carl Härlin.

Around the time they moved to this house, which stood at the edge of a forest and looked out over immense fields, Mathilda met the Mormon missionaries again: she heard that they would be holding a meeting nearby, and she wanted to go. So one night while Carl watched the girls, a heavily pregnant Mathilda left her home and its pear tree and potato cellar and lilacs and shed and cow and set off for the meeting.

Again she was moved by what she heard, and this time she asked to be baptized a Mormon. But now it was the missionaries who said no.

They wanted her to be sure. Or maybe they worried about Carl, who didn't seem interested at all.

Mathilda promised to study more, and after work she might stay up to read until one or two in the morning, easy enough in the long Swedish days of June or July. She also prayed twice a day in the forest around their home, hoping for a vision from God.

Her efforts were interrupted by the birth of her latest daughter and the urgency of the potato harvest. On the morning of September 21, 1887, Mathilda loaded 35 bushels of potatoes into the cellar for winter. That same evening she gave birth. She was soon back to studying, and now fasting as well, once for three days, which dried up her breasts so that the new baby drew only blood, probably from Mathilda's sore nipples.

The late nights and searching and praying and fasting and working put Mathilda in an ideal state to receive the vision she was hoping for. Two of them in fact.

Mathilda's first dream came in the short days of December 1887, on a night after the missionaries had visited her home.

In this dream her mother and several friends were running to her house to ask her the meaning of a great fire coming down from the heavens and burning everything in its path. Mathilda assured them that the fire would not burn her house. And it passed by as she said.

The second dream came weeks later. This time she saw a stream of light enter a large home, and Mathilda followed it inside. At the center of the brightly lit main room, she saw a woman in white, who called out *Right, right, right, right!* In another room, Mathilda saw a man dressed as a Lutheran pastor, with a black cassock and a golden cross on his breast, preaching to a large audience. She thought, *No, this is not right.* In yet another room she saw a lady in black instructing some eager listeners, but again Mathilda felt, *this is not right.* She decided to reenter the first room where the bright woman in white was still repeating *Right!* Two other people stood beside her now, and they waved a happy Mathilda in.

That did it. The visions convinced her that the Mormon Church was *right*, and she told the missionaries that after many months of study and searching she was ready to be baptized.

Mathilda told this as well to Carl, who replied that she should stop being so foolish and crazy.

A fretting Carl was probably the one who passed along news of the baptism to Mathilda's mother, because her mother soon came running to the Härlin house to beg Mathilda to be sensible. Then her mother cried and said it was all of the devil.

The rest of the family also tried to dissuade Mathilda, arguing with her until midnight once, and giving her a bundle of newspapers from the Lutheran mission in Utah that exposed the Mormons' latest crimes.

But Mathilda was determined, and she went through with her baptism anyway, in May 1888, at a nearby river, where a mixed crowd of fellow believers and people shouting at her not to give herself to the devil gathered to witness the event. Despite the shouting, Mathilda was immersed under water, in the Mormon (and Baptist) way, making her officially Mormon. It's not clear whether Carl or Mathilda's parents or siblings were among those watching.

Worse was yet to come for the couple's loved ones.

When Carl converted to Mormonism two years later, perhaps not coincidentally right after that church renounced its practice of polygamy, any tensions with Mathilda over religion eased. But those with his parents increased.

Causing even more trouble was Mathilda's desire to move to Utah, where many Mormon converts had gathered since 1847 to create their new society. Both the couple's families were distraught. *Let her go alone if she is so anxious*, Carl's parents supposedly said.

Carl decided to go with her. Perhaps he couldn't be a Swedish soldier and be Mormon. Perhaps he saw more economic opportunity in *Zion*, a word Mormon missionaries liked to scratch in the soot that collected on Swedish ceilings, to let it cast its spell. Most likely he just wanted to stay with Mathilda.

Around 8,000 Swedish converts to Mormonism (half the total in that country) emigrated to Utah by the end of the nineteenth century, though by 1891 the stream was already slowing to a trickle. Yet it was still strong enough to pull along Mathilda.

Surely it was a sad April day for all when Carl, Mathilda, and the four girls set out from Härfsta that year for Utah. They were not reconciled with their families, and never expected to see them again.

The 10,000-mile trip to Utah was easier than it had been thirty years earlier, as it could be made now with steamships and trains rather than sailing ships and wagons.

But it was difficult enough. Carl became seasick during the Atlantic crossing, and the four girls caught measles. Mathilda cared for them all. The family rested for a short time in New York (not at Ellis Island, however, which opened only the following year as an immigrant clearing center), before continuing by train to Salt Lake City, arriving there on May 13, 1891. Two days later, the youngest child, two-year-old Anna Maria, who had been sick during the entire 30-day voyage, died from measles.

Did Carl ever recover from this? Did he, like many struggling emigrant converts, feel that this was some sort of divine punishment, foretold by those back home who had warned him not to leave his native country and the religion of his fathers? Once in Utah, Carl never participated in any of the church's highest rituals.

Mathilda, on the other hand, always stayed steady, even when more children died. Even when one death hit her especially hard, that of a 16-month-old son who on his last day alive suffered 19 convulsions. Mathilda recovered, and preached the faith tirelessly to her children while working herself to death.

The family struggled during their first decade in the new land, bouncing around the Salt Lake Valley between ten different homes until 1905, when they finally built their own.

They also changed their name a final time. When the three Härlin girls first went to school in Utah, teachers told them that if they really wanted people to call them *Har-LEEN*, as in Swedish, rather than *Har-LIN*, as in American English, then they should add an *e* to the end of their name. And of course they should drop the foreign-looking *ä* in favor of plain old *a*.

Thus Carl Eriksson Björk Härlin became Carl Harline, and his wife and children were now Harline as well. And it explained why our friend at Ellis Island hadn't typed an *e*.

Mathilda Harline was not only a staunch believer, but just plain staunch. At age 47 she was thrown by a rampaging cow while protecting her children from it. She operated a loom and made carpets for sale, and sewed, cooked, washed, bottled, and gardened. And she bore a total of 13 children, eight of them in Utah. One son thought of her not only as his *best pal* but as the real Old Woman in a Shoe.

Carl farmed, as he had in Sweden, always having some hay to haul, and some pigs, chickens, cows, and a horse to tend. Though a quiet man, he was musical and liked to whistle, especially while he worked. Their youngest son, Leigh, born when Mathilda was 46, grew up to write a famous song about whistling while you work, when he was employed as a composer by Walt Disney in California. He also composed what became the Disney theme song, *When You Wish Upon a Star*, still sung by every Swede on Christmas Eve.

Carl and Mathilda's parents and relatives back in Sweden knew little about the successes and failures in America.

Carl had occasional contact with his family before he died in 1929. Mathilda sent and received occasional letters too, but these produced only a vague familiarity among the growing number of cousins.

Maybe the siblings and cousins heard about Mathilda's first stroke in 1915, which left her dragging one leg as she continued to work in the kitchen. Or her second stroke in 1921, which left her in a wheelchair, and for which she went thirty blocks to the temple every other day for a blessing, then afterward to a doctor for electric shock treatment and a massage of her numb limbs. Or at last the third stroke, which killed her, in 1922, at age 63, the same age at which her mother had died (a year after Mathilda left for Utah).

Most of Carl and Mathilda's nine children who lived to adulthood stayed in the Mormon Church, some rising to prominent positions or singing in the church's famed choir. But some, plus some of the grandchildren, were indifferent or dropped out altogether.

Carl and Mathilda's story moved me enough that I traveled to Sweden to see some of the sites and to meet some of the relatives.

Annika and her husband Bengt, who in the meantime had gone to the trouble of learning about my ancestors as well as their own, took me to see the stone ruins of the house where Mathilda was born and raised, the farm where Carl and Mathilda first met, and the stone ruins of the Härlin house near the forest—where Mathilda fasted and slaved, where baby Anna Maria was born just before the fateful trip to Utah, where Mathilda's mother begged her not to be Mormon, from where Carl and Mathilda set out for Utah, and from which I got my name.

They also put me in touch with numerous third and fourth cousins, most of them descendants of Mathilda's siblings. Any of the old resentments about the conversion to Mormonism or about leaving Sweden were by then forgotten, or perhaps not even really known, as we celebrated with a barbecue outside a typical Swedish barn painted red and white, and grew weary trying to figure out who was where on the ancestral chart.

But most relevant here is that Carl and Mathilda's story added depth to the Rolanduses' story. For Carl and Mathilda's story was also full of conversion—from Swedish to American, from Lutheran to Mormon, from Eriksson to Björk to Härlin to Harline. And it was full as well of ruptured relationships because of religion: I felt the sorrow not only of Carl and Mathilda in leaving home but of their parents in being left, because those parents were my family too, of course.

All this made the Rolanduses' loss of their son and brother, and Jacob's loss of his parents and sister, even more real, and personal.

# seven

 I said that I would leave the horse near the
border around midday.

A restless Jacob was anxious to move on.

He and Christian Vlierden breakfasted at the well-appointed table of their host, *Seigneur* (or Lord) Fildrack, and chatted politely with the ladies and young lord of the house. Though grateful for the hospitality, Jacob worried: it had long been daylight and he still had far to go across the flat landscape.

He at last asked Vlierden whether their host might be willing to send someone to show the fastest way to the closest town across the border. Fildrack was only too willing, and the guide rode with Jacob to the town called Hoogstraten, where they arrived sometime in the afternoon.

Vlierden continued riding south too, but on his own horse and ahead of Jacob—no doubt so he could claim that he hadn't helped (directly) with the escape. But even if he was blamed, Vlierden didn't mind: if it would remove blame from other Catholics in town, especially the clergy, then he was glad to be the scapegoat. Besides, he was off to war for who knew how long? People could say what they pleased.

While Vlierden rode on ahead, Jacob stopped in Hoogstraten to send his horse back to Boxtel.

He would rather have ridden the horse all the way to Antwerp, of course: he was still only halfway, and without the horse he was more vulnerable than before to pursuers, who would care little about the protection supposedly offered by an invisible and vague border. But Jacob had to return the horse, for the sake of the friend who had borrowed it—the young knocking nobleman, named Ravenskot. This young man had told the horse's owner that he needed it for a couple of days to conduct some business near the border; what he didn't tell the owner was that he planned to hand the reins to Jacob.

Making the situation even more delicate was that the owner, named Hugens, was the Reformed secretary of Boxtel's town council, and the best local friend of Timothy Rolandus. Hugens would be furious if he learned how his horse was actually used, and Ravenskot could be thrown in jail for his deceit. Jacob had to get the horse back when promised—which meant sending it now, and moving only slowly toward Antwerp, still beyond the horizon.

Jacob therefore instructed his guide to take the horse back to Fildrack's castle, where Christian Vlierden's trusty servant Faes (he of the injured but suddenly recovered foot) would come fetch it. Then, with some of the 25 florins in his purse, Jacob bought a seat on the next wagon to Antwerp, and put his trust in God.

If Jacob's fellow passengers were as ready to strike up conversation as those portrayed in the numerous printed dialogues of the time, then he would have had opportunity enough to explain just exactly how he came to be sitting there.

The ubiquitous canals and roads of the Low Countries were filled with boats and wagons on which crowded travelers, crammed cheek by jowl, eagerly sought out the views and news and stories of their companions. No doubt Jacob was reluctant to reveal much about himself, out of fear that he might leave clues for pursuers, and because he knew his fellow travelers' most assured prejudices against rebellious children.

He probably reflected quietly, or tried to sleep, or engaged merely in small talk, feeling the eyes of his fellow travelers upon him while he avoided theirs. They would have had a hard time imagining the spiritual struggle that had raged inside him for years now.

Jacob knew exactly when he had first begun to waver in the faith of his fathers.

It was long before he ever sniffed the incense of a Catholic Mass. In fact, it was six years before, when his father Timothy was ignominiously run out of town by his own Reformed flock (tiny though it was) and by his fellow Reformed preachers (brethren though they were). At least that's how Jacob remembered it.

The setting of this sorry scene was Ouderkerk, the small and picturesque village near Amsterdam where Timothy was first called as a preacher, in 1620, and where for nearly 28 years he served the community of some 40 Reformed believers. For most of those years, life was calm enough. There was always a little trouble from the inevitable assortment of local Catholics, who gathered illegally to worship, occasionally smeared the Reformed pulpit with feces, and once threatened Timothy with a formidable kitchen knife. But in Jacob's eyes the real trouble, and the end of the calm, came from Timothy's fellow Reformed.

Sometime in 1646, Timothy got into a big argument with several former members of the local church council, made up in the usual Reformed fashion of elders (who oversaw spiritual life) and deacons (who cared for the poor). According to the ex-councilors, the cause of the argument was that Timothy had borrowed money from the church's poor box without the council's permission, had arbitrarily removed the deacon who complained about it, and had treated the ex-deacon and his supporters with harshness unbecoming a preacher.

The ever-scrupulous Timothy, always sure of acting rightly, responded that he had indeed borrowed the money in question but had also paid it back with interest, had indeed suspended the deacon but only because of the man's irreverence and lies, and that he had in general acted justly toward all.

It was classic small-town church stuff. But that didn't diminish the seriousness of the matter for the parties involved, who were at each other's throats for the next two years.

Each side, certain it was right, sought the intervention of the classis of Amsterdam, to which Ouderkerk of course belonged. Timothy (and Jacob too) expected that body to take the side of their fellow preacher. Instead, the classis concluded that there was wrongdoing on both sides, and urged the parties to reconcile—which to Jacob was nothing short of betrayal.

When Timothy continued to insist to the classis that he had done nothing wrong, then took up more and more of the classis's precious time with his angry explanations and justifications, his brethren grew testy. Even the scribe abandoned the usually neutral and merely descriptive tone of scribes to note his disapproval of Dominee Rolandus's longwinded orations.

And when Timothy threatened to take his case to a higher jurisdiction if his brethren didn't support him, and when he claimed that they were treating him more as an enemy than as a brother—in fact much as the High Priest Caiphas had treated Christ—the classis decided that it had heard enough.

In the spring of 1648, it sent a delegation to Ouderkerk, with the task of interviewing all 40 members of the Reformed community on the general question of whether their preacher, Timothy Rolandus, was really fit for his task.

Timothy was humiliated. So were his wife and daughter and 15-year-old son. And there was more to come. When the delegates arrived, Timothy refused to acknowledge their authority or to tell them where each member of his flock lived, so that they might be interviewed; but the delegates imposed their will anyway by somehow arranging for young Jacob to go along and show them instead.

Did Timothy volunteer Jacob as a replacement for himself? Did the delegates suggest Jacob and Timothy reluctantly agree, thinking the boy a better alternative than some disgruntled member who might poison the delegates' minds further? However it happened, Jacob went along, and while the delegates walked or rode, he pointed out the homes of the Reformed. Then while the delegates went inside to discuss the suitability of his father, Jacob waited outside.

The boy would never forget this humiliation of his father, and himself, and his family.

After all the ruckus it caused, the delegation didn't even solve the impasse in Ouderkerk.

Instead the arguing dragged on for months after it left, and finally ended the old-fashioned way: with a transfer. One of Old Jacob's long-time preacher friends from Amsterdam, Jacob Triglandius, surely pained by the sight of his friend's son causing a spectacle each month in the classis, put his finger into his intricate web of connections and found far away from Ouderkerk, in the south of the Dutch Republic, a community that desperately needed a preacher. He convinced them to call Timothy, sight unseen and hearing unheard.

Everyone in the classis must have realized that this was not so much about a genuine calling as about simply getting Timothy out of Ouderkerk. But no one objected, not even the stubborn and principled Timothy. In early 1649, and despite sixty years of service by Rolandus men in the classis of Amsterdam, the Rolandus family, all with the bitter taste of exile in their mouths, set off to their strange new home.

Yes, Ouderkerk was certainly where young Jacob had started to waver.

The wagon to Antwerp with at least one weary traveler stopped for the night at a village along the way, where Jacob had his first sleep since the restless night before his departure.

Just as on that night, he didn't sleep long now, because another wagon to Antwerp was leaving at three in the morning and he wanted to be on it. At around eight, that wagon rolled into Antwerp, with Jacob aboard, and no pursuers in sight. He had reached his promised land.

# eight

[ I knew I had to try something else. ]

After settling down from the excitement of finding Carl and Mathilda, I was surprised to feel bubbling up from even deeper inside yet another story of conversion I knew.

How could any story be more meaningful than one involving your own grandparents?

Then I remembered that the Rolanduses' story had moved me even before I found Carl and Mathilda. Something else, someone else, had been working away inside me first, and it didn't take long to recognize that it was Michael Sunbloom.

Michael's story was harder to see than Carl and Mathilda's not only because it lay deeper but because it wasn't as obviously parallel to the Rolandus saga. Instead there were modern twists and turns that made it seem wildly different from any Reformation story. And it had a completely different ending besides.

But the more I thought about both stories, the more it seemed that in essentials they couldn't have been more alike.

In other words, Michael's story simply needed a little more converting than did Carl and Mathilda's.

• • •

In 1973, just before his twenty-third birthday, Michael Sunbloom broke his parents' Evangelical hearts by converting to the Mormon Church.*

It's another Mormon story, because that happens to be my heritage. But just about any religion will do here. Besides, Michael's was no ordinary conversion story. Sure, it started out as an old-fashioned familiar-looking Reformation-style family fight over religion, of which there are still plenty today, but it ended up as a new-fashioned fight instead.

I met Michael about a year after his conversion, in Valleytown, California, where we both lived. I had just graduated from high school, making me old enough to join the local group of Mormon Young Adults, a social organization for singles between 18 and 25.

Michael was the newly anointed president of that group, and he went out of his way to make me and other newcomers feel welcome. But things quickly went beyond duty between us, as we became close friends, despite the six-year difference in our ages. In fact he soon became the closest and most interesting friend I'd ever had.

He was of average height and weight, and wore his hair in the stereotypically long, sandy, parted-down-the-middle style of the 1970s (which also conveniently covered his sizeable ears). He was also typically well-tanned, which set off his bright and voluminous teeth. But what stood out about him were less visible things, including an easy laugh, an uncommonly clear manner of speaking (*it's called enunciation*, he once responded to someone who commented on it, as if enunciation were the most common thing in the world), and especially his ability to notice people.

Michael asked you a lot of questions about yourself, paid attention to the answers, and stored it all up—both to tease you and to point out your gifts, with unusual perceptiveness. Even when he teased (his preferred form of communication), you felt flattered that he had gone to so much trouble over you, and expressed his observations with such remarkable vocal dynamics. But the teasing was usually the prelude to the praise that followed, as he spoke in wonder about *incredible and unbelievably talented* people (including you) who to most others seemed perfectly ordinary.

---

* Michael Sunbloom is not his real name; neither are the names, and some of the places, in the rest of his story.

Maybe Michael did all this out of a sort of insecurity, because he wanted compliments in return. It was possible. But it felt like he was just a thoughtful person with an unusual ability to recognize gifts in people that most others didn't see. After I'd known him about thirty years, I was more convinced than ever of the latter.

I also learned during those first months of acquaintance that Michael was an accomplished cook, made more interesting conversation than any other friend I had, could organize and decorate and cater a dance better than most Young Adults had ever known, was an enthusiastic if somewhat clumsy tennis player (thanks to a chronic back problem that gave him a slight limp when he was tired), and most of all that he was a convert to Mormonism and the only Mormon in his family.

This last came out during a drive we made to the coast one weekend, from Valleytown in the central interior. Michael wanted to visit a Mormon missionary there who had previously been assigned to Valleytown and became close friends with Michael during that time. Would I like to go along? My parents, wary at first of my new and older friend, had been won over by this time and gave their approval.

We set out in his Porsche 914, a scaled-down version of a real Porsche, but still fine enough for him to call it his Celestial Chariot, an allusion to the Mormon notion of heaven. Along the way he told me about the missionary, named Elder Jones, which naturally brought up the subject of Michael's conversion to Mormonism. I asked him about it. When he finished telling his story, I asked whether anyone else in his family had converted with him. He said no, and then changed the subject.

It suddenly hit me that this was the first time Michael had ever mentioned his family around me, and that he, despite our friendship, had never bothered to introduce me to them (he already knew my family pretty well). I didn't even know whether he had siblings, or living parents, because he never talked about them. His silence seemed awfully incongruous for someone so tuned in to relationships.

I realized that when I thought about Michael he wasn't in a family, but alone, like an orphan, or a child who'd popped up from the cabbage patch, or, more fittingly, from some clam shell in the Botticelli paintings I would soon study in college.

Where was his Mom or Dad, and what were their religious sentiments?

The answers to these questions came only many years later, after I'd found Michael again.

His father, Michael Senior (who always went by Mike), was a sort of lapsed Lutheran. At least that's what Michael Junior thought. He wasn't sure, because Mike didn't have much religion growing up— unless drinking counted as a religion. Mike's father did that with great devotion. The Lutheran part only happened because his people had come from Sweden (in Swedish their name would have been Sundblöm) and, thanks to the Reformation, most Swedes were Lutheran.

Michael's mother, LuJean, whose people came most recently from Arkansas, was no more religious than Mike, unless hard work counted. Her work habits didn't give her much time for anything else, including church—although she did find time at age 16 to get pregnant. Not by Mike, but by some boy who soon disappeared. And pregnant not with Michael Junior, but with his half-brother David.

When LuJean's pregnancy started to show, her parents sent her to a home for unwed mothers, in San Francisco, where she stayed until David was born. When LuJean and David returned to Valleytown, they moved in with her parents.

Not long after that LuJean met Mike. He was 29, and she was 12 years younger, but LuJean fell for him anyway. A couple of years later, when she was 19, she was pregnant again, this time by Mike. And this time with Michael.

Maybe she named the baby after his father to encourage Mike to stick around more than the last guy had. If so, it worked. Sort of. Because Mike did sometimes come visit LuJean, even if at first he didn't pay a lot of attention to Michael or David. Then one day Mike found the Lord and decided that he should stick around for good, and marry LuJean, and be a father to both of the boys. Which was when LuJean started to find the Lord too.

When Michael thought about it later, he wasn't sure that his father really loved LuJean at that point, but he was sure that he believed in duty and loyalty (thanks to twenty bombing missions flown over Germany during World War II), and now God too. And that God would help him learn to love her.

So when Michael was three, Mike came to his in-laws' home and whisked LuJean and the children away to a new life. *Whisk* is probably an exaggeration, as it suggests a speed and elevation that weren't there. For a while, the new family simply moved in with Mike's mother, who had a little more room than LuJean's parents because Mike's over-drinking father was already gone (then died some years later, but no one bothered to mention it to Michael). Eventually Mike and LuJean bought a house of their own on the edge of town, in a place called Hillcrest Estates, a big name for a lot of modest houses on flat land.

Here in the new home, when Michael was five, was where the family started reading the Bible together every night, and where Mike and LuJean had the boys memorize selected verses: Michael was better at it than his brother and soon knew dozens, which caused some resentment, but otherwise they got along well.

Six years later, when I was five, my family moved to Hillcrest Estates too, just around the corner from the Sunblooms. We stayed only a year, and I don't remember seeing Michael, but I must have, because he was friends with the kid next door, Jesse Garcia, who liked to wrestle my big sister (she was a tomboy, but still a girl, which was the important thing). Sometimes he talked Michael into wrestling as well; that's why I know I saw Michael, even if I can't remember it.

Mike found his life's work as a gardener at the local college.

It made his skin hard, but for all his physical hardness he was a gentle man who rarely showed any anger. Hard-working LuJean kept working too, for a fancy millinery company out of Los Angeles called Hollywood Hats.

She and Mike found time for church as well, settling on a Pentecostal congregation. That church scared Michael, though, especially the speaking in tongues. So did the healing, which involved the preacher knocking someone on the forehead with the palm of his hand and the person then fainting, presumably healed.

Maybe Michael's fright was why Mike and LuJean changed churches, although more likely it was the scandal involving the organist and the preacher (who was forced to resign). Whatever the reason, the family switched to the big new All Folks Church at the other edge of Valleytown. It was still charismatic, but slightly more restrained than the last church, and a lot more people attended, thanks to the gifted preacher, Alvin Beeson, whom everyone just called AB.

Michael and his brother went to Sunday school and evening service every Sunday, plus Tuesday night Scouts, Wednesday Bible service, and Friday night lasagna. And of course the family kept reading the Bible together, even though it became harder to do every night as the boys' lives grew busier in junior high and high school.

Mike and LuJean hit their stride at All Folks, at least in regard to churchgoing. Because in another regard they eventually lost step altogether: namely, Mike resented LuJean's desire to work. She didn't have to for the family finances, and that she worked anyway hurt his sense of manliness.

Years of tension grew worse when LuJean started to travel a little for her job; Michael was almost done with high school by then and she saw nothing wrong with it. But that was it for Mike. He put his foot down: it was the job or him. LuJean chose the job, and to lessen the embarrassment of separation she transferred to a store in San Francisco, where she had spent some time while pregnant with David.

Mike stayed in Valleytown with the two grown boys, but he stopped attending All Folks, because he was embarrassed, too.

Michael Junior had just started college when the separation happened.

As in the past, school proved to be a sort of refuge for him. He'd always been good at it, the annoying kid in early grades who invariably sat in the front row and responded to every question from the teacher by madly flailing his hand about and yelling *I know! I know!*

But he was insecure in other ways, especially as he grew into his teens, and worried about being *dorky*, even fearing (thanks to his back) that he walked a little like Gumby. So he spent a lot of time reading, and became a bookworm. Still, he overcame a lot of his insecurity when he realized that people thought he was funny, and that they were easier to get along with when he pleased them, which came easy for him with peers or adults. His parents' friends long considered him to be *just the best little boy*, willingly washing glasses and helping with dinner when there was company.

As for church, Michael usually went along with his parents to All Folks. During high school, he'd actually wanted to stop going, but his parents told him he could make that choice only when he turned 18. Because he reached that birthday just as his parents were separating, he had two reasons to stop going.

After his mother left home, Michael noticed how much he missed her, and how helpless his father was around the house. Then suddenly, after two years away, LuJean came back. Mike was ecstatic, and became *more lovey-dovey than ever*, as Michael put it later—maybe even too much for Michael's tastes, who wasn't sure he bought it, and who always wondered whether his mother ever really loved his father after that time. But certainly his parents were determined to stay together.

To Mike's chagrin, the ever industrious LuJean went right back to work again. She had given up her job in San Francisco to come home, but that didn't mean she intended to give up working altogether. Mike must have realized by this time that she did it not just for the money, but to have a break from home, where she worked more for others than for herself.

Michael Junior felt chagrin as well about his mother's need to hold a job, but for different reasons than his father: her new job in Valleytown was at a nearby McDonald's, which mortified Michael. What would his friends think? But people loved her, he soon realized, especially at the counter, where she had a captivating smile and was a born entertainer. She had a way of making something pretty ordinary into something pretty great, even a burger joint.

Which went far toward explaining Michael, too.

Michael came out of his shell during college, and, though no longer attending All Folks, he became more interested than ever in religion.

In fact, his new interest was due largely to his increasingly active social life, as he started attending churches according to his girlfriend of the moment. Because he dated girls of several different persuasions (both Jewish and Christian), he learned more about religion than most teenagers do.

Sometimes church and social life were quite at odds, however, especially in the late 1960s and early '70s. His Catholic girlfriend, for instance, went so far as to take communion with Michael looking on from the audience, and then, quite against the expectations of her church or Michael, took him home afterward for sex.

He learned more orthodox traditions from his other girlfriends, and he came to like Episcopalian, Lutheran, and Catholic services best. In fact his positive impression of Catholic services was starkly different from the condemnations he'd heard at All Folks about *papists*, a sixteenth-century slur common in the Old Dutch Republic and the rest of Protestant Europe that was still being tossed about in such remote places as Valleytown, California.

Valleytown and the central valley had been the destination for many born-again Christians who fled the dust bowls in the 1930s, and their descendants still set the tone for religious life in the area. This was one reason Michael had always assumed it was okay to be prejudiced against Catholics. A second reason was that most Catholics around Valleytown were Mexicans, and just about everyone also assumed that it was okay to be prejudiced against them. Yet the Catholic services, and people, were more interesting and friendly than he'd expected, once he got to know them. Just as his friend Jesse Garcia was.

Still, he had to admit that he almost fainted every time the incense came out.

Within a couple of years, though, Michael left all the girlfriends, and all the churches.

For the last bit of college, his religion was partying. His roommate Ron was a big drinker and drug taker and ladies' man, and because Michael was a pleaser, and curious, he tried to keep up.

He didn't have Ron's stamina, though. At one too many parties, Michael passed out. The last time it happened, he was in someone's bathroom. Minutes after he fell to the floor, a girl came in to use the toilet, saw Michael lying there, and simply covered his face with a towel while she did her business. She ran into him again later that week at school and teasingly asked, *Remember me?* He didn't, and she told him what had happened, laughing all the while.

He tried to laugh back, but that was when he *knew it was bad* and he *had to try something else.*

# nine

Take thou thy lord's servants, and pursue after him,
lest he get him fenced cities, and escape us.
—2 *Samuel* 20:6

At about the same time that Jacob reached Antwerp on that early Tuesday morning of May 26, Timothy Rolandus was, just as Jacob feared, making plans to go after his son.

Various family members were, just as Timothy hoped, ready to go too: they would arrive shortly in Boxtel, or meet Timothy on the road. In the meantime, he had started asking questions around town to try and figure out just exactly where Jacob had gone, and just exactly who had enticed him to do so. As one of the prominent figures on the local scene, Timothy would have had little problem convincing the sheriff or a town councilor to help with his inquiries.

Leading a minor astray was at least as serious as stealing a horse. This explains why so many of Jacob's friends were willing to help behind the scenes with his escape, but not actually to be seen riding or walking with him—not the separate-traveling Vlierden, not the promised guide who dropped out at the last minute, not the hiding Ravenskot, not even the achy-footed Faes was eager to be spotted with Jacob on the road, day or night.

It wouldn't have taken Timothy long to learn that Christian Vlierden had headed south just hours before Jacob, and to suspect that there must have been a connection between the two events. It also wouldn't have taken long to learn that Vlierden's servant, Faes, was missing too (though not, as Timothy might have supposed, because he was following his master—rather, Faes was off fetching Jacob's horse).

Then suddenly, on that Tuesday, there was Faes again in Boxtel. Did someone see him with the horse before he could get it to its owner, Secretary Hugens? Did Timothy and, say, the sheriff corner Faes and make him talk?

Perhaps Timothy received intelligence as well from some local Catholic parent, who was worried about Jacob's example of rebellion against his father (even if it was in the name of true religion), and who therefore offered some tidbit of information, some fragment of a rumor someone had heard, about where Jacob was headed.

Whatever the order of events, however information was learned, Ravenskot was soon being arrested, and Timothy, convinced that Jacob was heading south, set out after him, with an entourage of perhaps half a dozen men. Among them was Secretary Hugens, still fuming about his horse.

No one could have blamed Timothy Rolandus if, while moving along the road, he entertained the wish that he had never brought his family to this strange new province called Brabant.

Of course after the debacle in Ouderkerk there had been little choice, but the situation in the family's new home was, unbelievably, even worse than in the old.

The biggest problem, and what made Brabant so strange, was that virtually everyone there was Catholic. No other part of the Dutch Republic could say that.

Timothy knew by heart how it had happened. The 17 provinces that made up the Netherlands (or Low Countries) had once been united under a common ruler, the king of Spain, and a common faith, Catholicism. But in 1566, some Netherlanders started rebelling against their king, and in some cases even against his religion: war was the result, and all unity crumbled.

During the 1580s, the seven northern provinces declared themselves independent from Spain, came to prefer the Reformed religion, and called themselves the United Provinces of the Netherlands, or more

The Low Countries, or *Nederlanden*, in 1648

simply the Dutch Republic. The ten southern provinces remained loyal to Spain, and to Catholicism, and were called the Spanish Netherlands.

But the struggle was far from over; in fact, it lasted another 60 years. During that time, families were split in two, by politics or religion or both, and then by distance, as massive migrations followed, much of it from south to north. Some provinces were also split in two, especially those that lay in the middle, such as Brabant, where much of the interminable fighting took place.

For most of the war, the Spanish Netherlands managed to hang on to sprawling, wealthy Brabant. But in 1629, the Dutch conquered a big northern chunk of the province, for good, along with some smaller holdings nearby.* Dutch rulers were elated, except for one thing: virtually all of their new subjects were Catholic.

Although it had been possible from the start of the Republic to be both Dutch and Catholic, most such people were spread around the land. In Brabant, however, Catholics were as dense as peat, and that made Dutch rulers worry. Could this many Catholics together in one place ever truly be loyal to their new state, especially when that state officially preferred the Reformed religion and outlawed Catholicism?

Perhaps to pacify Brabanders while the war raged on, rulers hinted that once the war was over, maybe an exception would be made in the new province and Catholic worship would be openly allowed. But when the war finally did end, in 1648, all such hints ceased.

Dutch rulers decided to treat Catholicism in Brabant just as it was treated elsewhere: as an outlawed religion. Monks were expelled from monasteries, priests and congregations were thrown out of churches, and churches were refurbished in Reformed style. Only one exceptional gesture was made toward the new province: the introduction of a small army of Reformed preachers and civic officials, whose task was to show locals the bright side of Reformed living, and to convert as many as possible to the true religion.

This was where Timothy Rolandus came into the picture.

Thanks to his troubles in Ouderkerk, and the intervention of Jacob Triglandius, Timothy was among the 56 dominees who wound up in Brabant shortly after the war's end. And oh how optimistic he and his

---

* The conquered territories together were called the Generality Lands, because they were run by the States General, the foremost centralized institution in the Republic. But Brabant was clearly the main prize.

new brethren all were! Surely the preachers' friendly manner and their message of irresistible truth would win over the Catholic populace, who surely remained in their false religion only because they had been blinded for so long by devious pastors and monks. And surely many of these pastors and monks would themselves convert, once they heard the truth.

And how heroic it must have felt, even to the bruised Timothy. After his ignoble departure from Ouderkerk, here was a chance to bring light to those in darkness, and to redeem himself. More mundanely, here was also opportunity at last for a reliable, improved income, which had always eluded him, yet which now was promised to every preacher who braved moving to Brabant.

It didn't take long to see how formidable the task would be. The new motley army of Reformed preachers in Brabant was too small, and pathetic, to win much ground. And the new Reformed communities in Brabant were tiny, even tinier than in Ouderkerk, and were all recently imported from elsewhere.

The Catholic communities, in contrast, were enormous, and angry that their precious churches had been confiscated for the sake of a handful of Reformed while Catholics had to worship nervously in cramped attics and barns, where smuggled-in priests illegally performed services while lookouts guarded the door. In revenge, local Catholics made life difficult for their new Reformed neighbors—interrupting church services, tying up church bells, ruining pulpits, filling in the locks on church doors with molten lead so that entirely new doors had to be made, and refusing to rent or sell housing to anyone who was Reformed.

The Rolandus family never did find a place to live in Timothy's first community in Brabant, called St. Michielsgestel. During Timothy's four years as preacher there, the Rolandus family actually lived some five miles away in Den Bosch, the chief city of Dutch Brabant and home of the newly erected Reformed classis for Brabant. The commute ate up a good chunk of Timothy's time (and perhaps his salary too) and made it difficult for him to know or enlarge his flock.

Then what disappointment when the promised salaries in Brabant turned out to be less reliable than supposed! And when the promised conversions never materialized! It's possible that no Catholic priests in the province ever became Reformed. And laypeople were nearly as stubborn: those very few who wanted to convert faced ostracism from local Catholics if they went through with it.

Within a couple of years after their arrival, the Reformed preachers of Brabant were all sighing from weariness and pleading with Dutch rulers to send more help or they might all just give up.

It never came. More preachers were not sent, despite the pleas. As promised, some of the preachers in Brabant did give up, and left. A few assigned to take their places from elsewhere never bothered to show up once they heard the discouraging stories.

And those who stayed—because they wanted to see it through, or had no prospects elsewhere—lowered their sights. They worried less about converting anyone, and settled for achieving a grudging coexistence with locals. Or they moved to some other town in Brabant where the Catholic population was a bit less aggressive, or the Reformed community a smidgen stronger, or living conditions a little better.

This last was what Timothy Rolandus finally found. After four years of no housing in St. Michielsgestel, Timothy perked up his ears when a position came open in 1653 in the nearby town of Boxtel—because Boxtel had a rectory for its preacher.

Other than that, it wasn't much different from the last place. In fact, in some ways it was worse. Timothy knew, for instance, that cantankerous Catholics in Boxtel had recently shot up the precious rectory, and narrowly missed hitting the last preacher as he sat working in his study. But at least there was a rectory, and a study, and a new office and kitchen too. Timothy hadn't known such things for years.

And so he put himself forward to his classis, in Den Bosch, for the post, and was granted it with little fuss. He moved his family there around July 1653.

He would come to regret it, for Boxtel was where real disaster happened. At least in St. Michielsgestel there had been no sign of dispute between Timothy and his flock. No sign of tension between him and the classis. And no sign of trouble with Young Jacob. But all that changed in Boxtel.

Moreover, the Catholics in Boxtel were highly aggressive, and even angrier than usual about the loss of their church—a surprisingly fine and large church for such a modest town, thanks to centuries of pilgrims leaving donations at the church's miracle-working altar.

Besides shooting up the rectory, and throwing rocks at its windows, Boxtel's Catholics had also recently put up armed resistance to civic authorities who came to shut down secret Masses. The locals didn't beat up those authorities until they were bloody and blue, or sew them in blankets, as believers in nearby Texel did. But they came close.

Catholics in Boxtel also made a point of frequenting the last openly Catholic institution left in town: the convent of Poor Clares. Unlike male convents in Brabant, which were simply closed after the war, female convents were allowed to continue until every sister had died out. Since that could take decades, believers took advantage while they could, and visited often, showing their defiance as well as their devotion.

Timothy did his best to get along with local Catholics. As the missionary guidelines for Brabant suggested, he was to learn their names, interact in friendliness, seek occasion for *affectionate conversation*, and use his Sunday afternoon sermons to preach on subjects meant especially for them. He also urged them to study the Reformed religion with open hearts and minds, for if they did so, he promised, then they would discover that only in this religion could they find the means to salvation.

But for all of his efforts, Timothy saw little fruit among Catholics. In the end he even came to despise many of them, for what they did to his son.


To compound his problems with Catholics in Boxtel, Timothy, just as in Ouderkerk, quickly had problems with some of the local Reformed as well.

In fact he blamed them for Jacob's ruin too—especially that scoundrel the schoolmaster. Any official Dutch schoolmaster, by definition Reformed, should have been the local preacher's closest ally. Yet within weeks, even days, of first arriving in Boxtel, Timothy had picked a fight with his, named Jan Gerard van Santen.

Part of the reason Timothy did so was due to his stubborn sense of rightness. But much of it was due as well to the difficulties of being a Reformed official in Brabant: namely, there was never enough income for any of them, and they tended to fight, even among themselves, for every penny they could get.

Timothy and the schoolmaster lived on adjoining lots, just north of the church. But they couldn't agree on the precise boundary between their lots, which appeared to be divided by a small barn and a plot of cultivable land. Timothy argued that both the barn and the plot were his, as his predecessor had used them. He had indeed, admitted the schoolmaster, but the predecessor had also paid a fee, because both actually lay on the schoolmaster's property. Timothy knew nothing of any such fee, and refused to pay it. He needed that barn and land.

But so did the schoolmaster, who received only part of his income from the state, and the rest from student tuition—and here in Brabant tuition was scarce, as few Catholic parents were willing to send their children to any official (Reformed) school. The schoolmaster was therefore just as willing as Timothy to fight for the property in dispute. He even enlisted in his cause the church custodian, who likewise was convinced that he had a beef against Timothy Rolandus.

With tiny audiences for the preacher, no students for the school-teacher, and little cleaning for the custodian, these men had a lot of time on their hands, and too often they spent it arguing with one another.

In August 1653, having barely introduced himself to the community, Timothy took his schoolmaster to court. By November the court reached its decision—in favor of the schoolmaster. Timothy was ordered to pay a fee to use the barn and garden, or hand them back.

Although Timothy was disappointed, he remained sure as ever that he was right. He also knew the notorious slowness of Dutch law, and that it might take months, even years, to see the verdict enforced. Thus he didn't pay a penny for using either barn or garden and decided simply to stay put until some officer showed up to remove or fine him.

Seeing Timothy's underhanded tactics, the schoolmaster decided to try some of his own—involving young Jacob Rolandus. Specifically, the schoolmaster began to attack Timothy's reputation by spreading unflattering tales about Jacob, who in the schoolmaster's eyes was just a little too friendly with local Catholics, more than a preacher's son ought to be.

One night in January 1654, someone placed a disturbing note on the door of the rectory. The note didn't survive, but reports said that it repeated rumors already circulating around town about Jacob. That he helped to sing Adoration, or the Sunday afternoon service, in the convent of Poor Clares. That he had asked the schoolmaster from a neighboring town to go along with him to this service. That he had told various *papists* in town he had no intention of becoming a preacher himself, as his father hoped. And more.

An infuriated Timothy immediately brought another lawsuit, this time for libel, against his rival the schoolmaster, whom he suspected of authoring the note. What really infuriated Timothy, in the end, was that the trouble-making schoolmaster turned out to be right. Not in the details, or the specific accusations, but in the essential truth: that something was stirring in the heart of Jacob Rolandus, and it was not, as his father had hoped, the Reformed religion.

In fact Timothy may have been the last to know.

No, Boxtel was at the moment not exactly a place that conjured up warm memories in the soul of Timothy Rolandus.

He hoped that he wasn't too late to catch his son.

He had to find Jacob before the boy did something foolish, such as enter a religious order, where his damnation would be assured. For some reason Timothy remembered that Jacob had once expressed admiration for the Capuchins; was that where he was headed? To the closest Capuchin convent? What a disaster that would be!

Why hadn't Jacob listened to him? Why had he ignored the counsel of Deuteronomy 13:6, which warned against being enticed away to *go and serve other gods, which thou has not known, thou, nor thy fathers?*

Timothy kept moving south.

# ten

[ The truth was refreshened from within me. ]

Michael stayed with his roommate through college, but he pulled himself together to get his usual good grades and a degree in elementary education.

The autumn after graduation, he started his first teaching job, at a school on the edge of sprawling Valleytown, where the heat waves rising from the pavement were a little less searing than those downtown.

He also cut back on parties—thanks to unhappy experience, his new job, and especially one of his old girlfriends, Joni, with whom he'd stayed friendly. She had recently joined a non-partying religion that Michael hadn't tried yet: Mormonism.

He had heard only some talk of Mormons while growing up, and at All Folks, but none of it was good. In his mind he simply assumed that Mormons were right down there with Catholics, if without as catchy a derogatory nickname as papist. But, said in the right tone, Mormon all by itself could be derogatory enough.

That Joni, a bright and open girl, liked the religion, and that various friends Michael met through her liked it too, surprised him, and made him curious. Around New Year of 1973, a few months into his first job as a sixth-grade teacher, Michael started looking closer.

Once again he was following a girl to church, and this girl for the second time.

Joni suggested that if Michael was serious about learning more then he ought to speak with the Mormon missionaries, who would tell him all he needed to know about the religion.

This was the usual way it went if you wanted to investigate Mormonism, as Mormons called it. Most Mormon missionaries by now were young men between 19 and 21, who ideally spent most of their two years as missionaries looking for and teaching investigators.

Michael had seen the missionaries, everyone had seen them, riding around on bikes, wearing white shirts and dark suits and nametags, and calling themselves Elder so and so. They weren't elderly, of course. It was just an ecclesiastical office they had borrowed, like other churches, from the New Testament. In fact most missionaries were young on purpose, because their difficult task required zeal, energy, enthusiasm, and a little naïveté.

Certainly youth had its disadvantages too. Such as naïveté, uninformed opinions, rigidity, and know-it-all-ism. But those disadvantages were much less pronounced in the missionaries who came to teach Michael—at least in one of them.

Missionaries always went in twos, for support and safety and to keep each other from straying, but they were hardly clones. Elder Garner, for instance, the senior of the two who visited Michael, was cosmopolitan, while his companion was rigid, and over the weeks and months of their meetings had to be pulled from the room more than once (by Elder Garner) to be told to ease up.

Michael prepared a long list of questions for each meeting, usually held at his apartment. The companion sometimes dismissed those questions, or took them as a sign of inhumility, but Elder Garner understood that they were reasonable, and searching. He also understood quickly that Michael responded to teasing, and Elder Garner was full of that.

It wasn't long before the ear jokes started, but Michael came right back with observations about Elder Garner's *gigantic* nostrils. And it escalated from there. They quickly became great friends.

Michael didn't get satisfactory responses from the missionaries to all of his questions.

In fact, he probably had more questions than any church could answer. But he heard enough, and had enough Mormon friends by now, to realize that many unflattering tales he had heard about the faith were spurious, or sensationalized, or if true troubled him less than he supposed they might.

Mormons didn't have horns on their heads (that one was easy, but it was amazing how long that rumor endured). They didn't practice polygamy any longer (not since around 1900), though some breakaway groups still did. They didn't, it was true, believe in the same sort of Trinity as most Christians (*three in one*); rather, they believed in a Trinity of three separate beings, and omitted the *one* in the traditional formula (Michael Servetus had been executed in Geneva 400 years earlier for omitting the *three*). But that particular doctrine had never mattered much to Michael, and the Mormons' kindly God-the-Father, circumscribed in a glorified body but still omniscient and omnipotent, appealed to him, because it seemed closer to the image he had of his own father.

It was also true, as Michael had heard, that Mormons would not ordain black men to their lay priesthood. All black people could belong to the church, but none could be part of its ministry. This was the hardest teaching of all for Michael, who by this time was known among his friends for his compassion toward any group that suffered prejudice; but because so many American churches were still segregated in practice, if not in theory, and because he liked so much else that he was learning about Mormonism, he put his negative judgment of the *Negro Policy* on hold for the time being.

More pleasing to Michael, and quite unexpected, was that many of the missionaries' teachings were not so drastically different from the Christianity he had learned growing up. Most fundamentally, Mormons too believed that salvation came through an atoning sacrifice by Jesus Christ, even if they disagreed with Protestants and Catholics (who also disagreed with each other) about the details.

Moreover, though Mormons were Restorationists (who claimed that Christ's original church had been lost through centuries of change, and required full restoration rather than merely a little fixing), they were not alone. Restorationist ideals, in one form or another, had roots that extended to the Middle Ages (such as among the English Lollards), the Reformation (elements of Calvin's theology, of Ulrich Zwingli's in Zurich, or of Puritanism and Anabaptism), and to various American churches (including the Disciples of Christ, Churches of Christ, Seventh-Day Adventists, or the sort of Pentecostalism that Michael grew up with).

Certainly these groups differed in their views of what needed restoring: Mormons included the *restoration* of some Old Testament practices not favored by others (most famously polygamy and temple rites). They also added the canonization of scripture besides the Bible (such as the *Book of Mormon*, which gave the church its nickname) and new appearances by heavenly beings (rather than just the biblical appearances). These beliefs, plus others, led many Christians to set Mormons at the edge of Christian respectability, or even beyond—to consider them as a cult rather than as Christians. But none of the beliefs troubled Michael: polygamy had been halted, the idea of the temple appealed to him, the additional scripture contained much that he already believed, and which Christian religion didn't claim supernatural events in its history? None of it really seemed strange to him.

In this Michael followed a common pattern of conversion detected by modern sociologists: namely, people tend to convert to what is mostly familiar. Not entirely familiar, of course, or there'd be no point in changing: rather, the familiarity makes potential converts comfortable enough to study further, and during that process they discover the new and different features that are appealing enough to provoke them to convert.

The two most provocative new features for Michael were not the high theological stuff about the Trinity or additional scripture or other such issues. Rather, they were ideas he had never heard before, and that struck him to the core when he did hear them.

One was the Mormon twist on eternal life, which took eternal to include not only endless life after death, but endless life before birth. For as long as he could remember, Michael had felt that he had always existed and always would. Upon hearing this idea, he thought: *Talk about the truth ringing clearly within your heart, or should I say refreshened from within me.*

Here was a sense of conversion beyond those commonly understood: not merely *turning around*, as suggested by the Latin root *convertere*; not merely undergoing a change, as in conversion's usual sense of changing from one thing to another; not merely a conversion table, as in finding an equivalent form; but rather conversion as discovering what you have always been, or believed.

It wasn't a new phenomenon. The classical thinker Plotinus thought of conversion as *a return to origins*. And the Amsterdam preacher Jacob Triglandius, Old Jacob Rolandus's friend, grew up Catholic but upon reading Reformed theology for the first time immediately felt at home: as he put it, he had *already been reformed, before I knew the doctrine of the Reformers.*

The second provocative idea for Michael was the belief that family bonds could continue after death. Popular Christian culture often held the same belief, though various churches Michael had attended taught officially that family bonds would dissolve at death. He liked the Mormon teaching, for despite his own family's hiccups, Michael had always felt close to them, and he liked the idea of continuing together.

Though the familiar and new ideas mattered to Michael, in the end what moved him most of all were the people he had already begun meeting in the new faith. Here he followed another fairly common pattern of conversion: namely, relationships come before doctrine. You start by meeting some friends in the new religion. You like those friends, and become interested in their beliefs. You then study those beliefs, and if you like them too (and you may be predisposed to like them, given your new friends), your connection to those friends becomes so strong that you want to join them.

How long that connection remained, of course, and on what conditions, were other matters, as Michael would learn. But at least in the early stages of conversion, including his, the promise of new relationships was crucial.

To the missionaries, Michael was ready to convert. In fact while many missionaries spoke of their most promising investigators as *golden*, Elder Garner and his companion wrote melodramatically, in their weekly report to superiors, that Michael was *platinum*.

Whatever precious metal he was, Michael did indeed want to convert. Only one thing made him hesitate, even briefly, and that was another relationship he cared about: that with his parents. What would they think?

# eleven

 The provost of the Jesuits gave me hope that
he might help me, if possible.

Jacob probably came into Antwerp through its easternmost gate, for just inside that gate he took a room at an inn called the Little Mill.

Although awake for most of the past two nights, he was still too wound up to rest. After setting down his bag in a safe place, he decided to start immediately on the crucial business of finding new friends.

Armed with names and addresses given him by friends in Boxtel, he asked his hostess for a couple of directions, then set out into the large and impersonal city.

For most of the sixteenth century, Antwerp was the economic heart of all the Netherlands, as ships from every part of Europe made their way to the city's expansive and welcoming harbor on the Schelde River.

Then the war with Spain ruined everything. Before the war began in 1566, some 100,000 people lived in the half-moon shaped city. By 1589 that number was down to 42,000, thanks mostly to emigration. (Between 1585 and 1625 more than 100,000 people emigrated from southern to northern Netherlands, and many of them came from Antwerp.)

By the time of Jacob's arrival in 1654, Antwerp had recovered something of its old sheen. But most important to Jacob it was, despite past vacillations, decidedly Catholic, symbolized by the gigantic statue of

Our Lady at the center of the town hall—a statue that never would have been allowed by Protestants.

In fact Antwerp was a favorite destination for tens of thousands of church-deprived Dutch Catholics, especially those from Dutch Brabant, just across the border. Prevented from worshiping openly in their own land, many journeyed here when they could to engage in the beloved rituals of their religion without having to look over their shoulders. On some feast days, some observers claimed that the small boats of Dutch Catholics covered the Schelde so densely that it looked more like a forest than a river.

Jacob hoped to find a sympathetic reception here too, of a more lasting sort.

His first call was at the Franciscan convent, or *friary*, where the deposed Catholic pastor of Boxtel had promised to send a letter of introduction to the superior, telling him to look out for a young Dutch refugee.

But when Jacob knocked at the friary's door, the superior responded that he had received no such letter. He might have heard something about a refugee from a colleague in another friary, but he recalled nothing more.

Jacob tried next at the Jesuit house, to which a Jesuit he knew in Den Bosch had promised to send a similar letter. Here the reception was warmer but still cautious. The person who answered the door knew nothing about any refugee, but a second Jesuit suggested that Jacob speak with the *provost*, or head of the house (Jacob always called him by the Latin term *praepositus*), who came out to walk with him in the garden while Jacob told his story. The provost gave Jacob the impression that he might be willing to offer some help, if possible—a wonderfully vague offer.

Finally Jacob called at the hospital, because the former pastor of Boxtel had promised to write here too. Happily, the pastor of the hospital had indeed received a letter, plus 25 more florins for Jacob. But he had no time to talk and asked Jacob to come back the next day.

That was enough for Jacob's first day in the city. He went back to the Little Mill to rest, at last. There was still no sign of his father.

Early on Jacob's second morning in Antwerp, a Wednesday, Christian Vlierden came by the Little Mill to say farewell, before heading farther south to war.

Did Jacob realize that this was the last time he would ever see his best friend? If he did, there was no time to mourn, for he badly needed new friends here in Antwerp if he hoped to stay for good. His dwindling florins would keep him only so long.

Thus Jacob spent his second day much as he did his first: in search of new friends. His experience today was much the same, too: some people were warm, some were cool, and they were most likely to be friendly if a letter of introduction preceded or accompanied him. Unlike in villages and small towns, most people in cities didn't know each other, and some were only too ready to take advantage of the unsuspecting. Consequently, many people were inclined to be a little wary of a new face; a letter from a trusted source helped to dispel that wariness.

A *Mevrouw* (or Madam) Verbeek, reassured by a letter Jacob handed her, promised to put in a good word for Jacob with the local Jesuits, whom she knew well. She also introduced him to an exiled Dutch canon (a distinguished priest attached to a particular church) named Johan van den Bosch, a kindly, pious man who had many contacts of his own now in Antwerp and who promised to share them with Jacob, though he hardly knew the boy. The canon even went along on some of Jacob's visits, to lend credibility to the new arrival. Friendly as well was yet another contact of the deposed pastor of Boxtel: the pastor's own brother, who was a pastor himself, near Antwerp, and who invited Jacob to dinner that very night.

Such encouraging receptions were what Jacob had in mind when he fled from his home. Surely he had been warned in advance that not every Catholic in Antwerp would be thrilled to see him—that's why he needed specific contacts. But had he really believed it? How could his new fellow believers not embrace him after the sacrifice he had made for the faith? That his appearance at someone's door might provoke suspicion, rather than sympathy, was probably still hard for the young refugee to swallow.

Such was the plight of the convert, to whatever faith.

Although the Reformation was 130 years old by then, and conversion a common enough occurrence, it was always unsettling—and not only to the convert, whose heart was battered in the process, but especially to everyone around, in the old faith or the new.

Those left behind in the convert's previous faith wouldn't even call what happened a conversion, preferring instead such unflattering labels as *apostasy* or *leaving the road of the ancestors*—as if the point of one's existence was simply to do as ancestors had done (at least the ancestors who were favored).

Those in the convert's new faith, though delighted that an other-believer had come to the right side, and though trumpeting the news in pamphlets and sermons, sometimes seemed more interested in the propaganda value of the convert than in the convert personally, more in congratulating themselves for belonging to the irresistibly true church than in welcoming the new believer. For even while noising abroad the good tidings of conversion, old believers kept watching the convert with a wary eye.

People on all sides understood that, as Saint Augustine himself had pointed out, half of conversion was always aversion, and most people were uneasy with the aversion part. Even the famous convert Saint Paul was held in suspicion by his new faith community (Christian disciples didn't believe his story at first) and in contempt by his old (from whom he had to make a daring escape).

The Reformation too, for all of its occasional radicalness, was at heart yet another great age against change, of any sort—in government, society, church, or the family. Reformers on all sides (Luther included) bent over backward to claim that they weren't really changing anything, but merely returning to origins. And parents of all faiths condemned minors who converted against a parent's wishes, because such children threatened a vital link in the great chain of authority that gave order to heaven and earth: kings over subjects, lords over peasants, magistrates over burghers, and parents over children. Children who converted on their own either literally or figuratively left their family too.

This helps to explain why one scholar later wrote that the two greatest taboos during the Reformation were converting to another religion and marrying someone of another religion. This was why most people then (and later) stayed put in the faith of their parents, even in a town such as German Augsburg, where Lutheranism and Catholicism were both perfectly legal and thus conversion was legal as well. This was why in Reformed Geneva inheritance could be conditional on remaining Reformed. And this was why in France, which had no such inheritance law, parents still found a host of clever ways to ensure that heirs continued in the faith of the father and mother or they would not be heirs at all.

Conversion was a pain for families as well as for the convert.

Prejudice against converts was also due to the old Christian sentiment that real conversion took time.

If every convert was potentially unstable, the recent convert was especially so. Who could tell how deeply rooted new converts were? How steadfast could an underage convert be, since he had left his parents and the religion of his birth? Could a convert be trusted, after breaking one taboo, not to break another? That could be known, again, only after many years.

In seventeenth-century minds, true conversion didn't follow the sudden model of the apostle Paul, struck on the road to Damascus. Instead it followed the gradual model of Saint Augustine's *spiritual discernment*, or the slow *spiritual stages* of Saint Benedict.

On the Protestant side, Luther did have a dramatic spiritual experience in a monastery tower, but only after years of struggle beforehand. Calvin spoke simply of his own *gradual enlightening*. And classis after classis in the Dutch Republic rejoiced at the conversion of monks and priests to the Reformed Church but also warned everyone to beware the tricks and instability of such fellows, who *often* and rapidly went back to their former religion.

Catholics such as the famous Cardinal Borromeo of Milan instituted special *catechumen houses* to aid those converts from Protestantism whose families had abandoned them and left them destitute. But charity wasn't his only motive: he also wanted to provide a long period of probation and acclimation to ensure the retention of the new convert.

That some converts in every faith did return to their original church only reinforced prejudices against them. Up to 20 percent of converts in religiously mixed Augsburg, for instance, found it too hard to shake their birth religion and thus returned to it.

The practice of most people was therefore to wait and see about converts—and then wait and see some more.

In fact, Jacob would have to prove his reliability over and over again, in Antwerp, and for the rest of his life.

Part of how he was received depended, of course, on the people he met, some of whom were by nature more accepting than others, such as the saintly Canon van den Bosch. But much of it depended on Jacob himself, through demonstrating the earnestness of his conviction, which took time, but also through telling the story of his conversion and escape, which gave a clue to the depth of his conviction.

The genre of the conversion story appeared during any great age of conversion. Every story contained some element of the original Latin *convertere* (again, to turn around, or to turn in some other direction), but the specific meaning of the term might change according to time. In the ancient and medieval world, conversion meant turning from paganism to Christianity. In the Christian middle ages, when there was little changing of religions, it mostly meant turning from the world to a deeper life in Christ, usually by entering a monastery. In philosophical or scientific circles, conversion meant the radical transformation of an inferior substance to a purer substance. But in the age of Reformation it especially meant turning from one church to another—and the new printing press made it possible for not only the most famous converts but even the most obscure to publish their stories to the world.

Jacob had a good story, and he surely told it often during those first days and weeks and months, in full or abbreviated form according to the occasion and the interest of the listener, in order to help establish his Catholic bona fides.

# twelve

[ My parents did NOT want to hear about it. ]

When he first began studying Mormonism, Michael imagined that the things he was learning about the religion would interest his parents as well.

Since the All Folks days, they had remained firm believers but still hadn't found a permanent church. When Michael learned about such ideas in Mormonism as lasting family ties, he eagerly shared them with Mike and LuJean, thinking that maybe this idea, maybe this religion, might be the solution to their search.

But his parents weren't interested at all. In fact they were dumbfounded that Michael was studying Mormonism seriously. Surely their gifted son was too intelligent to be duped by this cult, which surely drew its steady flow of converts only from among the gullible.

Michael was stunned. How could his parents make such a judgment when they hadn't looked into the subject closely, hadn't consulted any sympathetic sources, hadn't gotten to know any Mormons personally? Instead they had merely heard rumors about polygamy and accepted the label of *cult* (and everything it implied) slapped upon the faith by others.

Michael was stunned again when he also tried telling his parents about such Mormon ideals as abstinence from alcohol and drugs and tobacco and nonmarital sex—because he imagined they would be pleased that he was giving them all up, after his years of partying. But again they wanted nothing to do with Mormons, even the parts they might agree with.

Especially Mike seemed unable to bear seeing Michael so happy in something that Mike thought was so wrong. This wasn't how he'd envisioned life going for his talented son. Mike had found the Lord and was sure that Michael, despite his recent spiritual wanderings, would find the Lord too. But you couldn't find the Lord through a cult such as Mormonism, Mike was sure of that.

Though hurt by his parents' reaction, Michael persisted with Mormonism anyway, and to their dismay he decided in March 1973, some three months after beginning his study, formally to convert.

As with all converts, surely other factors besides pure religious zeal were operating on Michael, such as his stage of life. As a 1979 study of conversion put it: *The transition to young adulthood is particularly marked by a call to ideological commitments and conversion-related orientations.* But whether a conversion was mostly the product of zeal or the Holy Spirit or the need for independence from parents, young adulthood was indeed the peak period for joining (and quitting) just about any religion, at just about any time in Western history.

Almost 23, Michael Sunbloom was no longer a minor, so he faced no legal obstacle to his decision. The opposition of his parents was a personal obstacle only; still, he cared deeply about it, and hoped that with time they would eventually drop their antagonism. Maybe they would eventually even join him when they saw his happiness. So he went ahead.

To declare his conversion, Michael would have to be baptized again. Mormons didn't recognize the validity of baptisms performed by other churches (most other churches returned the favor and rarely recognized Mormon baptisms either). And the Mormon baptism was, again, of the fully-under-the-water sort, rather than the common Christian method of sprinkling. Baptismal fonts (essentially big bath-tubs) were set up in Mormon churches just for this ritual, and were located at the end of a large room where friends and family could come watch the big event.

But Michael knew that his family wouldn't be there watching. Elder Garner, who was to perform the baptism, knew this as well, and that it hurt Michael, even though many new friends would indeed be in attendance. To lighten the mood, and to help make the day a happy one, the Elder came prepared.

Dressed in the usual white pants and shirt worn by males during the ritual, Elder Garner descended the three or four steps that led into the font, and made a quick motion toward his face. In water up to his waist, he turned to face Michael, also in white, who was descending next. On his way down the steps, Michael raised his eyes briefly at Elder Garner, then nearly fell into the font trying to suppress his laughter.

The Elder had stuck two whole cherries in his already prominent nostrils, to accentuate them. At their angle, the audience of 30 or 40 people, sitting quietly and somberly according to custom, could not see exactly what was happening, and just before performing the ceremony Elder Garner discreetly removed them. He explained afterward that he had done it out of Christian charity: he didn't want Michael to feel alone in his self-consciousness about his ears, which, though normally hidden by his poofy hair, were bound to shock everyone when he came up out of the water soaking wet.

It was just the touch Michael needed that day.

Yet it still wasn't enough to remove the sting of his parents' absence, or their opposition.

Since Michael no longer lived at home, his parents couldn't exactly throw him out. They probably wouldn't have anyway. But they didn't want to hear a word about what Michael most liked to discuss: his new religion and friends.

Michael visited home still, if a little less frequently, because the Mormon issue, even if not discussed, loomed silently over everything.

Once while at home, Michael got a call from a cousin who had heard about the conversion. He took the call in the kitchen, where the phone hung on the wall, and where Mike Senior and LuJean happened to be eating. When the cousin started asking about Mormonism, and what in the world had moved Michael to convert, Michael hesitated, stepped as far into the hallway as he could (the old phone cords stretched only so far), and took the risk of answering.

Big mistake. The enthusiastic chatter grew too much for Mike. This never violent man suddenly picked up the large tub of cottage cheese next to his plate and flung it angrily at the phone, splattering curds everywhere and putting an end to the conversation of the astonished Michael, who stuck his head back around to examine the damage.

It wasn't quite as dramatic as the distraught father of the ancient convert Perpetua, who threw himself upon her *as if he would tear my eyes out* to persuade her to quit her new Christian faith and thus avoid the martyrdom that awaited her. Still, Michael had never seen his father so angry, about anything.

He made sure never to bring up Mormonism again around his parents, or to bring his Mormon friends around, who would surely be treated coldly.

Some of Michael's old friends were dealing with the conversion no better than his father.

Upon hearing the news, roommate Ron promptly threw Michael out. In fact he wouldn't talk to Michael for ten years afterward, and only then because Ron's sister became Mormon too.

Other friends were less dramatic, and simply disappeared.

At work, where Michael was still a rookie teacher, a few of his colleagues soured on him. He soon realized that when he started gushing in the teachers' lounge about some upcoming church activity, a few teachers would leave the room—especially two of them.

Once, after Michael returned from a weekend conference with other Mormon young adults, one of those two, a male math teacher, crudely asked, *Did you f—— those Mormon women?* The other, a female, later apologized for the rudeness of her friend, but not on his behalf. And both stayed unfriendly toward Michael.

Such hostility toward his new faith always baffled Michael, even many years later, after he had left it. But maybe the hostility, from whatever source, shouldn't have surprised him.

He believed that he was following Jesus, and Jesus had warned in Matthew and again in Luke that this might mean upsetting people close to you. *Suppose ye that I am come to give peace on earth? I tell you, Nay; but rather division.* Father against son, son against father, mother against daughter, and so on, said the texts. You even have to *hate* them to follow Jesus, they continued.

But the sting of division and loss was eased by Jesus's subsequent promise: *Every one that hath forsaken houses, or brethren, or sisters, or father, or mother, or wife, or children, or lands, for my name's sake, shall receive an hundredfold.* There would surely be new friends (he'd already made some), and new family too—a new sort of family defined by Jesus himself: *Whosoever shall do the will of my Father which is in Heaven, the same is my brother, and sister, and mother.*

This didn't mean Michael wanted to give up his parents, not at all; in fact, his Mormonism had only intensified his desire for a close relationship with them. But this verse did mean that he could deal with their hostility, and that of old friends, by recalling the promise of the hundredfold. In other words, new relationships didn't merely help pull him to the new religion (as occurred with many converts), but also gave him the courage to go through with conversion when old relationships objected (as occurred with plenty of converts).

He wasn't going from some relationships to none, but from some relationships to even more. He had far to go to reach that hundredfold, but he had made a start, and he also held out hope that his parents would one day at least see how much his faith had helped him.

If Michael had to stay silent at home about his new religion, around his new friends he could talk about it as often and as enthusiastically as he wanted. He even told them that he felt not only that he had always existed, but that he had always been Mormon: it had simply taken him 23 years to realize it.

# thirteen

 Father saw that I was beginning to become Catholic.

The full version of Jacob's conversion story, which he adapted according to occasion, went like this.

After his early troubles with the Reformed in Ouderkerk, in 1648, Jacob turned away from the church for good when the family moved to Boxtel, in 1653.

Ironically, he hadn't even wanted to go along on the move. At 20 years of age, he was eager to be off on his own—perhaps in Amsterdam or Leiden—to study. The last thing he wanted to do was continue studying with his father, as he had already done for years. But Timothy said that it would be for just a while longer, so Jacob reluctantly complied.

Thank God that he did, he realized later, for it was in Boxtel that he found the truth.

It all started here, as it did for so many converts, with his friends. As long as his father *kept* him in Boxtel, Jacob's new friends would necessarily be Catholic, for there were no Reformed believers his age. Jacob had probably never known any Catholic well before—not during his 16 years in Ouderkerk, where Catholics constituted a minority, and not even during the last four years when the family lived in overwhelmingly Catholic Den Bosch: because that city was the center of Reformed operations in Brabant, it offered some socialization within the faith.

Boxtel, like every other small town in Brabant, offered almost none, at least for someone Jacob's age. The preachers sent into these Catholic wilds knew this in advance, of course, but they girded up their loins and took their families along anyway. How were they to persuade Catholics to true religion if they didn't go among them? It would not even be surprising if Jacob first met his new friends in Boxtel through his father, who was trying to build good relations with local Catholics.

Within months of arriving in town, Jacob found three especially close friends, all from the noble Vlierden family: the son Christian (about Jacob's age), and two daughters, Anna Margarita and Magdalena.

Christian still lived at home, at a castle in town. The daughters, along with some 20 other religious women, lived in the town's convent. Jacob visited with all three of the siblings there, and, because the Vlierden sisters were beguines (women who lived a pious life but who had more freedom than nuns to move outside convent walls), he could meet them elsewhere as well.

Yet the Vlierdens, claimed Jacob, never tried to convert him. In fact they refused to speak with him at all about their religion, out of respect for his father, or out of plain fear: as Catholics, they could be punished or fined for proselytizing. And the sisters, as part of the Catholic religious establishment, could lose the pensions they were granted by the religious settlement of 1648—for those pensions were conditional on good behavior, which surely did not include enticing the minor son of the local preacher to convert. Even when he asked the Vlierden sisters simple questions about conventual life, Jacob said, they were reluctant to answer.

There was one matter of religion on which at least Christian Vlierden felt free to speak: the scandalous lies told by the Reformed about Catholics.

Jacob was soon convinced not only that the Reformed were telling lies but that Reformed preachers were the chief liars, including here in Brabant. Despite all the lovely sounds the preachers made about getting along with their new neighbors, and despite the general practice of religious toleration in the Dutch Republic, where Catholics and Reformed and Mennonites and Jews learned to live in relative peace, the Reformed preachers (in Jacob's opinion) clung all too fiercely to long-cherished but false notions about Catholics and then flung them about as if they were gospel truth.

Like many Reformed children, Jacob accumulated these notions from his earliest years. And like many Reformed adults, he had simply assumed that they were true. What sorts of notions? That most atrocities during the recent Netherlandish wars, for instance, had been committed by Catholics. That the pope would *rather have his priests keep whores than marry*. That the pope told his *whore-chasers* they could earn salvation simply by performing enough Masses. And that the pope insisted that all emperors and kings stand beneath him, *kiss his feet and ass, and carry his shit pot*.

These particular claims were found not only in libelous news rags and irresponsible gossip but in a highly respectable source: the back pages of the original handwritten Bible translation done by Old Jacob Rolandus.

There in an educated script, right after the gospel of John, was a ribald dialogue between the pope and Christ, with the pope saying the most astonishing things. It was very possibly written there by one of Jacob's uncles or cousins, for several of them became preachers and one of them surely inherited that precious Bible. Other learned Reformed preachers said similar things about Catholics during meetings of the synod and classis. And so did Jacob's intelligent sister Maria.

Jacob knew that Catholics believed equally preposterous stories about the Reformed. A favorite one said that Calvin had been sent to prison for sodomy, another that Luther was conceived when his mother had intercourse with the devil—a most unimmaculate conception—and a third that the Reformed held the Lord's Supper at night so as to conceal their orgies.

But Jacob came to believe that Dutch Catholics were burdened with *ten times more lies* than the Reformed, lies designed to portray Catholics in the *most abominable light*.

The two times that Reformed preachers told *hurtful and abominable lies* about his father only confirmed Jacob's suspicions about the willingness of the dominees to speak falsely.

The first time was of course in Ouderkerk, when the classis of Amsterdam accepted and repeated the lies of Timothy's enemies. The second time was in Boxtel, when Timothy's new classis, in Den Bosch, did exactly the same thing.

When Timothy brought his lawsuit for libel against the schoolmaster, in early 1654, the classis squirmed. No classis wanted the leading Reformed lights in any town clashing in public, especially not in Brabant, where amused Catholics could have a good laugh at the spectacle. Couldn't Timothy settle things in private, asked the classis? But of course the preacher, sure as ever that he was right and unwilling to compromise, would not.

And so the classis started to meddle. In April 1654 it summoned the schoolmaster to tell his side of the story. The man appeared as requested, and insisted that Timothy's accusations against him were false, while his own accusations against Timothy were true—including those regarding the Catholic leanings of young Jacob.

Timothy missed this meeting, surely on purpose, for he could guess what was coming, and he didn't want to be within earshot when the schoolmaster told his lies. The official excuse he gave for his absence was that he had injured his shin, and he even sent Jacob to Den Bosch to tell the classis so. But the classis was impressed enough by the schoolmaster's story that it ordered Timothy to appear and respond anyway, within five days, bad shin or not.

Timothy complied. No one recorded the details of his meeting, but Jacob at least wrote down his opinion of it: once again the classis believed the *godless and the lying* more than it believed one of its own, and acted as if Timothy was to blame for the entire mess in his community.

Why Timothy would continue to support such a faith was beyond Jacob, but he himself had seen enough. Although even his mother and sister also had some unkind words to say about the classis at this time, at least in private, it was Jacob who took the conflict most to heart. His father's treatment in 1648 and again in 1654, plus the pull of Jacob's new friends, all caused the young man to open his mind to the possibility of studying another religion—which in Boxtel could only mean Catholicism.

●　●　●

There was one more reason Jacob decided to study the Catholic faith: Timothy's frequent exhortation to local Catholics to consider that their own religion might be wrong and another right.

Jacob took that suggestion to heart, but the other way around from what his father had intended: maybe his own Reformed religion was wrong.

Since his friends wouldn't tell him about their faith, Jacob asked them at least for something to read—something from the Catholic point of view, for he knew the Reformed point of view only too well. The choices were legion by this time, as thousands of religious works had been published in the 130-some years since Martin Luther had nailed up his 95 theses. Almost all of these works were combative, meant to pick a fight with rival religions rather than merely to explain their own. Typical Catholic titles included *Calvin Beaten Down*, *Dispute of Martin Luther with the Devil*, *Midday Sun for the Deep Darkness of the Reformed Church*, and *A Catholic Shield Against Heresies*.

The tract Jacob's friend Christian Vlierden brought to him was titled *The Light on the Candlestick*, written by a layman from the Spanish Netherlands who called himself simply *the Flemish Peasant*. In fact the author, named Arnout van Geluwe, really was a socially undistinguished Fleming, which was the point of his prolific output: if he, a mere peasant, could so easily and clearly and often demonstrate the superiority of Catholicism on every imaginable point, then it only reinforced the truth of that faith.

Although no simpleton, Jacob was indeed a beginner in the religion of his friends, and the down-to-earth style of the Flemish Peasant served him well as a starter. So did the fact that the Flemish Peasant had once been Reformed himself, and therefore knew right where to strike.

The tract's basic question was this: which current church, Catholic or Reformed, best matched the original Christian Church? In some 60 pages, full of quotes from ancient Christian authorities, the Flemish Peasant willingly provided the answer. The *Reformed* religion was just another name for a long line of recycled heresies that had been condemned more than once over the centuries, while the Catholic Church was Jesus's original.

This answer, and the evidence for it, stunned Jacob. Although his initial purpose had been informational, he was now moved to take a closer look at Catholicism, especially the numerous ancient authorities cited by the Flemish Peasant, for everyone, Catholic or Protestant, could agree that the church was *pure* during its first 500 years, and the words of these ancients, *the Church Fathers*, were therefore crucial.

Fortunately for Jacob, almost all of the authors he needed were available right on the shelves of his father's *very large and costly* library in Boxtel. No doubt to the surprise of his family, who knew Jacob's recent indifference toward his studies, he began lugging books from that library up to his own room. And what a harvest he found! There, just as the Flemish Peasant promised, were statements supporting the need for miracles and vows and saints and other favorite Catholic practices long criticized by the Reformed.

If Timothy was pleased at first about Jacob's sudden studiousness, he began to worry when he sensed what lay behind it: the Church Fathers were a favorite source for any Christian beginning to doubt his or her particular brand of the faith, so rich and varied were their writings. Timothy therefore forbade his son from taking any books from the library—especially those by the Church Fathers—when he, Timothy, was not present.

Fearing that Jacob was *beginning to become Catholic*, Timothy also began to go on walks with his son, now *talking sweetly*, now threatening, trying to undo the damage caused by Jacob's friends or Timothy's own library, and trying to keep Jacob away from that blasted Vlierden.

Timothy's vigilance could extend only so far, however, and while he was busy stopping up one hole in the dike he inevitably missed others.

Restricted in the library, Jacob started seeking out live Catholic teachers. Plenty of priests still lived in Brabant, including around Boxtel, despite the official ban on their faith. Some were there legally, because they had been in office at the time of the Treaty of 1648 and were therefore allowed to stay as long as they, again, caused no trouble. But many were there illegally, often from outside the province, and these tended to be even more active than their lawful counterparts in secretly serving sacraments and preaching, or privately talking to such searching souls as Jacob Rolandus.

Local Catholics knew where to find the underground priests, and Jacob simply had to ask the Vlierdens or one of the many new friends he had met through them. On Easter Sunday, April 5, Jacob learned that a priest was hiding at the moment in the castle of the nobleman Ravenskot. Jacob immediately sent a note asking whether the priest might have any time this coming Tuesday to offer instruction in a few foundations of the faith.

The priest agreed, and on the appointed day Jacob rode to the castle, near the tiny village of New Halder, with his friend Anna Margarita van Vlierden, as if to pay a social visit. On the way home from that meeting, Jacob and Anna Margarita ran into the other Vlierden sister, Magdalena, who was on her way home from Den Bosch, where she had found another priestly teacher for Jacob: this one belonged to the Jesuits, a religious order renowned for its ability to instruct newcomers to the faith.

If Jacob liked the idea of the Jesuit, he must have wondered how it would ever come to pass. For Den Bosch was a couple of hours away from Boxtel by foot, and his already suspicious father would be sure to notice such a lengthy trip. For the next week or so Jacob continued to study simply with local priests, seeing them on the pretext of social calls.

Then, *as if from heaven*, Jacob got his chance, thanks to Timothy's bum shin. When Timothy asked Jacob to ride to Den Bosch to tell the classis that Timothy could not attend its meeting, Jacob dutifully did so. But after going about his father's business, he went out to conduct some business of his own.

As instructed in advance by Magdalena Vlierden, Jacob first sent a note to the Jesuit saying that he was in town. Then he made his way to the prearranged meeting place, a tavern called the Emperor, located on the Fish Market, and sat down to wait.

It didn't take long for the Jesuit, 46-year-old Father Jacob van Gerwe, to arrive.

To many Reformed, Jesuits were the worst of the whole Catholic bunch. Old Jacob had complained about them often, telling magistrates in Amsterdam that Jesuits were the most numerous and bothersome of all the Catholics in town, not to mention the most diabolically effective at luring people (especially teenagers and young adults) to their infernal religion.

One of Old Jacob's colleagues was harsher still, employing every slur he knew against them in one sentence, calling them *scorpions, snakes, parricides, arsonists, spies, and traitors*. A second colleague tried a couple more (*hyenas and butchers*), and compared Jesuits *to the shit which the anti-Christ has shit*.

Such hostile sentiments were precisely why Father van Gerwe and the other 90 Jesuits covertly at work in the *Holland Mission* (which actually encompassed most of the Dutch Republic, not merely its dominant province) kept a low profile. They traveled by night, used aliases, and disguised themselves as colporteurs and peasants and ordinary burghers and physicians in order to serve the sacraments and preach. And of course when they talked with such prospective converts as Young Jacob Rolandus, they did so in the shadows of places like the Emperor tavern.

By 1654, Father van Gerwe had been laboring in the Holland Mission for 18 years. His superiors considered him judicious, prudent, intelligent, and eloquent. Thus he knew well not only how to survive in the Dutch Republic, but how to approach someone like Jacob Rolandus.

It was after all Father van Gerwe who had suggested that Jacob's friends give him *The Light on the Candlestick* to read, and who had probably provided a copy himself through Christian Vlierden. Now the Jesuit continued in person his instruction of the eager student, amid the flickering firelight of the Emperor.

This first meeting with the Jesuit was even more satisfying than Jacob had expected—in fact it was his most satisfying meeting yet with a priest.

In his new journal, which he seems to have begun about this time and which he kept partly in code in case his family discovered it, Jacob wrote that Father van Gerwe *gave me contentment in everything*. At sessions with other teachers, Jacob had made no such comment, saying only rather neutrally that he had *received instruction*.

But now, after only a single meeting, Jacob was persuaded. He wrote that on the way back to Boxtel he could think of his family's church as only a counterfeit and misguided version of the original religion founded by Christ. It was no Reformed Church but a *Deformed Church*.

Jacob had several more secret meetings with Father van Gerwe. At least two of them were again made possible by Timothy: once he was away from home denouncing the schoolmaster yet again to the classis, and once he asked Jacob to run yet another errand.

Jacob didn't record all of the topics discussed in these meetings, but surely they included the usual things that riled up Protestants and Catholics, including miracles and vows and saints and relics, and of course how a minor might justify converting to Catholicism against the will of his parents.

Anyone hearing Jacob's conversion story would have certainly wanted to know this last especially. The Jesuits were experts at answering it, and Jacob probably first heard from them the justifications he would soon use himself.

He (and all Catholics), Jacob would soon insist, were not the ones guilty of rebellion or innovation. Rather, those labels belonged to Jacob's great-grandfather, Roeland Jacobsz Uyttenhoven, who rashly left the faith that his ancestors had followed for centuries. Jacob was merely returning to the original and true tradition.

Moreover, who could forget Jesus's famous saying that whoever wanted to follow Him had to love Him even more than brother or sister or mother or father? This trumped *honoring your parents*, or at least gave it new meaning. Dear as parents were, God must be dearer, Jacob was sure.

And finally, it wasn't as if the forsaker of parents and family would be left alone by God. For God would welcome him into His own better family, as in the 27th Psalm: *When my father and my mother forsake me, then the Lord will take me up*. Jesus promised the same thing in Matthew: *Whosoever shall do the will of my Father which is in Heaven, the same is my brother, and sister, and mother*, and the true disciple would receive a hundredfold of new earthly friends into the bargain.

Jacob probably had learned these biblical texts even before meeting Father van Gerwe, but now he felt their specific application to him— now they seemed vital.

On April 24, only ten days after his first meeting with Father van Gerwe, and at the end of another afternoon tutorial, Jacob formally converted.

He did this by placing his hands in the hands of the Jesuit and making a profession of faith: this explicitly recognized the authority of the pope, the truth of the Catholic Church, and the validity of its sacraments, and for the big climax condemned Protestantism as a heresy.

This quiet scene was much less dramatic than the one at the profession of the famous Catholic convert Henri IV of France, which included five bishops, an overflow crowd of more than 10,000 people, and the release of countless white doves from the church's belfry when the king spoke the magic words. But Jacob's profession was meaningful enough for himself. When he went home, he was in his own mind Catholic.

Ten days later, in early May, Jacob secretly sought out the former pastor of Boxtel, Laurens Timmermans, at the home of a locally prominent Catholic. There, quite against the law and the wishes of Jacob's parents, Pastor Timmermans performed other rituals to seal the conversion. He listened as Jacob made a general confession of sins, in preparation for his first Catholic communion. Then, the next day, a big prayer day for the Reformed, Jacob found time after his father's morning sermon to meet Pastor Timmermans again and actually take that communion. The Vlierden sisters were there too, to share in the joy.

After the Catholic communion, Jacob went on a walk. To think? To settle himself? Whatever the case, he was back at the Reformed service by two, for Timothy's afternoon sermon. There he sat among the usual handful of Reformed believers, in the choir of the once magnificent church of Boxtel, appearing to be one of them, but on the inside feeling quite Catholic.

He couldn't go on like this much longer.

The whole process of conversion was obviously stressful for Jacob.

He studied in secret. He sought out teachers in secret. He kept his journal in code. And the thought of being separated from his parents in the eternities (because of their false religion) caused him to burst regularly into tears.

Maybe he was as torn as Sir Henry James in England, who suffered so much stress during his conversion that he became mentally unbalanced, or as Madame de Fontrailles in France, who wrote of her deep *interior agitations* before her conversion. But however stressful the process may have been, Jacob converted anyway.

Even more stressful proved to be what to do about his conversion. Jacob realized quickly that he was hopeless at what contemporaries called Nicodemism, after the New Testament character Nicodemus, who in public was a Pharisee but in secret came to Jesus for instruction.

Catholic and Protestant clergy alike mostly condemned Nicodemism, promising those who engaged in it condemnation to hell, and equating it to *playing Bo-peep with God almighty*. Plenty of ordinary believers thought otherwise, however: especially those who preferred a faith that was outlawed in their particular country found it absolutely necessary to behave discreetly. They might attend the services of one church but believe in another, declare allegiance to one faith but secretly prefer another, and they did so to keep their lives, or property, or status, or family relationships intact—such as the French girl, daughter of a zealous Calvinist, who hid her conversion to Catholicism for seven long years, out of fear that her father would die from sadness if he found out.

But Jacob wasn't made of such stuff. Like his father, he was highly principled, which easily led to the drawing of clear lines and confrontation. He found Nicodemism an abomination (here was something on which he could agree with John Calvin), even a threat to salvation, and thus knew that he couldn't go on keeping his faith secret.

One possibility was to tell his parents of his conversion and then hope that they would allow him to practice his new faith discreetly, as most Catholics in Brabant were forced to do anyway. But even if he considered this, he decided against it: it was one thing for Timothy and Catharina to speak cordially with Catholics every day in town, but quite another to house a Catholic under their roof, even if that Catholic was their flesh and blood—in fact *because* he was their flesh and blood. Parents simply assumed it was their right to choose the religion of their child, and to direct their children in all things, *so long as they were children*. His parents would fight him, he decided.

Foreign visitors to the Republic marveled at the well-functioning households in which the husband was of one religion, the wife of another, and the children of a third or fourth. But foreigners missed that even in mixed households parents still felt it their right to determine their children's religion. Boys might be assigned to the father's religion and girls to the mother's. Children might be raised in the mother's religion here and the father's there. Or every other child might be baptized in the mother's faith and the rest in the father's. But it was the parents who did the choosing.

Foreigners also missed in their fleeting glimpses of mixed families the tensions that could still exist in such a household—especially when the household was headed by a preacher. A preacher's family was supposed to set the example for all families in town, Reformed or otherwise. The dominee's son, especially one named Rolandus, simply could not be Catholic. Once people knew that Jacob had converted, his family would become a disgrace among the Reformed and a laughingstock among Catholics.

Moreover, even if his parents somehow allowed him to live at home and practice Catholicism out of their sight, they would still expect him to participate in the family's Reformed rituals around the table. And this he could no longer do in good conscience.

As Jacob wrote in his journal, his Catholicism, if revealed, would be an unavoidable *inconvenience* for his entire family. Thus, he concluded, he would not tell them, and he would not live at home. He had to leave altogether.

Yet the thought of leaving was painful too.

How could such an action honor his parents? He could find biblical support for leaving their false religion, and for choosing God even above parents, but he could find none that allowed him to dishonor his mother and father.

To leave them would cast a still darker shadow upon their already damaged reputation—as if they were so tyrannical that their son had to flee in desperation. It would also cast doubt on whether Jacob cared for them as much as he claimed. For though he might repeat to everyone in his hearing that he honored his parents in his heart, if he left them physically he could never fulfill one of his society's most crucial and tangible forms of honoring parents: caring for them in their fast-approaching old age. There was no reconciling that.

Jacob found the nerve to leave home only when his father started pushing him. Somehow Jacob got wind that Timothy was thinking of sending him away to live with Reformed relatives, in more Reformed areas of the Republic, where the boy might be rehabilitated. Much as he wanted to leave home and be out from under his father's thumb, this was not what he had in mind. Thus Jacob decided to leave on his own terms, before Timothy could act.

Yes, his leaving would cause a scandal for his family. But staying home would do the same, as people would inevitably discover his conversion, and his presence would serve as a constant reminder of Timothy's failure as a parent.

Not to mention that staying at home would put Jacob's soul in peril: he would find conflict with his parents, he would have to pretend to be Reformed, and he would not be able to practice Catholicism as he pleased.

Therefore, he wrote, *I followed my conscience*, and decided to heed what his father had often told him to do: to obey God more than man. What Jacob understood by that was not what Timothy understood, of course. Timothy, like John Calvin or Martin Luther, would have regarded what Jacob called his conscience as merely a *conscience in appearance*, because it was not in harmony with scripture, as Timothy understood it. But Jacob was determined.

On May 6, just days after his first communion, and with thoughts and emotions swirling inside, Jacob resolved to leave home, *quietly*.

On May 16, realizing he needed help to do so, he started telling some of his friends, many of whom were ready to lend that help.

On May 25, at two in the morning, he jumped out his window, over the schoolmaster's fence, and rode as fast as he could to Antwerp, where he now found himself.

And that was his story, so far.

It was moving enough that when he had the chance in Antwerp to tell it in person to his hero, the Flemish Peasant, the man included an abbreviated version of it in a new tract featuring 56 recent converts to Catholicism.

Jacob hoped that in whatever form it was told, then or later, others would see that his conversion was genuine.

Later observers would be less convinced that there was such a thing as *genuine* or even *false* conversion, in the sense of conversion being wholly pure or wholly cynical. Converts' motives, they would conclude, are always mixed, and at least partly unconscious.

Surely there was more to Jacob's story as well—more than the parts he or others bothered to record. His conversion probably included, for instance, a strong dose of the old father-son conflict. Jacob's placing of the blame on the classis for his own loss of Reformed faith, or saying that the idea to convert actually came from things his father said, or even his leaving behind at home his copy of the Dutch Bible translated by his grandfather while taking with him his father's Hebrew Bible, might have been ways to mask less conscious and less speakable feelings of resentment, as the mores of the day made it difficult for a child openly to disrespect his elders.

And was it any coincidence that the most likely age for conversion, then or later, was young adulthood, right when someone like Jacob was trying to find his own way?

Or maybe Jacob acted mostly on unconscious impulses that he inherited through birth and training from his father and grandfather, especially their strong streak of self-assured and self-righteous stubbornness. Timothy showed his during his battle in Ouderkerk, Old Jacob his during the translation of the Bible, when he chose to do that work rather than to reconcile with his wife, certain as he was that she was wrong about their most recent dispute. Both men paid the price for their commitment to truth, as both in the end were alienated from their flock or family—but pay it they did, so sure were they. Maybe Young Jacob was driven by the same trait when he converted.

But this is all guesswork, as is any inquiry into any conversion. Unconscious forces don't necessarily negate the reality of a conversion, nor can conversion be reduced to generational conflict or cultural structures. They simply make the process more complicated to explain than the classic stories of conversion suggest.

In the end, conversion may be as inscrutable as love, or God. Perhaps it is therefore enough to know that Jacob did convert, in April 1654, and then left his home and family a month later.

# fourteen

[ If nothing else, teaching is a prime opportunity to develop love. ]

His ties to family and old friends weakened, even severed, Michael continued seeking out the promised hundredfold of replacements.

He began at school, among his students, with whom he spent most of his time. Although these were never relationships of equals, they mattered deeply to Michael. And his new faith made them matter even more.

Despite the fears of a few fellow teachers, Michael never proselytized his sixth graders (although one of his Mormon students couldn't stop calling him *Brother Sunbloom*, according to the Mormon custom of address, which Michael hoped no one else heard).

Rather, his faith gave him a new sense of connection to his students, even a kinship, for he now saw them as his *spiritual brothers and sisters* rather than as young strangers. The thought made him more determined than ever to connect with each. *It's very obvious that I'm very capable of reaching every one of them in some respect, to some degree, during the year*, he said in one outburst about his joy at having been led to teaching.

In fact Michael rapidly developed a reputation as someone who not only cared about students, but knew how to convey that care.

One way he did so was through his imaginatively decorated classroom, more a theme park than a study area.

Photographs of the room show that there were no generic School Safety posters tacked to the walls, but only lively, original creations. Michael used the weeks before school started to layer each of the room's many bulletin boards with nine large sheets of illustrated paper, one for every month of the school year, every sheet containing a new theme and background for a given subject (such as history). When a month ended, Michael tore down that sheet to reveal the next month's theme. Most of them featured Michael's gift for comic art. One board, devoted to spelling, included a group of cartoon figures dreaming about brightly colored vocabulary words that changed every day. Others featured map games, Concentration, math activities (such as Math Rap), and a neatly constructed reading chart in the days before computers and printers made neat construction easy.

Even the blackboard was a work of art, covered with his clear and vibrant handwriting that managed to make homework assignments look almost inviting. The final touch was the continuous border, around the top of the room, made of large snowflakes designed by students.

And this is not to mention the extra holiday creations that filled the few remaining spaces. Whether it fit the latest educational fashion or not (and it probably did), it was thoroughly Michael.

Michael also reached kids through the learning activities he created, for which the decorations were mostly the backdrop.

Every day began, for instance, with a search for the mystery question about the previous day's work. Upon entering the room in the morning, students ran to lift desks, peer under chairs, search behind the encyclopedia on the bookshelf, and so on, until they found all the partial clues and pieced them together to find the answer.

For math they might play Let's Make a Deal! and for English they wrote an hour a day based on topics and pictures selected from a folder entitled *Write Away*. There was no time lost, no sitting around waiting for the bell to ring to start or end the day. No Boredom Allowed.

That theme carried over to the extracurricular activities Michael organized. Once a year he rose at four in the morning to lead his students on a field trip to Yosemite National Park, only a couple of hours from Valleytown. Each Halloween he and another teacher took four students chosen at random to the haunted house Scream in the Dark, where the students loved to be terrified.

To placate those not chosen, Michael and the two other sixth-grade teachers took three students out to lunch every Friday. You could go only once, but everyone got to go, unconditionally: there were no contests to win, no grades to achieve. The three whose names were drawn invariably ran to the parking lot to claim a seat in Michael's two-seated Porsche; after he removed the convertible top, they happily crammed into the passenger seat (no seatbelt laws yet), thrilled at the thought of going out to lunch, and in such splendor.

Perhaps Michael's greatest specialty was skits, with his tastes an odd mix of cabaret, camp, and television programming from his 1950s childhood. Later, when he moved away from the United States, he would say that American culture reminded him of one big halftime show. If so, he contributed to that show in no small way.

The Christmas program was the most regular venue for his skits. The first year he wrote and directed the sixth-grade contribution to that program, and the second he ran the entire show: six skits, assorted choirs, and all the staging. When the soundman, a student, was expelled from school the day before the show, when the props were stolen that same night (by the soundman?), and when the star lost his voice on the morning of the show, Michael had to scramble.

His creativity saw him through, but he lost eight pounds that week and got a total of five hours of sleep, because everything had to be, as usual, just so.

All the decorating and fun and creativity and getting things just so were partly for Michael's sake, of course.

He didn't want to be bored any more than the students did. And he always was a little fussy about his surroundings, still the *best little boy* who washed up dishes without a spot.

But in the end it was mostly for the students: this was how he expressed his affection for them, tried to give them confidence, and worked to make the alienated feel accepted. And most kids responded.

In fact the emotional attachment he developed with his students was what he enjoyed most about teaching, and it grew even stronger after his conversion.

Yet that attachment was also what eventually drove him from teaching. The problem was this: every summer his relationships with students ended abruptly, and predictably. They sometimes came by and said *Hey Mr. Sunbloom!* But it wasn't the same.

Every year Michael insisted that this was his *best class yet*, and every year as the end loomed he choked up at the thought of losing *my kids*, again. These endings, and not the grading or the noise or the grind or the intractability of 11-year-olds or even the unreasonable expectations of parents, were what wore him down.

The endings were especially hard with those students who grabbed his heart most—usually the disadvantaged and slow, or those with a wit to match his own—such as Vincy, Javier, and Leo.

Vincy was bald, the consequence of an illness. Michael's approach to this was indirect: by helping the other kids see that in some way they were all different from everyone else, Vincy became just another special kid, rather than a different kid needing special attention.

Javier was far behind the rest of the class academically, but he had a warmth Michael responded to, and a bluntness that sounded more like Brooklyn than Valleytown. After being prodded once again for his homework, Javier responded in a way that made Michael try to restrain his laughter: *Hey man, let this fella slide! Every time I forgets my homework, man, it's the big bust.* That Javier called Michael *the Heavy* only increased his affection for the boy. As did Javier's pleading, on the day he was chosen for Friday lunch, that they drive slowly down his street so that neighbors could see him in full glory standing on the seat of Michael's Porsche.

Then there was Leo, a bright smiling kid who informed Michael that he had been selected as one of Leo's best friends, but not to *let it out of the bag* because Leo had *an image to keep up*. Michael told a friend, *You can't begin to know how much something like that means to me.*

Michael also had a soft spot for students who were hard to reach, often because of *coldness and lack of affection in their home lives.*

These students *needed to be reassured that they possess qualities that are truly respected and admired by those around them.* And Michael was, again, unusually able to find those qualities.

*God is love,* Michael told himself often while working with his students. It wasn't a thought unique to Mormons, of course, but it was through Mormonism that the thought came most alive for him. And he usually managed to express it in entertaining ways.

Meaningful as Michael's relationships with his students were, he of course needed peer relationships even more, and he sought out the hundredfold of them especially at church.

He met new people at regular worship services on Sundays, but mostly at activities of the church's Young Adult program, such as dances, service projects, trips to the coast, and Sunday evening *firesides* (usually involving a guest speaker and some music, which happened not around a real fire but at the church building).

He also met numerous Mormon missionaries, who liked to take the outgoing and articulate Michael along on their visits to investigators, so that they could meet a real live ordinary Mormon. In the process, Michael became close friends with several missionaries, including Elder Jones, the one Michael and I later went to visit on the California coast.

Michael usually enjoyed meeting investigators and helping to teach them, though the meetings sometimes turned ugly. One night the missionaries, knowing Michael's background at All Folks, took him to meet an apparently interested couple from that church. But the couple didn't really want to learn about Mormonism: they wanted to condemn it. For two hours they railed that Mormons would burn in hell and gnash their teeth in eternal torment.

An increasingly upset Michael finally interjected, *What gives you the right to pass such judgment?*

*Our righteous authority,* came the reply.

Michael reminded them that the meek, not the vicious, would inherit the earth, then added, unwisely, *and so you will be left out in the cold.* Which of course only got Michael and the missionaries thrown out of the house.

Soon afterward, a chastened Michael found a new favorite scriptural verse, in the first book of John. It reminded him not only of how harshly this couple had judged Mormons, but of how harshly he had judged them in return. *If a man say, I love God, and hateth his brother, he is a liar: for he that loveth not his brother whom he hath seen, how can he love God whom he hath not seen? And this commandment have we from him, That he who loveth God love his brother also.*

Michael committed it to memory, and to heart—and good thing, because he would need it often in the months and years to come.

Despite some unpleasant moments, Michael liked his time with the missionaries so much that he began to think of going on a mission himself.

The only problem was his age. Most Mormon missionaries went out at 19, and Michael was already 23. Yet some as old as 25 did go, so it wasn't impossible. Michael discussed the matter with his bishop, the leader of his congregation, who like Michael happened to be both an educator and an adult convert. But to Michael's surprise, the bishop advised against it. The problem wasn't so much his age but that he was far more mature than most missionaries, and had already begun a serious career. The church would benefit more, said the bishop, if Michael stayed home and continued working with local missionaries, and helped to build the Young Adult program. *Besides*, the bishop added with a twinkle, *your mission now is to get married*, a message the new convert Michael had heard repeatedly since becoming Mormon.

A bit disheartened, Michael took the advice. He had been around enough missionaries to know that the bishop was right about maturity. But he regretted not going on a mission.

The bishop was also right that Michael's talents could be put to good use locally. Michael not only accompanied the missionaries but began to find investigators for them, including a fellow teacher at his school named Kathy, who soon converted to Mormonism with her husband. Michael baptized Kathy himself, while a missionary baptized the husband. Later, when Kathy had a baby, Michael bought the baby a special gown for the blessing ceremony and sent Kathy a dozen roses.

Then, in the spring of 1974, about a year after his conversion, Michael was asked to be president of the Mormon Young Adult program for all of Valleytown, which officially numbered some 150 members, although only half of them were actively involved.

He was overwhelmed by this *calling*. Yet never was anyone better suited to the task, and never was any task at church better suited to Michael. Through it especially he would find the promised hundredfold of new family and friends.

Including me. For it was soon after he accepted this new responsibility that I met Michael Sunbloom, greatest Young Adult president in the history of Valleytown, and maybe of all Mormondom.

# fifteen

 I told father that I would gladly go with him,
but my conscience wouldn't allow it.

Jacob had little control over whether his fellow Catholics in Antwerp accepted him and his conversion story, of course.

All he could do was show through his living that his conversion was sincere, but living took time.

In the meantime, he continued to seek out friends, and to revel in his newfound freedom to practice his religion openly. As he moved about the city in those first days after his arrival, he frequently ducked in and out of its abundant churches and chapels, to pray or to attend Mass— things he had done only in secret in Boxtel.

If Jacob's newfound joy was enough to help him forget his worries for the moment, then he was quickly shaken to remembrance on only his second day in town, toward noon, when a coach pulled alongside him on the street.

Jacob recognized the faces inside: they were two Catholics from Boxtel, obviously here in Antwerp on business. One, named Gerrit van Loo, owned the coach, while the other, Jasper Beyaerts, was the former dean of the now disbanded *chapter* of Boxtel (a group of priests meant to add luster to important churches). After an exchange of greetings, the dean conveyed some unsettling news: just moments before, and just a few streets away at the Horse Market, he had spoken in the flesh to none other than Jacob's father, Timothy, who believed that Jacob was here in Antwerp and had already become a Capuchin.

Jacob didn't have time to puzzle out how his father had learned his whereabouts; at the moment he simply had to get off the street and find help. But where to go? And who would help him on such short notice? He hardly knew anyone.

He couldn't return to the Little Mill, just inside the eastern gate, where his father had also probably entered the city. It was too obvious, and how could he be sure the proprietors would protect him?

Dean Beyaerts, who knew people enough in Antwerp, certainly had sufficient influence to help Jacob. In Boxtel he would get into deep trouble for doing so, but in Antwerp he could at least try discreetly. Yet the dean seemed little inclined; in fact when he told Jacob that Timothy was in town, it seemed more a chastisement than an offer of helpful intelligence—because soon afterward, the dean reportedly told others that Jacob was a *brat* for running away from his parents (a sentiment no doubt aggravated by the knowledge that Jacob's escape would be blamed on the clergy of Boxtel, including the dean, who would all suffer financially for it). In the end, he offered Jacob nothing.

The eternally friendly Canon van den Bosch was willing to help Jacob, even to shelter him, but he was more pious than powerful, and right now Jacob needed more of the latter.

Desperate, he turned to the Jesuits, given his friendly reception there and Mevrouw Verbeek's intercession on his behalf—and of course his good experience with his teacher back home, Father van Gerwe.

Antwerp was full of Jesuits, some 125 of them at any given moment during the seventeenth century.

That they were regularly and furiously condemned not only by Protestants, as expected, but also by their fellow Catholics was a reflection of their success and influence. One person claimed, for instance, that a Catholic lawyer named Tongerloo was prone, in whatever setting he might find himself, to blurt out a stream of invective against Jesuits that included the words *rascal, scoundrel, knave*, and worse. And the lawyer was far from alone in his sentiments.

Jacob didn't care: thus far the Jesuits had offered him more kindness than any other influential entity in town. And so in his present difficulty he went to see them.

Once again the provost was helpful. He suggested to the anxious Jacob that if he truly didn't want to return to Boxtel then he had better lie low, for the border would provide no protection to a minor caught by his own father. Jacob heeded that advice, and took cover, and Timothy and his party searched Antwerp in vain most of that Wednesday. Late that same day, they decided to divide into two groups and move on.

Timothy led one group south to Brussels, while his friend Secretary Hugens led a second group back to the town of Turnhout, on the road between Antwerp and the Dutch border, in case they had somehow passed by Jacob on their initial trip to Antwerp.

After four days of fruitless searching, Timothy returned to Antwerp, still convinced that Jacob must be there.

It was Sunday, May 31, one week since Jacob's flight.

Timothy, at 60 years old, was no doubt weary by the time he got back to the city, because, short of money as ever, he had done at least part of his traveling on foot. But he was also as stubborn as ever: after returning, he spent the remainder of the day not resting, but traversing the streets of Antwerp, still looking for his son.

When he retired at last to his room that evening, there was a note from Hugens, who wrote that he too was headed back to Antwerp because he had learned that Jacob was indeed in the city, staying at a place called the Little Mill. Once again Timothy put off resting, and headed directly to the tavern. Now they had him!

How had Hugens learned this? Jacob always suspected that it was thanks to Dean Beyaerts, who on his way back to Boxtel must have run into Hugens on the road and told the secretary about his brief conversation with Jacob in Antwerp—showing again that he had more sympathy for parents than for an underaged co-religionist.

The scene in Antwerp is easy enough to imagine: an aging father in the fading daylight and lengthening evening shadows, moving across the uneven cobblestones as fast as his elderly legs would take him to the inn at the eastern gate of the city.

Fortunately for Jacob, he was out when his father arrived. Timothy waited for some time, but finally decided to go get some sleep, then return early the next morning and catch Jacob by surprise.

There was one hitch: Timothy had explained his business to the inn's hostess. She might tell the boy that his father had been there looking for him, and he would leave before Timothy came back the next morning. Timothy forbade the hostess from saying anything, hoping that her empathy for this bereft parent would move her to comply.

But the hostess decided to favor the son above the father. For when Jacob came in even later that evening, she told him exactly what had occurred. A grateful Jacob quickly grabbed a few things and threw the rest into a locked trunk owned by the hostess: he would come back for it later. Canon van den Bosch had already said that Jacob could stay with him, so he headed there, despite the late hour.

Before leaving the inn, he told the hostess not to fret about having defied his father: she should freely tell Timothy, when he came calling the next day, that Jacob already knew he was in town and had planned to leave the inn that night anyway.

By the time an eager Timothy arrived early the next morning, he was of course too late to catch his prey. He could not have been pleased with the hostess.

While Timothy stewed at the Little Mill that morning, Jacob went to the Jesuit house once more for advice.

This time the Jesuits took the most cautious road possible and suggested that Jacob go to his father in person—and even return to Boxtel with him. Jacob would hear nothing of returning, but he did agree to go speak with Timothy, that very afternoon of June 1, on condition that two Jesuits accompany him, for protection.

The meeting was arranged through the hostess at the Little Mill. Timothy told her where he would be; soon afterward Jacob and the two Jesuits came to the Little Mill to find out, then they proceeded to the meeting place.

When Jacob entered the room where Timothy was waiting, both began to sob. Timothy assumed from this, Jacob later wrote, that his son was expressing contrition for leaving. Based on this assumption, Timothy said, after the outpouring of emotion, that Jacob must now absolutely follow him back to Boxtel.

But Jacob surprised his father. His tears were not from contrition at all, but rather from sorrow that he and his father were at odds. He replied that he would love to follow his father, but his conscience would not allow it.

When Timothy began overruling him, Jacob was speechless—as if, like many a grown son, he was paralyzed by the conflicting emotions of wanting both to respect and to separate from his father. Seeing Jacob's state, the Jesuits tried to speak for him, saying something about the boy being free to choose for himself. Predictably, Timothy exploded at them.

The Jesuits struck back, by mentioning one of the biblical texts about loving God above even one's own parents. Timothy snapped that the Jesuits ought not to compound their reputation for stealing minor children by adding yet another unbecoming blemish.

In fact Jesuits, like other religious orders, did sometimes accept minor children, without parental permission, provided the child was 16, the *age of discretion*, and the minimum age to take religious vows. But this didn't assuage the anger of even Catholic parents, who singled out aggressive Jesuits for the practice. The Frenchman Michel Ripault watched three minor sons become Jesuits against his will, despite his best efforts in court to remove them. Another French Catholic, Guichard Coton, promised his 19-year-old son Pierre that he would *exhaust his wealth* to punish those Jesuits who had *seduced* the son. Other Catholics called Jesuits *false fathers*, and their seminaries *dividers of families*. Now the Reformed Timothy, who had never liked Jesuits to begin with, could chime in with these Catholic parents.

While the Jesuits and Timothy escalated their arguing, Jacob could bear no more: he had suffered enough unpleasant confrontations with his father, and so he ran out the door. Timothy saw Jacob leaving, but too late, and started chasing, but too slowly.

Jacob ran all the way to the Jesuit house, *to hide a bit*. He also *cried violently* at the thought of his aging father chasing after him. He might have cried more had he known that this would be the last time he would ever speak with his father.

Later that evening of June 1, under cover of darkness, a drained Jacob made his way to his new accommodations at the home of Canon van den Bosch.

The canon tried to offer comfort, saying that on this very night he had heard several hundred angels above the house, singing half an hour long, *Glory to God in the Highest Heaven*—a sure sign that God was pleased with Jacob's steadfastness in his new faith and that his sorrows would one day turn to joy.

Maybe it was enough to help Jacob sleep that night.

# sixteen

[ The theme was No More Strangers. ]

Michael's reign as Young Adult president lasted for two years, as long as a Mormon mission.

It was only fitting, for he regarded his new task as his mission, and he invested as much energy in trying to make the lives of his new friends interesting and meaningful as any white-shirted, short-haired elder invested in trying to convert someone.

Between the spring of 1974 and the spring of 1976, Michael created some of the most memorable events ever seen in the rarefied world of Mormon Young Adults. In fact the events were memorable enough, and increased the sense of fellowship enough, that some who had planned to go away to college now thought about going to school locally, to be part of it all.

The Thanksgiving feast Michael dreamed up, for instance, was by several accounts the best activity of all, as he transformed a plain church gymnasium into what he called *an authentic pilgrim village*, complete with stocks, autumn garnishes on walls and tables, and a lot of unpilgrim-like food and entertainment—including servers (starring Michael) dressed in tall black hats, knickers, vests, and gold-buckled shoes, who introduced each course with a cabaret-style song (words composed by Michael), and all supplemented, of course, by a line of cheerleaders (Michael always found a way to work in cheerleaders) dressed as pilgrims who brought down the house.

If it sounded to outsiders like dreadful innocent merriment, it must be remembered that before Michael came on the scene the activities were sometimes just plain dreadful, even for insiders. Michael's creations were a revelation for these college students who had to find their fun without alcohol. Some outsiders even started attending the activities: the Thanksgiving feast itself drew 180 people—notable because even during the summer, when those going to distant colleges came home, there were at most 150 Mormon Young Adults in Valleytown. People were obviously coming from surrounding towns, or locals were bringing friends from other faiths.

Michael also scheduled at least monthly a Saturday daytime activity that involved fun, or service, or learning, as well as weekly Sunday after-noon get-togethers at rotating homes (the brainchild of Michael, so that he could be around his new friends as often as possible), and a monthly Sunday evening fireside, where Michael could indulge his weakness for syrupy semipop religious music and for hearing people gush about their spiritual experiences.

Other activities included Project Share, a Great Pumpkin Chase at Halloween, a three-day winter retreat at Yosemite Park, buses to Mormon Night at Disneyland, and a Mormon version of Mardi Gras in the church hall (his severely tamed replica of Bourbon Street included a Dixieland band, fully clothed street performers, and booths that offered pralines, beignets, and virgin mint juleps). He also orga-nized, as often as possible, group excursions to San Francisco or Los Angeles to see *Saturday's Warrior*, the new and excruciatingly senti-mental Mormon musical, which he saw at least as many times as he had seen *The Sound of Music* (nine), and which made him weep just as much. And at last, for his swan song, he organized a big semiformal dance, with the usual themed decorations and good food and big crowd and, he claimed, *the best band in the valley*.

Few presidents had ever made the activities as appealing as Michael did, or made the Young Adults feel so included and valued. Only one activity (the winter retreat at Yosemite) was formally called *No More*

*Strangers*, after Paul's famous saying in Ephesians, but it was the unofficial theme of all activities.

Michael was no more a stranger either. By the time he was *released* as president in the spring of 1976 (with many thanks from ecclesiastical leaders for how he had caused the Young Adult program to grow, not to mention how good he had made those leaders look), he had increased his new relationships even more than a hundredfold. And he was already a legend.

I saw only some of Michael's creations in person, because for most of his time as president I was away—first for my freshman year of college, and then (after one more summer in Valleytown) for a Mormon mission in Belgium.

But the occasions that I didn't see I heard about, from my parents (who always mentioned when Michael called), or from other Young Adults, or of course from Michael himself. He wrote often to tell me the latest, as one of his other talents was writing letters—composed on personalized stationery, then sent in envelopes covered with colorful stamps and hand-drawn, unflattering caricatures of me that could only have puzzled postal workers.

One day he had his class of 27 sixth graders write to me, with each letter separately addressed and stamped, so that I set a mission record for letters received in one day.

In his own letters, Michael wrote mostly about Young Adults, though he always ended with effusions about what a gifted missionary I must be, and that he considered me to be more a brother than a friend. And of course he told me news about school, and his tennis game, and his new girlfriend Susie.

After many months of casual friendship, he and Susie had begun dating steadily in mid-1975. For a while, it looked as if she might be Michael's ticket to exiting Young Adults gracefully (by getting married), rather than anticlimactically (by simply turning 26, as Michael would in July 1976). They got along easily, and Michael liked Susie's family too, although he didn't bother introducing her to his parents: he knew the thought that he might actually marry a Mormon would only alienate them further.

Coincidentally, Susie once met Michael's mother, LuJean, without realizing it. She and a friend started telling Michael about *the cutest and funniest woman* who had served them lunch that day at McDonald's. Michael inquired a little more about the location and the woman's appearance, and laughed when he realized they were talking about his mother. But that he couldn't properly introduce Susie to her stung him.

It hurt even more when Susie began to waver in her affection for Michael. In the spring of 1976, she told him about her uncertainty—caused mostly by lingering feelings she had for *her missionary*, who had left some months before she started dating Michael and who would return home in about a year. Michael had known the missionary, and liked him, but that didn't make her hesitations easier to bear.

Despite having dated numerous girls over the years, Michael joked that the closest he had come to marriage was when he served as best man at the wedding of his old missionary friend, Elder Jones. Michael was honored to have been asked, and traveled 1,500 miles to carry out his duties. But he also wondered aloud to everyone how in the world young Elder Jones had married before he did, and when his own lucky day might come—surely it would be before he turned 26, he insisted.

But it didn't work out that way. While Susie gradually pulled away from him in the spring of 1976, Michael began to withdraw from Young Adults and the church. By the time I came home from my mission, in August 1977, Michael had been out of the church for many months, and was about to leave teaching, and Valleytown, and (it felt) me, as well, as if our presumably close friendship had been a dream or illusion.

When I asked around about what had happened with Michael, no one really knew: some simply shook their heads, perplexed that someone once so devoted could *go inactive*, the dreaded label Mormons use to describe anyone who has stopped attending church and whose fate can only be bad. His hundredfold of new friends and family, which he had hoped would last long, disappeared even faster than it had formed.

That's not how things usually went for legends. I couldn't imagine what had gone wrong.

• • •

Although I was certainly naive in general and in particular, I did know that Michael's Mormon experience had included a few bumps. It always takes a while for a newcomer to figure out local culture, and maybe Michael never did figure it out completely.

Things that some Mormons thought important, for instance, such as wearing your hair short, were trivial to him. One Sunday after the monthly testimony meeting, during which Michael had publicly and emotionally expressed gratitude for his new church and for how kindly people had welcomed him, his bishop could only say, *It's too bad about your hair*.

For the 1970s, Michael's hair wasn't unusually long—just long enough on the sides to strategically cover his ears. In fact, it wasn't any longer than most other Mormon boys and young men of the time were wearing theirs. But to this bishop, and other side-parting, well-oiled, close-cropped men of his generation, long hair was a sign of worldliness, rebellion, and effeminacy. Though merely regrettable atop the head of most young men, it was absolutely lamentable on the Young Adult president.

That exchange, and others like it, made Michael feel that the bishop missed everything important about him. And it made him feel that perhaps some of the new relationships he had formed at church were more superficial, and conditional, than he had supposed.

Another tightly combed middle-aged bishop, while preaching to the Young Adults on his favorite subject of provident living, fished around briefly for an example of its opposite, and found one in Michael's baby Porsche. He didn't condemn the car outright, but while turning his head toward Michael he remarked unfavorably on *certain cars our Young Adults drive*. He said it with a smile, as if it were a gentle joke, but it didn't work on a practiced joker like Michael, who was stung by the public censure, especially because unlike most Young Adults he had a career and could afford at least this version of a Porsche. Again he felt that his more important qualities, and efforts, had been overlooked.

But was this really enough to drive him out, I wondered? Even then, such annoyances seemed to me the sort of quirkiness you might have to work through in any church, if you wanted to stay in.

More serious for Michael, I knew, and for many other Mormons, was the church's *Negro Policy*—especially given the Mormon belief in the divine origins of all human beings. To designate one group of those humans as inherently inferior made as little sense to Michael as did the U.S. Constitution's original determination that a black person was only three-fifths equal; the church's policy likewise seemed to Michael a vestige of old human prejudices rather than the result of divine decree. (In fact the policy was dropped in 1978, but too late for Michael.)

Yet most serious of all, I was sure, was Michael's looming exclusion from Young Adults. He knew that the upper age limit of 25 was meant to protect younger women from older males, but to him the rule seemed pointless: he would never think of preying on them. (The upper limit was changed to 30 some years later, but again too late for him.) The Young Adults were his connection to the church, even his church family. To lose them forever only compounded the sense of separation he suffered from losing his students every June.

Michael celebrated his fateful twenty-sixth birthday, in July 1976, in Europe, probably because he wanted to be far from Valleytown when it happened. Being far away removed some of the pain, especially when *far* meant Europe—which he had studied eagerly in college, had always endowed with a *mystical quality*, and had long wanted to visit. During the months before this first trip there, he not only mourned Susie and the Young Adults but read his old textbooks *for fun* and worked a second job cleaning offices to help cover the costs of the trip.

That birthday, and that trip, marked the transformation of Michael's simple discontentment with Mormonism into outright disaffection.

I detected it in the letters he sent to me in Belgium, afterward. They arrived less frequently. They mentioned his love for people and for God but no longer his love for the church. They recounted that he was spending most of his spare time on extracurricular activities at school, not on church.

More explicitly, the letters expressed resentment of gossip circulating at church about him and Susie—that somehow she had rudely dumped him, or that he had been unkind to her. In fact they were still on perfectly friendly terms.

But most of all, his letters recounted happily how close he was growing to his parents again—good news indeed, though I correctly guessed that this was only happening because of their joy that Michael was leaving Mormonism.

When I didn't hear from him at all during the last few months of my mission, I sensed that his disaffection from the church was complete. Why hadn't he just told me? Because so much of our bond had been forged at church and he didn't want to disappoint me? Because he thought me too young and zealous to grasp his crisis?

Probably both. When we saw each other briefly after I returned home from Belgium, it felt like the last time I would see him—not only because he told me that he might be moving away soon, but because there was a new strain between us: the openness was gone. Even his teasing had lost its zing, and that was the surest sign of all.

I felt that I knew him no better than did any other Young Adult in Valleytown, though I probably regretted more than most that we were now strangers to each other again.

# seventeen

I will place the love of God before the love of parents,
since Christ himself taught us this truth.

If Jacob found any comfort on the night that Canon van den Bosch
heard angels, Timothy, lying in a strange bed in a strange city, certainly
did not.

He regarded the disaffection of his son, from the family and from the
true faith, as an unalleviated disaster. Certainly nothing for any angels
to sing about.

In retrospect, Timothy could see the signs of trouble easily enough,
starting with Jacob's increasing orneriness about his studies. But what
else could he have done? They both knew that no one around was better
qualified than Timothy to teach the subjects Jacob needed to become a
Reformed preacher himself: Greek, Hebrew, and Latin. And so even
when Jacob put on his sour face, or gave *ugly answers*, or stormed out
of the house, even when he grumbled to his sister about their father,
Timothy kept suffering and sweating over those languages with his son.

To little avail. Jacob once blurted to Maria, *I don't want to learn
from my father, he can pester me as often as he pleases. I won't do it
and will not do it, even if father stood on his head and spread his feet!*
Then around his twenty-first birthday, in January 1654, he repeated it:
*I want not to and shall not study with my father.*

How many 21-year-olds in any time or place could happily study with
their father for so long? Some Dutch boys went to university at around 17

or 18, but certainly by 21 young men of the educated classes were usually gone from home. Both Timothy and Old Jacob certainly had been.

Why wasn't Jacob as well? Timothy had promised that studying with him would be for a short while longer, but didn't explain why. Was it the old family cross of insufficient funds? Perhaps, but there were special scholarships available for the sons of dominees.

The bigger problem was this: those special scholarships assumed that the recipient would study for the Reformed ministry, and it was becoming clear that Young Jacob wasn't sure he wanted to do so. Just as the curséd schoolmaster had said.

Had Timothy insisted absolutely that Jacob become a preacher?

There's no direct evidence that he did, but the hints were everywhere, starting with the family's history, and Jacob's very name.

Others popped up repeatedly during their miserable tutorials, when Jacob or Timothy pulled down from the shelf a copy of the new Dutch Bible translated in part by Old Jacob, or Hebrew Bibles and Greek Bibles and reference works that had once belonged to him.

Still other hints lay all around the Rolandus home, which like other devoutly Reformed homes was probably decorated with favorite Reformed images and texts from the Bible: Jacob's ladder, Jonah fleeing Nineveh, Moses on Sinai, Solomon in his temple, Potiphar's wife tempting Joseph, the prodigal son, and still other figures adorned furniture, books, tiles, fireplaces, utensils, watches, tablecloths, chests, chairs, serving trays, cradles, desks, hearth shields, and even shoehorns.

There were also Reformed prayers at table, and the reading aloud of Reformed devotional books and the new Bible. And there was Timothy performing his usual and primary task, preaching twice every Sunday, where Jacob was always faithfully in attendance. If those weren't enough, Jacob could look around at the sons of other preachers, including his cousins, and see that many of them were becoming preachers as well, just as their families expected.

Yes, there were reminders enough to Jacob of his heritage and the hopes his father had for him. Their relentless presence may well have contributed to his growing resentment toward his intended calling, and to his finally declaring that he could *no longer roll at father's feet.*

But still Timothy had persisted, even to this very moment in faraway and foreign Antwerp. Jacob was still a minor, after all, and didn't yet know what was best for himself. After the recent heartbreaking encounter with his son, Timothy seemed ready to settle for Jacob simply coming home. He wouldn't push him any longer to become a preacher. He might not even press him to quit Catholicism. If only he would come home.

He just wanted Jacob home.

When Jacob awoke on June 2, the day after his heartbreaking confrontation with his father, he found the provost and another Jesuit waiting at his door.

That Jesuits were now coming to Jacob rather than the other way around suggested that they felt implicated in his great matter. Though always willing to lend aid where they could, and to stand up for minor religious refugees who truly wanted to stay in the land, they did not wish to suffer false accusations. They wanted to make clear to all exactly what Jacob was thinking.

Thus they asked him straight out whether he wished to return home with his father. When Jacob said that he did not, the Jesuits went immediately to tell this to Timothy, and to see whether they *could assuage his spirit somewhat.* But when the Jesuits found him, at his new lodgings in the Little Mill (where he had no doubt installed himself in the hope that Jacob would return there), and repeated the sentiments of his son, Timothy refused to believe them, much less allow his spirit to be assuaged. To the contrary: he reviled and blamed the Jesuits as before, and threatened to take Jacob away by force if necessary.

Upon leaving, the provost promised that he would persuade Jacob to return to his father, but if the furious Timothy heard this comment it was doubtful that he believed it.

Mindful of his promise, the provost went back directly to Jacob's room.

Both the provost, Joannes Blocklant, and the other Jesuit with him, Remigius Happaert, were originally from the Dutch Republic, just like

Jacob. Those origins, plus their many years of labor in the Holland Mission, helped them to understand thoroughly what it meant to be Catholic there: hard, but possible, and requiring discretion. Thus they asked: couldn't Jacob practice his religion quietly, like so many others in Dutch Brabant? Especially since Timothy had supposedly told the Jesuits, in the course of their last heated conversation, that Jacob could keep his Catholicism if he would return home?

But again Jacob said that he could not: his *soul would be in peril* if he did. Satisfied, the provost asked a favor: would the boy then please return with them that afternoon to hear out his father and uncle, who was also along with Timothy, a final time? And would he then, in their presence, put onto paper his decision and hand it to his father personally?

Jacob agreed, and the two Jesuits sent their servant, named Ignatius, to arrange another meeting with Timothy—this time with Jacob in tow.

Hours later, when the Jesuits came by to get Jacob, he declared that he didn't want to go after all. One horrifying encounter had been enough. He did not wish, he explained, to cause another *alteration* in his father.

But there was another reason too: the servant Ignatius, while setting up this meeting, had overheard members of Timothy's entourage (which numbered at least seven) discussing how they could take Jacob by force. On his way home, Ignatius went past Jacob's room and repeated what he had heard.

That was why Jacob would not go see his father again. He had, however, prepared the document requested by the provost, and now handed it over. But this didn't really solve the problem for the Jesuits: Timothy hadn't believed them when they had repeated Jacob's words, and he wasn't going to believe them now if they simply brought a note supposedly written by Jacob. He would insist, again, that his son was not acting freely.

This was precisely what happened. The Jesuits reluctantly went to deliver the letter without Jacob, Timothy read it, and angrily declared that his son could not possibly have written such a thing. Yes, it was in his hand, but it must have been dictated to him.

Look what it said! It claimed that Jacob's conversion, and his flight to Antwerp, were not his own doing, but God's. And that if he had done evil by obeying God rather than his earthly father then he would confess and repent it. But for now he relied on those favorite texts of all converting Christian children, Matthew 10:37 and Luke 14:26, which demanded loving God even more than parents.

If that wasn't evidence enough of compulsion, there was more: the letter also asked Timothy for financial support so that Jacob could study in Antwerp. After all, it continued, Timothy would benefit personally from those studies, for as Jacob learned the true religion in detail he would gladly write it all to his father so that they both *might arrive together at the true fold whose great shepherd is Christ Jesus.*

Finally the letter closed with Jacob's promise always to pray for his father, mother, sister, and friends, and his acknowledgment that the provost wanted him to go back to Boxtel, but he could not, because of the quarrels that would arise at home. It was signed, without a hint of irony, *your most obedient son.*

By eight-thirty that evening, Timothy, Jacob's uncle, and a nephew were at the door of the Jesuit house waving Jacob's letter around and accusing the provost of being its true author. And they demanded to see Jacob immediately.

The provost denied that he had written the letter, and said that Jacob was not there. He also promised again to convince the boy to return home.

Later that night, the provost tried keeping his promise, summoning Jacob once more for a talk. But once more Jacob would hear nothing of returning. At this point, the provost, weary of arranging meetings and drawing up documents, simply told Jacob that he had then better keep to his room and off the streets, for his father was determined to find him.

For extra safety, Ignatius came by that evening to accompany Jacob to lodgings in the home of yet another pastor, in case Timothy managed to learn Jacob's whereabouts.

June 2 had been yet another long and wearing day for all of the Rolandus men.

•　•　•

By the time Jacob sent his note to his father, the search party from Boxtel had been away from home for over a week.

On June 3, the following day, five of the men decided to return home. Maybe the note convinced them that it was hopeless to keep trying. Probably they couldn't afford to stay away from work and obligations much longer. Only Timothy and his brother-in-law (Jacob's uncle), determined to make one last attempt, stayed behind.

A couple of days later, the brother-in-law, named Leeners, came to the Jesuit house and asked for yet another meeting with Jacob. The provost passed the message on, and Jacob agreed to meet, on two conditions: that a Jesuit accompany him, and that his father not be present (surely another wound for Timothy's already riddled soul).

The Jesuits offered one of their own rooms as a meeting place, but Uncle Leeners insisted on a neutral setting. Hence the Jesuits asked a Miss Wijnants, who lived nearby, whether she wouldn't mind allowing the use of her home for this critical purpose. She agreed.

On the appointed day, Saturday, June 6, the Jesuits sent the reliable servant Ignatius, plus a man named Knuyt (perhaps a Jesuit, more likely a friend of the Jesuits), to fetch Jacob and accompany him to the Wijnants home. Once they arrived, Jacob and Knuyt waited in the parlor, and Ignatius went to fetch Uncle Leeners at the Little Mill.

While Ignatius walked back to the meeting place with Uncle Leeners, Timothy followed surreptitiously at an inconspicuous distance.

After knocking at the door of the meeting place, Uncle Leeners and Ignatius were let in by the maidservant, who shut the door behind them.

Timothy crept up and waited just outside the door for his opportunity.

The maid tried to show the uncle into the parlor, where Jacob and Knuyt were waiting. But the uncle declared, oddly, that he wished to stay in the front hall and for Jacob to come out instead. Jacob did so, accompanied by Knuyt, and greeted his uncle. Uncle Leeners stated that he wished to speak with Jacob alone. After an assenting sign from Jacob, Knuyt returned to the parlor.

His uncle began reasoning *sweetly* with Jacob, but when he could not persuade the boy that his conversion and flight were a mistake, and that his new protectors the Jesuits were dangerous, Leeners' mood soured.

As the conversation deteriorated, the maid came back through the front hall in order to go out. When she opened the front door, Uncle Leeners suddenly flew at Jacob, grabbed him by the neck and upper arm, and tried to push him out the door, yelling at the same time to the waiting Timothy, *My brother! My brother! My brother! I've got him, help me!*

Although Timothy stood just outside, the maid shut the door so quickly that he wasn't able to get in. Jacob started crying again over this latest awful scene, and yelled for his friends in the parlor, who burst into the front hall. Ignatius and Knuyt approached Uncle Leeners and warned of the consequences facing those who committed violence in another's home: Miss Wijnants could press charges, if she pleased.

Still the uncle would not let Jacob loose. Instead he yelled that Jacob was his flesh and blood! Which was truly the crux of the matter. But mutual flesh and blood weren't enough to persuade Jacob, who now asked his friends to free him. They did so forcibly, and shoved the uncle out the door.

Jacob and his two companions left quickly through a rear exit.

Surely Timothy never imagined, when he played with Jacob as a boy, or when striving mightily to raise him in the fear of the Lord, or when recounting to his son the heroes of the Rolandus family, or even when thanklessly teaching Latin and Greek to Jacob the teen, that it would come to this: he, Timothy, cutting a sad figure on a dirty street in distant Antwerp, because his son, seduced by those devils the Jesuits, had shut the door in his face.

Timothy left for Boxtel almost immediately after this horrific event.

# eighteen

[ I threw myself to my knees to find sanctuary. ]

I heard only occasionally from Michael over the next decade, mostly in the form of postcards containing the barest of information, quite in contrast to his once overflowing letters.

He mentioned in the autumn of 1977 that he was serious about quitting teaching, though he didn't really say why (and even though he and two co-teachers had recently been asked to make a district-wide presentation about their methods).

He mentioned months later that he had grown so enamored of Europe and travel that he had interviewed to become a flight attendant with Pan Am, had finally gotten that job in December 1977, had resigned from teaching that Christmas, and had started his training the next month.

And finally he mentioned in 1979 that after a year he had also given up being a flight attendant and moved to his dreamland, Switzerland, where he taught English at the local Berlitz School and shared a flat with a Swiss friend named Stefan, one of the *finest individuals* Michael had ever met.

I had to admit that this hurt a little, because Michael had always made me feel that *I* was his finest friend. Yet Stefan, whom Michael had mentioned a couple of times in his letters, was obviously even more so, if he'd made Michael feel welcome enough to move across the world.

Michael's old girlfriend Joni, who had introduced him to Mormonism, went on a tour of Europe around that time and dropped by to see him. When she returned to Valleytown, I was eager to hear the latest from her. Michael was thriving, she reported, living in a lovely apartment just fifty meters from Lake Zurich. He missed his family and friends, especially *sitting down for chats* with his dad. But he was a popular teacher at the Berlitz School, and Stefan was as fine a person as Michael said.

None of that surprised me. But was there anything Mormon still about Michael, I wondered? *Not really*, she said. I finally accepted that he had left the church, and that the complaints he had made about it must have indeed been enough to drive him away.

But I was wrong: they had not been enough. There was something else he wasn't telling me, or anyone else for that matter, including his family. I learned about it only many years later, when Michael and I were friends again.

That he held something back for so long shouldn't have surprised me, I suppose. Sometimes the people presumably closest to us are the last to know about what's going on deep inside, at least if we know they'll disapprove, for we don't want to disappoint them, or suffer their censure.

Jacob Rolandus didn't tell his family that he'd become Catholic until after he left them. Michael didn't tell me about his struggles with his family over Mormonism, even when he finally started mentioning his family to me. And I had hardly told Michael everything about me— such as that I wasn't as gifted a missionary as he imagined. So why should he have told me from the start that being forced out of Young Adults at age 26, and enduring complaints about his hair, and suffering unkind chatter about him and Susie, and holding nagging doubts about certain church policies were not the real reasons for his defection? And that the real reason was his gradual realization of his own homosexuality?

Here was what the normally loquacious Michael wasn't saying about why he quit the church and quit teaching and started flying and moved to New York and then Switzerland.

Soon after becoming Mormon, Michael grew alarmed over the turmoil he started to feel in body and soul.

Some of it, though at first terrifying, proved to be simply confusing and embarrassing. For instance, in spite of having become celibate, Michael suddenly and inexplicably developed symptoms that resembled (he knew from health classes) venereal disease, as it was then called. He was flabbergasted, something like those medieval monks who began to wonder whether they had only dreamed of being seduced by witches in the night.

Michael sought out his doctor, protesting that it was impossible for him to have VD. The doctor agreed: instead Michael merely had *prostatic congestion*, or an excessive buildup of sperm. But Michael's relief turned to panic when he heard the remedy, the same remedy the doctor prescribed to all celibate men with Michael's condition: masturbation. This wasn't what he wanted to hear, since he knew his church regarded it as sinful. Even though the episode had nothing to do with homosexuality, he left the doctor's office feeling confused, not to mention more anxious than ever that something was wrong with him.

Making him most anxious of all on that score, however, was his confusion about Susie. He loved being with her, certainly felt love for her, and gushed about her to everyone who would listen. The confusing part was his irrepressible realization that he was more profoundly attracted to males (in a general sense) than he was to her, or to any female. He didn't know how to understand this attraction, or how to think about it, or what name to give it, or how to talk about it with anyone—thus there was no chance he would act on it, especially not because he first sensed it while with the various missionaries he so frequently accompanied to their meetings with investigators. He mostly just tried to ignore the feeling, but it kept coming back, undeniably, disturbingly.

In high school he had had no girlfriends, just friends who were girls. In college girlfriends started finding him, and he sometimes had sex with them, never considering that there was any other option—not when the entire world seemed to consist of couples who were male and female.

True, he had always ended up preferring to be friends (real friends) with his girlfriends rather than a couple. And true, he had long recognized that some men were more attractive than others—but he supposed anyone could see that. He never inferred from such things that a man was a romantic possibility. And he was as little aware of homosexual activity around him as he had been of Mormonism: he barely knew that either existed, and most everyone he knew assumed that both were bad. Michael had simply assumed the same.

Ironically, it was only when he became a celibate Mormon with no sexual outlet that Michael became aware of his attraction to men. He would later meet people who had recognized such an attraction from childhood, but he had not: his sexual feelings were dormant at best. He had always socialized primarily with girls because he felt more comfortable with them than with most boys, not because of any strong sexual attraction. Even when his feelings for men finally stirred, in his early twenties, they didn't take clear shape, certainly nothing so blatant as desiring sex. The only explicit sexual image in his mind, as a Mormon male, was not to engage in unmarried sex with a woman. Sex with any man was literally unimaginable.

Though he wasn't alone in his confusion about his feelings, he certainly felt alone. He was aware of no one, inside or outside the church, who felt as he did, or who even talked seriously about it. Homosexuality was so widely assumed to be wrong that it required no real discussion at all—precisely what gave the assumption its strength. A disapproving comment here, a snide remark there, said everything.

That assumption was planted within Michael as well, from his early years, and not so much through anything he heard at church (frequent railing from the pulpit against homosexuality became commonplace only in coming years), but through the usual slurs.

The most memorable occurred when he was a boy, standing in the milk aisle at Van de Kamp's supermarket with his mother (again a dairy product at a crucial moment in his life). LuJean and her friend were discussing someone, when suddenly the friend picked up a carton of milk, leaned over to LuJean and furtively said: *He's just like this milk—homo.*

Michael heard that comment, as well as whispers later on that some senator was *homo*, followed by shushing and under-the-breath talking. Neither time did Michael know exactly what the word meant, but he understood absolutely that it was bad.

As he grew older, Michael learned plenty of other things that reinforced popular assumptions about homosexuality, including from formal laws and even science. The American Psychological Association classified homosexuality as a mental illness until 1973—the very year that Michael became Mormon (though the declassification didn't register with him at the time).

Efforts to legitimize and understand homosexuality intensified around that date, especially in nearby San Francisco, but those efforts elicited far from positive reactions in Michael's social and religious circles. And Michael was mostly oblivious to it all anyway, as San Francisco and homosexuality were other worlds; he had enough to occupy him in his new church.

Thus for many months, even years, after his turmoil began, Michael simply forged ahead with what he knew best—which was that a young Mormon man, especially the president of the Young Adults, should do a lot of good and date girls and for his final act get married.

Michael was taking the classic approach followed by many in his shoes, Mormon or otherwise: seek distractions from unwanted feelings by keeping too busy to act on them, or even to think about them.

He devoted himself more than ever to school, and Young Adults, and his new friendships. He bore fervent public testimony at church meetings and to prospective converts that he knew *the church*, despite its imperfections, was *true*. The strategy worked well enough for several years, at least in public.

In private, especially toward the end of those years, he was some-times on his knees for hours, weeping and praying to God to remove his sexual feelings: they simply could *not* be right and God *surely* had not created him that way or meant for him to feel that way. He also fasted numerous times, without food and water for 24 hours, to figure out how to get over it.

Always a great solver, Michael was sure that he could solve this too, if he just put his mind and will to it.

Continuing to date Susie, and continuing to gush about his feelings for her, were the most promising solutions of all, he thought. He told me, and others, how *super neat* she was, how close he felt to her, how he was sure he was *moving ahead of the competition*, how he thought he was *ready for the big question*, how he saw them getting married, how he had prayed about marrying her and felt sure that the answer was affirmative, and how devastating it would be *if she ever dumps me*.

He fretted aloud when Susie's girlfriends started telling her to do just that, and to wait for her missionary: her inability to make up her mind about Michael was a sure sign to break up with him, they said. He fretted some more when he heard from other young Mormon men that they too had received affirmative answers to prayers about this girl or that, and yet the relationship had fallen apart anyway.

But privately, during the weeping hours, Michael was already doubting that he wanted to go any further in the relationship. When Susie announced in the early summer of 1976 that she had decided to go away to college the coming autumn, Michael secretly felt relieved, though he kept telling people, including me in letters, that he hadn't given up on her.

Expressing his feelings for Susie and repeating his hopes for marriage with her was heartfelt, in a very real sense: he wanted it all to be true. By saying such things to others, he hoped he would come to feel them, and that others (and he himself) would know he was normal.

Yet Michael's feelings toward men were not going away, and thus neither was his stress. One possible (and mortifying) manifestation of that stress occurred while he was at a movie with Susie: for no apparent reason, he fainted. It might have been his usual lack of sleep and over-activity, but the emotional and physical drain caused by his struggle against his sexual feelings didn't help.

A more obvious manifestation of stress was that Michael, even while publicly pursuing Susie, even while putting together his final creations as Young Adult president, decided in the spring of 1976 to seek help.

He was sure that his parents wouldn't be able to provide it, despite their good hearts.

And he was pretty sure (a couple of tentative attempts with ecclesiastical leaders proved him right) that he wouldn't find much empathy at church, only condemnation, however kindly it might be expressed.

This wasn't uncommon during the 1970s, in most any church. One British study soon afterward showed that although 61 percent of gay believers had turned to their particular church for help in understanding themselves, almost none felt like they got any, making them feel only worse, or alienated.

From his own hard experience, Michael knew that plenty of people had outlandish ideas about Mormons. But he also knew by the little said at church on the subject that plenty of Mormons (like plenty of other people) had outlandish ideas about homosexuality. He was as baffled by his co-believers' simple assumptions about gays as he had been by his parents' negative assumptions about Mormons: how could they, he wondered, make such judgments when they hadn't looked into the subject closely, hadn't consulted any sympathetic sources but only hostile ones, and hadn't gotten to know any personally?

He finally looked for help elsewhere.

# nineteen

 That evening Ignatius came to tell me that Father was in the land again.

One can only imagine the anguish in Boxtel as Timothy, returning from his heartbreaking attempt to bring Jacob home, walked empty-handed through the door of the rectory and met the eyes of his hopeful wife and daughter.

But the dominee, despite his weariness and disappointment, wasn't finished yet. Within a few days, he hit the road again—not with abduction on his mind this time, but the courts. His world's laws and assumptions regarding the strength of parental rights offered him one final hope for getting back his son.

His destination was The Hague, capital city of the Dutch Republic and some 60 miles northwest of Boxtel. There he gained an audience with the States General, the highest political body in the Republic (in theory), which on June 17 passed a resolution condemning the *captivity* of the minor Jacob Rolandus in Antwerp.

The resolution recounted how deceitful papists in Boxtel had lured away Jacob, taught from childhood by Dominee Rolandus himself. Once snared, the boy fled by night to Antwerp, where he fell into the traps of the even more deceitful Jesuits, who were holding him at this very moment by force. When the dominee pursued the boy to Antwerp, the Jesuits arranged a meeting under the pretense of reconciliation, then had the nerve to say to the boy, in the father's presence, *Don't you love*

*God more than your parents?* The resolution called upon the governor of the Spanish Netherlands to return the stolen boy to his father. And it declared that until he was returned, the pensions of all remaining Catholic clergy around Boxtel, granted to them for life by the settlement of 1648 on condition that they *carry themselves quietly and well*, would be frozen like a Dutch canal in winter.

The clerk of the States General handed the signed resolution to Timothy so that he could take it personally to Brussels, capital city of the Spanish Netherlands. The dogged Timothy then set out for that city, 100 miles to the south—his fourth major journey within weeks.

He had reason to hope that he would be heard in Brussels, just as he had been heard in The Hague. The sanctity of a father's rights over his minor children was something on which both Catholics and Protestants could wholeheartedly agree. Just recently, Timothy had in his own classis helped to censure another preacher's minor son who, without his father's consent, had dared to exchange a promise of marriage with a young woman. The censure lamented that the young man, by acting on his own in such a weighty matter, had disobeyed God, the church, and his parents.

Timothy knew that his Catholic counterparts in Brussels, despite myriad religious differences with the Reformed, would have judged the case in precisely the same way.

The provost of the Jesuits in Antwerp knew this as well.

That was why, when he learned around June 30 that Timothy was in the land again, this time to plead his cause in court, he grew alarmed, and immediately called Jacob to him.

But the provost was also sure that in a few cases, including Jacob's, there were limits to a father's authority. If a child, for instance, had reached the magical *age of discretion* (around 16), and had done a disputed deed of his or her free will, then it was hard to persuade any court to undo that deed.

Timothy understood this too. In the case of the censured minor son above, for instance, Timothy's classis ruled that, though the boy had disobeyed his father and deserved censure, and though his promise of marriage was regrettable, the promise itself was so binding that it transcended all other concerns—even his father's authority. The boy was ordered to go through with the marriage anyway.

There were similar decisions on the Catholic side, and not only in cases of marriage but of conversion, for which a minor's rights were stronger still. In France, for instance, French courts ruled that a boy as young as 14 and a girl as young as 12 could convert without parental consent, and that at age 16 a minor of either gender could enter a monastery or convent without consent.

The Dutch Republic had not decreed a specific minimum age for conversion, but in practice it too would probably leave alone those minors who had reached the age of discretion and had acted freely.

The provost was therefore confident that Jacob's case was sound, but he had to demonstrate it in Brussels. For unless refuted, the resolution by the Dutch States General could prove every bit as dangerous to Jacob as having his father and uncle and cousins out on the streets trying to grab him. This wasn't because the Dutch had any jurisdiction in Brussels or Antwerp, of course, but because here after the war the two neighboring states wished to maintain good relations—and any perceived indifference in Brussels to the rights of a Dutch father over his son could poison those relations.

When Jacob arrived at last, the provost suggested that they travel immediately to Brussels, 30 miles south of Antwerp, so that Jacob might tell his story in person to the same authorities who were about to hear Timothy.

The two travelers were in such haste that when they missed their final connection by canalboat they made the rest of the journey on foot. Arriving around two on the afternoon of July 3, they soon found their man, Jean Leroy of the Grand Council (or Supreme Court), who by then had already heard Timothy's version of events twice—the second time just hours before Jacob's arrival.

After Jacob told his version, Leroy was persuaded more by the son than by the father. He advised Jacob to tell his story again, to a notary this time, then send copies of the sworn document to the States General in The Hague and anyone else who might need persuading.

That should be enough to take care of things, thought Leroy, who had seen enough such cases in his long career.

The meeting with Leroy completed, the provost left to take care of other business in town, suggesting before leaving that Jacob meet him around seven at the docks, where they would catch the canalboat back to Antwerp.

Jacob had never been to Brussels, and he started wandering through its unfamiliar streets. Upon turning one corner, he suddenly saw in the distance his father with a small entourage. The men weren't looking Jacob's way, so he turned quickly into another street. After that, he wandered more carefully, before finally heading to the docks, where as agreed he met the provost and another Jesuit from Antwerp.

Still the tension wasn't eased: to reach the big boat heading to Antwerp, passengers first had to take a small boat, which made five or six trips out in total. How was Jacob to know whether his father or cousins were already on the big boat, or might board it after he did?

Jacob waited to go out on the small boat until what he thought would be its final trip—and for extra safety he ducked into that boat's cabin. Yet even before it left shore, Jacob's fears were realized: at the door to the cabin there suddenly stood his cousin, Daniel Ravens, beckoning to him to come outside. Jacob stayed inside for the moment, fearing what his cousin might do, or that Timothy stood behind him. Finally Jacob went out with the two Jesuits, bade his cousin hello, and asked about his father's health—but Daniel refused to say where Timothy was. Anxious again, Jacob went back inside until the small boat was away from land and no one else could board.

Once away from shore, Jacob went out again to chat, so that his cousin wouldn't accuse him of *alienating friends*. He asked about the health of mutual friends, which Daniel reported was good. But when Jacob tried to converse further, Daniel began *acting like a fool, ridiculing, cursing, and giving wrong answers to every question*, to the point that people started staring. Jacob gave up and went back inside once more.

On the big boat to Antwerp, Jacob tried conversing again, but Daniel played the fool again, causing the skipper to ask whether

Daniel was drunk or just soft in the head. Jacob finally had to warn his cousin that ridiculing another's faith (at least the Catholic faith) wasn't allowed in this land, and that there were plenty on board ready to seize him if Jacob gave the word.

That shut Daniel up, and he didn't say another thing until Antwerp, where they all disembarked and went their separate ways. Still, it was an unsettling journey for Jacob.

Two days after arriving in Antwerp, Jacob did as Jean Leroy had advised.

On July 7, 1654, under solemn oath, he dictated to a notary three documents, containing the testimony he had given to Leroy but broken now into several parts. (He had first shown a draft of the documents to the provost, who suggested making their tone a little *sweeter* toward Timothy.)

One document declared that no one had persuaded Jacob to leave his parents, no one had compelled him to stay in Antwerp, and no one had prevented him from speaking with his father there. A second told his conversion story, in brief form. And the third specifically refuted all accusations that the Catholic religious of Boxtel, namely the Vlierden sisters, had persuaded him to convert or helped him to escape: how could they, when they wouldn't even answer his questions about their faith? Moreover, said the third document, he had never helped serve Mass or any other service at the convent, but went there only out of neighborliness and in the presence of someone else.

Clearly Jacob felt responsible for the suffering the Catholic clergy of Boxtel were now enduring because of their frozen pensions, and he wanted to remove all blame from them. That Jacob neglected in these documents to name any of the Catholic priests who had instructed him, or to mention that the Vlierden sisters had arranged for some of his instructors, were in his mind apparently justifiable omissions. It would have branded them as villains, when to Jacob they had been his angels.

When the documents were signed and sealed, Jacob dispatched them—one to the Dutch States General, one to the burgermeester of Antwerp (who didn't want to be accused of illegally harboring a minor), and one to a Catholic priest in Boxtel who was trying to thaw the pensions of his fellow clergy.

Around the same time, Jacob sent another private letter to Timothy, *humbly* asking that his father please stop his pursuit, personally and in the courts, for *I am assured, with God's grace, to finish my life in this one and only salvation-giving church.* Jacob prayed that God would watch *over my dear father, for the sake of his piety,* and he assured Timothy *and my dear mother and sister* of his affection, but really Timothy must stop.

Besides traveling to Brussels to help Jacob defend himself, the provost of Antwerp lent his substantial support in another way.

Namely, he had legal documents prepared in the event that Timothy's lawsuit went forward in Brussels or The Hague. These documents assembled various precedents supporting the right of minor children to convert, and testimony that the Jesuits of Antwerp had done nothing to force Jacob Rolandus to remain in their city.

The documents admitted that there were indeed legal reasons on Timothy's side: all nations upheld a father's authority over minor children as a part of *natural law*. But there were even stronger reasons on Jacob's side, which boiled down to this: after 16, a child's rights grew stronger, especially in regard to conversion, and especially conversion to the *true* church. If a Catholic father could not act against a son who had entered a monastery at age 16, reasoned the documents, how much less could a *heretical father tear his son away from the true church?*

Here was a narrow opening indeed in the monumental edifice of parental rights, but it was enough for Jacob, and it was secured with a list of reasons too long to mention here. Everything was ready for the expected battle.

In the end the provost's preparations were unnecessary. By late August it was clear that there would be no trial or further inquiry, in The Hague or elsewhere, regarding the conversion and flight of young Jacob Rolandus, and thus no flinging back and forth of fat legal documents made even fatter by the large writing of notaries and lawyers paid by the line.

Were Jacob's notarized statements enough to satisfy the Dutch States General, which had heard dozens of distraught parents of converts by this time and therefore recognized a case of genuine coercion when they saw it? Or did Timothy finally give up when he saw Jacob's latest documents, convinced at last of the fall of his son?

Certainly Jean Leroy and the authorities of Brussels and Antwerp were satisfied that Jacob had acted freely, whatever private sentiments they may have harbored against disobedient children.

Timothy never chased Jacob again, and Jacob would never come home after all.

# twenty

[ Especially the blatant crap hurts my feelings. ]

The first place that Michael found some help in dealing with his newly discovered feelings was among a few of his oldest friends: books.

He had always been a great reader, and books could be consulted in private, so that no one had to know what he was up to. Soon he was devouring the works of well-known thinkers who had written not so much about homosexuality but about self-acceptance and self-knowledge generally.

Paul Tillich wrote of the *courage to be*, or to act *according to one's true nature*. Affirming that nature meant affirming your uniqueness, and that takes courage, said Tillich, for the things that make you unique are precisely the things that tend to draw disapproval. Yet self-affirmation is not selfish: rather, it allows you to love others in the most complete way you possibly can.

William James had a similar message. Conforming to what most people around you do, listening to other voices, even respected voices, could bring the temporary relief and comfort of social acceptance, but it would not lead to full growth of the unique individual.

And from Erich Fromm's *Art of Loving* Michael learned the importance of self-knowledge for healthy relationships: *Mature love is union under the condition of preserving one's integrity, one's individuality*.

Those were a start, but he still wasn't sure what his *true nature* or *integrity* or *individuality* were. Did self-acceptance really mean accepting how he felt, or did it mean making himself acceptable to himself and others? Maybe you could justify anything you did by saying it was the result of self-acceptance. Could self-acceptance really extend to something as widely and confidently condemned as homosexuality?

Michael needed something more specific on that subject, but there was no easy Internet research at the time, no convenient list of books or of counselors who specialized in homosexuality, and no simple way to ask the advice of people he trusted without jeopardizing his relationship with them.

One day in the spring of 1976, just when he was being let go as Young Adult president, he saw in the newspaper a number for a hotline devoted to helping people who had questions about homosexuality. He decided to call it.

Even though he spoke with only a disembodied voice on the line, Michael was able for the first time to verbalize his attraction to men. From that call he was put in touch with a therapist in southern California, as Michael thought it best to *solve my problem* far from home and then return to Valleytown with people none the wiser.

But his secret therapy over the following months didn't *solve* his feelings at all, at least not in the way he had anticipated. The counselor, more attuned than laypeople to the latest developments in the understanding of sexuality, taught Michael (through discussion and scientific literature he gave him to read) to see his feelings in a new way—as not necessarily a problem.

No, Michael did not have homosexual feelings because he had done something horribly wrong or been subjected to some horrible situation or event.

No, he did not feel this way because he had a dominant mother and an absent father (even if that discredited theory had possessed general validity, it certainly wasn't true in Michael's case).

No, he was not attracted to guys because he had been dumped by girls. Except for Susie, whom he perhaps only kept pursuing because he knew she wouldn't ultimately choose him, Michael had always been the one to quit his earlier relationships, usually because he preferred to be friends with the girl.

What about the late emergence of his sexual feelings, and his sexual experiences with women? Didn't that suggest he might be reading things incorrectly? Not necessarily, responded the counselor, as studies had already suggested that although some people were consciously homosexual from childhood, some couldn't discern their feelings until about 25. Strong socialization and Michael's inclination to please had pushed him to date girls, and he had responded, perhaps in ways beyond the abilities of many gay men, but those relationships still hadn't been enough to make Michael feel whole.

Most people in Michael's circle at the time, skeptical of or even hostile toward psychology, might have passed off the counselor's words and the latest findings in sexuality as fads, as part of an anything-goes social agenda, as evidence of a decline in morals and the growth of a culture of permissiveness—even though the same people might readily accept the latest findings in medicine or televisions or washing machines or heterosexuality. Some would even have passed off the sessions with the counselor as brainwashing, or *converting* Michael to something he had not previously been.

Back at home and out of the comfort of the counselor's chair, not even Michael himself was sure what to think. Though he was not afraid of psychology, and had taken classes in it, he still worried that he was merely justifying his feelings, or that they weren't genuine. He also still found it difficult to contradict those many older people around him whose opinions he respected.

But over the next many months, Michael came to accept more and more that his feelings were as natural to him as heterosexual feelings were to most others. Such self-acceptance made a lot more sense, and made him feel a lot more whole, than his efforts to *cure* himself had—in fact those efforts had only given rise to a growing sense of self-loathing, and he wanted nothing more to do with that.

There wasn't an explicitly religious component to this counseling, partly because most of it was based on scientific research, and partly because most churches were not yet trying to grasp the implications of that research for longstanding religious views of homosexuality.

Yet ironically it felt more religious to Michael to admit his feelings than to condemn them. *I can stop praying to change*, he remembered thinking. Just as he felt that he had always been Mormon once he became one, so he was beginning to feel the same way about his sexuality once he admitted it.

Still, it was gut-wrenching to accept these feelings, because it would in effect mean giving up Mormonism. That was something he didn't really want to do, despite the issues he had with the faith. Leaving the church would also mean leaving most of his Mormon friends too, he was sure—especially if they learned the real reason for his departure. In later decades, the church would clarify that homosexuals could remain in good standing and accept their feelings as long as they didn't act on them (the eventual policy of various churches). But in the 1970s even this possibility wasn't yet clear. You had to be one or the other, either a Mormon or a homosexual.

Michael would have rather chosen both, but in the end he chose his sexuality, believing that only in an intimate relationship would he find his greatest fulfillment, and reach his full potential as a human being. He decided to keep his real reason for leaving the church to himself, and to exit as quietly as possible. Yet that wouldn't be easy: after the reputation he had established, people were bound to notice, and they would speculate. He could hardly bear the thought of the gossip sure to follow, and sure to be even worse than the gossip already spreading about him and Susie: *especially the blatant crap hurts my feelings*. That thought alone was enough to make him think twice about quitting.

If it was hard for Michael to ponder giving up Mormonism, it was just as hard for him to ponder giving up his heterosexuality, for one of the things that had most attracted him to the church was the ideal of family togetherness, forever, with kids, and the image he had of himself as a husband and father in such a family.

Even though studies showed that it was generally easier for converts to quit a religion (especially during the first five years after converting) than it was for those born into it, even though another study showed that a church leaver was most likely to be young, single, male, highly educated, liberal, and mobile (like Michael), even though Michael knew that other converts quit too (in Utah itself two in five converts to Mormonism quit the church for good), and even though he knew that plenty of Mormons *disengaged* for a period of time (78 percent of Mormons in a 1979 study had dropped out of activity for at least a year in their lives), he liked being Mormon. Except for his homosexual feelings, he had no serious reason to quit, especially since momentum seemed to be growing for a change in the Negro Policy.

That leaving a religion is as complicated as joining it (or staying put in it) is reflected in the vast number of terms scholars have invented to describe the various levels of activity: practicing believers, fringe believers, attenders, non-attenders, partial leavers, total leavers, disidentifiers, switchers, dropouts, defectors, disaffectors, deconverters, disengagers, leave takers, disaffiliates (four types), unchurched (six types), returnees (four types), and more. Church cultures have plenty of less formal terms too: ceased to meet, lapsed, active, inactive, falling away, converts, apostates, backsliders, slackers, gone over to Rome, practicing, non-practicing, semi-practicing, cultural Mormon, cultural Catholic, cultural whatever, and so on.

But such complexity and nuance weren't much help to Michael, who was faced with a simple binary choice: he had to be in or out of the church.

What helped ease Michael out of Mormonism were precisely the things that had allowed him to leave his family's religion and become Mormon in the first place: a growing conviction about the reality of his feelings, and the prospect of even more promising relationships in the new if still uncertain life ahead.

Two of the most important relationships appeared in those tumultuous middle months of 1976—just after he had finished his counseling, just after his reign as Young Adult president ended, and while he was still publicly expressing hopes about Susie and trying to stay Mormon. More precisely, both relationships emerged as a result of his first life-altering trip to Europe that summer.

# twenty-one

 During his prayer before the altar, the canon learned that my father, mother, and sister would become Catholic within two years.

As Timothy ceased his efforts to bring Jacob home, Jacob settled into his new life in Antwerp, amidst a new circle of friends and adopted family.

Certainly the Jesuits continued to be the center of that circle, as they again offered crucial support that made it possible for Jacob to stay in town, and to flourish.

Early in August 1654, the provost helped Jacob find a room of his own, away from the temporary lodgings with Canon van den Bosch. Over a two-week period, there emerged one place that was too expensive, a second that was too mean, and a third that was just right. It was in the home of a widow named Josina Franx, who lived just around the corner from the Jesuit house. Jacob could move in the first of September.

When the great day came, Jacob thanked the canon for his hospitality and offered to pay for his time there, but the canon refused, saying that he wished only a reward from God. A grateful Jacob asked for a blessing and promised to stay in touch.

After the provost's manservant Ignatius helped carry Jacob's meager possessions to the new quarters, Jacob went by the Jesuit house to thank the provost too, for all of his good care. And well Jacob should, for the provost had not only found Jacob's room but would pay the first year's room and board of 200 florins.

The provost also arranged for Jacob to attend the Jesuits' advanced school in Antwerp, starting with the new academic year on October 12. The Jesuits by now were famous for their secondary schools, called *colleges*, which offered teenage boys six years of grammar, rhetoric, and logic (all in Latin), plus the novel attraction of free tuition. But in some places, including Antwerp, the order also ran advanced schools, often near an existing university or that would become the heart of a new university itself. The advanced curriculum included a full year's review of the secondary curriculum (simply called Letters), two years of philosophy, and four years of theology. Though intended primarily as a training ground for new Jesuits, the advanced schools might take in outsiders such as Jacob too.

During August and September, Jacob prepared for his upcoming classes, using books given or lent him by Father Happaert and other new friends. Because his Latin was already strong (thanks to his long-suffering father), and because he wanted to learn his new religion thoroughly and quickly (beyond what he'd learned from the Flemish Peasant), Jacob skipped the year of Letters for the time being and enrolled directly in several theology courses. He plunged into his preparation and his new courses with great enthusiasm, far more than he had ever shown when studying under his father. His new professors showed just as much enthusiasm for this *youth with rare gifts*, who lacked only *true faith* because of his upbringing in a *heretical household*.

Yet some of their enthusiasm was due precisely to that upbringing, because despite it Jacob had found the truth anyway! He was a shining example of the irresistible pull of Catholicism. The annual history of the Antwerp house (required of all Jesuit institutions) was only five pages long for 1654, but one entire page was devoted to *the son of a Reformed preacher* and grandson of the famous Bible translator who converted, fled from home, and came to the Jesuits of Antwerp for help.

The annual report for the entire Jesuit province of Flanders, sent to Rome, likewise highlighted Jacob's conversion, out of the two to three hundred other souls won by the province that year.

Initially adrift after his flight from home, Jacob now had new lodgings, new friends, and new studies to anchor him.

During those early months in Antwerp, Jacob also became anchored in the customs of his new faith.

He attended Mass daily, assisting when possible, and also attended sermons daily—even more frequently than when he was Reformed.

He confessed frequently, which in the Reformed tradition he had done only to God but which he now did to a priest, for confession was one of the Catholic Church's seven grace-bestowing sacraments.

He communed as frequently as he confessed, which was far more often than he had communed in the Reformed Church (at most once a month). He also found new meaning in the Eucharist: now the wafer and wine were Christ's own flesh and blood rather than merely a symbol of each.

He fasted more frequently than the few Reformed fast days he had observed in the Dutch Republic, and in fact he sometimes fasted entire days, spending a good part of the time at church, in prayer.

And he engaged in still other devotions that as a Reformed boy he had never known at all. He walked in processions holding a torch. He went on pilgrimage, including a short pilgrimage for his friend Anna Margarita van Vlierden, who was sick back in Boxtel, thanks, feared Jacob, to her frozen pension. He also asked Father Happaert for a piece of a relic, which the father obtained. And Jacob even bought that classic Catholic object of discipline meant to instill even more piety: a hair shirt—and this during the warm summer, at a moment when he had very little money to buy anything.

There was a small problem regarding his baptism. Most Christian churches, except for the Anabaptists, accepted each other's baptisms as valid. But the bishop of Antwerp, like some other Catholic bishops, questioned the validity of any ritual performed by Protestants. Hearing this, the provost of the Jesuits took Jacob aside and baptized him privately, with the provisional formula established for such cases, *If you are baptized, I do not baptize you, but if you are not baptized . . .* and so on.

That baptism allowed Jacob to receive a sacrament he was certainly missing: confirmation. On the appointed day for the ceremony, which had to be performed by a bishop, the bishop of Antwerp anointed Jacob and a few children with the usual oil, and like the children Jacob wore a cloth around his head until noon to keep the oil from running. Like them as well, Jacob received a special gift to help remember the occasion, but unlike others his gift came not from his parents or godparents. Rather, Jacob's protector and father figure, the provost, gave him a golden cross on a chain, to wear around his neck from that day forward.

All this, plus his growing circle of new friends (though not yet a hundredfold), helped Jacob to feel fully Catholic, and part of a new family.

So enthusiastic did Jacob become about his new faith that he felt a desire to practice it full time, by entering a religious order. He revealed that wish one afternoon to an old friend from Boxtel, who was passing through Antwerp. The two had attended Adoration together in the Jesuit church, then afterward strolled in the garden for a long while, speaking of *holy things*. During that conversation, Jacob uttered his deepest desire: to one day become a Jesuit himself.

Here was Timothy Rolandus's greatest fear: that Jacob would become not merely a Catholic, but part of its clergy—and a Jesuit at that. Soon after revealing that desire, Jacob spent another entire day in the Jesuit church, confessing, communing, praying, and fasting.

He knew that the Jesuits would test him, and make him wait. But the path he was to follow seemed clear.

Despite Jacob's new friends and family and purpose, he couldn't entirely escape the shadow of his past life.

Because Antwerp was a crossroads for travelers and traders from all directions, not to mention a favorite destination for Dutch Catholics, Jacob regularly encountered people from back home during his time in the city.

Canon Schellekens, from the disbanded chapter of Boxtel, and more sympathetic to Jacob than was the chapter's former dean, came often to Antwerp and brought news and letters from old friends. A Mevrouw Verbeek of Antwerp, who had a sister in the convent of Boxtel, made her home a meeting point for numerous visitors from Brabant, and regularly invited Jacob to come by when a mutual friend called.

Jacob was far less enthusiastic when he bumped into relatives in Antwerp, or those few other Reformed acquaintances who passed through, as these were inclined to badger him for having left parents and faith. More than once he looked out his window at the unsettling sight of a cousin or an uncle walking past.

Cousin Daniel Ravens, the one who had pestered Jacob on the canalboat from Brussels, now went even further by spreading gossip about him, starting at the Little Mill, where Jacob was well known. Over mugs of beer there, Daniel recounted some of Jacob's teenaged follies—warning that *once the papists get to know* him they would weary of his silliness and drop him. Just the previous year in The Hague, for instance, Jacob had run around the streets in a ridiculous costume of fur and a flaxen beard, screaming and yelling. In Daniel's opinion, Jacob was a little crazy. When the hostess later told Jacob all this, he grew embarrassed and explained: he and Daniel had been in The Hague for a wedding, and while at the home of another cousin, who was a furrier, Jacob had tried on one of the fur coats and an old hat. Daniel then egged him on to go show the costume to yet another family member, down the street. That was all there was to it.

Another visitor Jacob would rather not have seen was the steward of Boxtel (appointed by the States General to oversee ecclesiastical accounts there), a devoutly Reformed man named Cuchelinus, who bragged while in Antwerp that if he could have a word with *that scoundrel* Jacob then he would tell him a thing or two. When he finally did meet Jacob, however, at the home of a mutual friend, *the windbag* had nothing to say except a curt *hello*.

Jacob also ran into a couple named Gaillert, Reformed neighbors of the Rolanduses' in Den Bosch, and *hard believers* who spoke *very broad and wonderful things* to him. The woman even said that she discerned from Jacob's visage that he was sick, which was surely the judgment of God. She promised to pray that Jacob would see the light. He calmly promised to pray the same for her.

Even less pleasant for Jacob than encountering certain people from home was the disturbing news he heard of the latest events there.

One evening at Mevrouw Verbeek's, Canon Schellekens told Jacob that the pensions of the clergy of Boxtel, including the canon's own, were still frozen. But Jacob was not to worry: not one member of the clergy (not even Dean Beyaerts?) blamed him for their misfortune. It's doubtful that this assuaged Jacob's lingering guilt. News in mid-September that the pensions had been released at last surely brought great relief—until he heard a few days later that two pensions were still frozen after all: those of the Vlierden sisters.

Surely this was his father's doing. Timothy might have given up hope for getting Jacob back, might have ceased trying to persuade the States General to pursue the boy, but it was almost certainly he who managed to extract this final concession from the States General as a way to punish those he blamed most for Jacob's conversion and flight. And suffer the sisters did: for before the end of September Anna Margarita van Vlierden died of the illness that had afflicted her since the freezing of her pension.

That many saw her death and her frozen pension as no coincidence was confirmed by the next disturbing rumor to reach Jacob: Anna Margarita's surviving sister, Magdalena, was supposedly threatening to shoot Timothy. Jacob didn't believe the rumor, and laughed at the idea of Magdalena shooting anyone. But the guard being posted outside the rectory in Boxtel was real.

The news Jacob heard of Christian Vlierden was no better. No one knew where he was, or what had become of him. Gossip said that he had been killed in battle. His horses and his servant Faes were certainly dead—had Faes died in jail or of natural causes? As for Ravenskot, he was still in jail for the stolen horse.

Finally, the sheriff of Boxtel (who was Reformed) was said to be at odds with Timothy because Timothy had accused him of complicity in Jacob's escape. The angry sheriff in response said that if Jacob was a papist then it was Timothy's fault—and as an extra measure the sheriff ordered a halt to the repairs on the rectory's leaky roof, so that rain kept running inside.

All of these tidings put a damper on Jacob's joy in his newfound faith and home. But most dampening of all was the news that Jacob heard about his parents.

A driver he met in Antwerp in late July 1654 said that he had recently been in Boxtel and seen the extraordinary sight of 14 or 15 preachers coming and going at the rectory. Were they there to console Timothy? To offer help and advice?

Timothy certainly needed consoling, and more of it as the months went on. In September, he missed the monthly meeting of the classis in Den Bosch, something he almost never did. His low spirits were no doubt the cause, but the classis reprimanded him anyway for his absence and for not even bothering to send an excuse. People in Boxtel noticed too, and whispered that Timothy wasn't right. Surely it didn't help his spirits, or Catharina's or Maria's, to learn that his nephew, the other young Jacob Rolandus, had just taken his first position as a preacher.

Not even a (brief) reconciliation with the schoolmaster during this low time cured Timothy. Feeling sympathy, or guilt, over Timothy's condition, the schoolmaster tore up all the documents from the lawsuit over the barn and threw them into the fire, in Timothy's presence. But nothing really helped.

Just as parents suffered over the deaths of their children, so Timothy and Catharina suffered over the loss of Jacob, which seemed like death. Or worse: at least a dead child had hope of resurrection, while a Catholic Jacob was doomed.

Despite so much unsettling news, Jacob pressed on with his new life in Antwerp. The pain of this world was temporary, after all, while his quest was heaven.

Still, pain was real for the moment. Old Canon van den Bosch, he who once heard angels rejoicing at Jacob's flight from false religion, tried once again to comfort Jacob and offer him hope.

While the two sat in the canon's rooms after lunch, one day in the late summer of 1654, the canon expressed his certainty that Jacob's father, mother, and sister would become Catholics within two years, and would even come visit Jacob in Antwerp; there was no doubt about it, said the canon, because it had been revealed to him during his prayer at the altar that morning.

All the boy's worry and sorrow and doubt would then be swallowed up in joy, and all the struggles worth it.

# twenty-two

[ I was more interested in seeing my holy land than in
finding my dreamboat. ]

Michael almost didn't make that fateful trip to Europe in the summer of 1976. In February he bought a ticket for a group tour that was to leave in July, but in April the tour was canceled. Moreover, his promised travel companion, the former Elder Jones, canceled as well. Given the late date, Michael doubted that he would find replacements for either.

But he did, thanks to the stately Penelope Johnson, who Michael simply called Mom J. Michael had met the elderly and widowed *Sister Johnson* in 1975, when he came by to ask whether the Young Adults might be able to help her with any cleaning up around her yard. Not that her well-ordered home on a quiet, dignified street in Valleytown really needed much cleaning up, or that she couldn't find workers herself. But, rather, she enjoyed the company, and saw something in Michael that she liked, so she readily agreed.

Michael likewise sensed a kindred spirit in her. She too was a fairly recent convert to Mormonism. She too possessed not only a curious mind but (for all her stateliness) an irreverent sense of humor. And she too had a passionate interest in other places and cultures, an interest that had taken her to all corners of the world. Much of that travel she had done with her husband, but in recent years she had gone alone as well, often as an expert genealogist for her new Mormon Church.

On the day of the cleanup project, Michael spent more time listening to Penelope's tales of Rome and Paris than he did raking leaves, and their friendship took off from there. Perhaps his still somewhat strained relationship with his parents at the time led him to cultivate more aggressively than he ordinarily might have a close relationship with a woman almost old enough to be his grandmother. Perhaps her recent widowhood and the fact that she never had children of her own led her to be more attentive to Michael than she otherwise might have been. Whatever the case, the two visited often after the work project.

It wasn't long before she was encouraging Michael to pursue his interests in other places and cultures, which was how he had mustered the nerve to register for the summer 1976 tour. When he told her in April that the tour had been canceled, she drew upon her experience and suggested an alternative company. Then she added that, if Michael didn't mind, she would like to go along too.

He was overjoyed. Just when it looked like the trip had fallen through, he would actually be going on a better tour than the one originally planned, and with a seasoned companion as well—a companion, he didn't know at the time, who would also serve as a guide into his new life.

Traveling that summer across England, France, Germany, Switzerland, Austria, and Italy was as thrilling as Michael had imagined.

He wrote to me rapturously about the wonders he had seen so far, including the *Sound of Music* sights in Austria, but he went on most about Switzerland, which he wished the Mormon pioneer leader Brigham Young had found instead of Utah: Michael was *totally in awe* of what he had seen there.

There was only one annoyance to the trip, he reported: namely, Penelope's reversion to her pre-Mormon habit of drinking wine with dinner. Michael watched in disbelief at first, then in irritation, as she calmly ordered and downed a chablis here or a rosé there. He minded the wine less than the hypocrisy: she should be either in or out of the church, he fumed to me, and quit pretending to be Mormon at home if she didn't really want to be.

That very assessment, however, caused Michael to reflect on himself: he kept telling himself that he was in, but deep inside he knew that he was already edging out thanks to his own more serious conflict.

He was reminded repeatedly during the trip of that conflict, thanks to what he later called *the overt homosexuality* of hotel staff just about everywhere they went, which even the inexperienced he recognized. He had taken the trip partly to get away from his feelings but soon realized that it was not exactly the best remedy, as the travel industry was *rife with well-mannered young men*, as he called them.

It didn't help when the worldly wise Penelope, who had never discussed Michael's sexual issues with him, commented on the number of male hotel staff *sniffing around* their table. He was mortified by the attention, and her observation, and responded by saying that he wasn't interested. He was here to see Europe.

Michael was jarred out of his non-interest by an encounter with the second important person in his new life, whom he met while the tour was in Lucern, Switzerland.

While raving to me in his letters about the wonders of that land, Michael neglected to say that the greatest wonder of all had been not a majestic mountain or inspiring building or picturesque Alpine village, but a person.

As Michael and Penelope walked down the street near their hotel in Lucern, a tall blondish young man walking toward them made eye contact with Michael and smiled. Straight-faced, Michael returned the stare briefly, but grew alarmed when the young man didn't look away. After passing by, Michael, still alarmed, turned around and saw that the young man, still smiling, had turned to look back as well. Panicked, Michael quickly led Penelope into the hotel.

He emerged again about an hour later, to read before dinner in the park next door. As he walked the short distance to the park, a car with its blinker on suddenly pulled alongside: behind the wheel was the same young man Michael had seen earlier, who was again smiling. But Michael didn't slow down; as soon as the car turned the corner, he headed into the park, evading his admirer. Then he sat on a bench and opened his book.

Just when he thought he was safe, Michael heard footsteps and looked up. There was the young man coming toward him. When he was only a few paces away, Michael, to his own mortification, nervously blurted out, *Are you homosexual?*

The question reflected not only Michael's nervousness but his lingering uncertainty about himself, for had he felt more self-assured he would have spoken casually, or at least used the already preferred English word *gay* instead of the clinical term he chose. The multilingual young man understood perfectly anyway, even if the question's bluntness made him stumble a bit and chuckle. But he quickly defused the awkwardness by calmly introducing himself as Stefan Keller and beginning an ordinary conversation.

Michael overcame his nerves and was smitten almost immediately, allowing himself for the first time to be attracted to a specific man. It was not only Stefan's sophistication that impressed him, but his kind manner. For though the six foot three inch Stefan with his styled blond hair and clipped mustache and fine features was at first glance the poster boy for the stereotyped Aryan superman, when he opened his mouth the gentlest voice imaginable came out.

That voice was a reflection of Stefan's entire person, and made it all the more painful for Michael when he eventually learned that just a few years before their meeting Stefan had been beaten severely on a London street (where he did part of his training as a chef) because a neighbor found out that he was gay.

Despite the multiple fractures to his skull, Stefan remained quite matter-of-fact about his sexuality: it had simply been part of him for as long as he could remember. Like many young boys, he had had a crush on his first-grade teacher—but his teacher happened to be a man. He didn't fret about his feelings then, or afterward, and he was self-assured enough to help Michael feel more at ease about himself too.

By the end of their conversation, several hours later (Michael missed dinner), Michael felt that he had had a spiritual experience—*talk about "the truth shall set you free,"* he thought. He knew that his friends from church wouldn't have seen his experience that way. They were more likely to remind him that the devil himself could appear as an angel of light. But to Michael the sense of truth and wholeness that overcame him when he admitted his feelings was the same sense he had come to know while engaging in the rituals and activities he had loved in the Mormon Church. And it seemed just as imperative to him to accept it as genuine.

Michael and Mom J left Lucern the next day, and he had no serious expectations about seeing Stefan again. They exchanged addresses and promised to write, but in those days before email and cheap phone calls it took more determination than most people possessed to stay in contact at such distance. Still, Michael was grateful for the experience, and the momentary relief and peace and confirmation it gave him. He and Stefan had only spoken, no more, but the conversation lit *an emotional ember* inside Michael, and made him feel more complete and content than he had ever felt with any woman.

Yet afterward, he still couldn't completely admit his feelings to himself. For in a letter he sent to me just after this earth-shattering meeting, there was no mention of Stefan. Instead there was a good deal of wondering about whether he would be married in the next year or two, and the usual expression of his fading hopes for Susie.

# twenty-three

 The brother of my mother's maid gave me a letter from my sister.

If Jacob took heart at the canon's glorious vision of a reunited and Catholic Rolandus family, he could hardly be blamed for wondering how it might ever come to pass.

Except for his father's attempts to abduct him, no one in Jacob's family had been in touch since his escape three months earlier. And no one of them showed any sign of wanting to learn anything about Catholicism.

Then just days after the canon's revelation, the Red Sea finally parted and opened a way.

On a Sunday in late August of 1654, while a torch-bearing Jacob walked near Antwerp's great market in yet another procession, he felt a tug on his coat.

He turned and saw to his surprise the brother of his mother's maid. There was little time to talk, but the fellow managed to convey greetings from Jacob's sister, Maria, and to say that she wanted Jacob to write. Here was the chance Jacob had been hoping and praying for!

Maria, who loved Jacob even as she mourned his fall, must have finally wearied of having no contact with him, of knowing nothing about his state of mind and soul. Hence, when she heard from their maid that the maid's brother was going to Antwerp, she cornered him.

At about the same time, Maria also tried to contact Jacob through his only Reformed friend, the schoolmaster Gerart van Hogerlinden, from the nearby village of Cromvoort: would he please write her brother and pass along her greetings, she asked. The schoolmaster did so (though he spent most of his letter chastising Jacob). But the maid's brother reached Jacob first, on the street in Antwerp.

After relaying Maria's message, the brother added that he had to return to Boxtel right away: would Jacob like to send something now? Pulled along by the procession, Jacob replied that he was obviously busy at the moment, so could the messenger ask Maria to write a letter instead?

A week later, Jacob got that letter, through the same messenger.

The fellow left it at the home of a mutual friend, who told the Jesuits, who sent Ignatius to tell Jacob, who hurried across Antwerp's cobblestones to fetch it.

He read the brief note eagerly. *My brother, Greetings from me your sister. The youth with whom you spoke has whispered your greeting to me, and that I should write you, so please let me know with a short letter where you are lodging, for I do not wish my letters to fall into any hands but yours, and it would also not be good for you. May God watch over you, your sister, Maria Rolandus.*

Thus began the heart-wrenching correspondence between this devoted brother and sister.

Over the following three years, they exchanged more than a dozen letters, partly to tell the latest news, but mostly to try to persuade the other to the true church. In the process they would debate all of the usual issues that divided Protestants and Catholics: saints, grace and works, the sacraments, and so on. And thanks to an increasing array of controversy books, which enabled anyone who could read to find in one handy place what his or her faith taught on every imaginable point of doctrine, not to mention how to poke holes in the doctrine of rivals, the siblings would trot out the same arguments and counterarguments, proofs and counterproofs, that had already been on parade for decades.

But these tired old arguments, heard with numbing frequency since the dawn of the Reformation 130 years before, suddenly took on fresh urgency when traded between flesh and blood. It was one thing for

Martin Luther to condemn religious rivals to hell, and quite another for a loving brother and sister to do so.

Woven into, or punctuating, the latest proof of a particular doctrinal point were countless expressions of affection between Jacob and Maria—requests to write soon, hopes of seeing each other again, vows to stay in touch, promises to pray for each other and love each other no matter what. But most moving of all were the tears they shed as they pondered the awful eternal state that awaited the other if the other did not repent.

Bottomless sorrow at the thought of a sibling's most assured damnation was not the only way for religiously divided relatives to express love for each other. But it was the way chosen by Jacob and Maria Rolandus.

The day that Jacob received Maria's note, September 1, he sat down in his brand new lodgings to respond.

A new cross hung over the foot of his bed. A can of ink, a stack of paper, some candles, and a forest of quill pens (all thanks to the provost) lay ready on his writing table. Close by on a shelf (thanks to other friends) stood the latest Catholic handbooks, including a favorite, Martin Becanus's *A Compendium of the Controversy Manuals of This Time Regarding Faith and Religion*.

Jacob had to get his letter right. He prayed that God would guide his pen to say those things that would move his sister, and through her their parents, to see the errors of the Reformed religion. Then, in his small, paper-saving script, he launched optimistically into the task of conversion.

He recounted to Maria how the good God had pulled him, unworthy creature, to His Church, so carefully preserved over the centuries until the present.

He expressed his hope that God would grant him the grace to endure in his new faith, the truthfulness of which was obvious to anyone who would study sincerely and see through the lies told about the Catholic Church, especially by the Reformed Church, for the FOY *religion* (a French word literally meaning *faith* but which was also used as a slur against the Reformed) *is founded on lies after all.*

And he explained that he had no greater purpose than to love and serve his father and mother and sister; indeed, what better way to show his love than to demonstrate those lies, so that they could see for themselves?

Yes, he repeated, it was true: he loved them all deeply. Those who saw his conversion and flight as signs of disaffection couldn't be more wrong. He had left his family (and their faith) only because he had to love God even more. *God is my witness how sorrowful it is to me that my joy has brought this sadness as well, that I must live here as if alienated from father and mother.* It wasn't only the physical alienation that made him sad, but his alienation in the eternities if his parents insisted on clinging to their false religion. That thought was too heavy to bear, and he could only comfort himself with the hope that *the good God will hear my prayers and protect them, and see the sincere piety of my father, just as He looked favorably upon the good works of Cornelius, even though he was pagan.* Surely Timothy's sincerity had to count for something.

Jacob closed by saying how happy he was that Maria had given him occasion to write, that he eagerly awaited news of them all, and that he hoped God would strengthen his parents in their old age.

When finished, Jacob went, as he would with almost every letter meant for Maria, to show the provost what he had written, to be sure that he'd said things in the way most likely to persuade her, and his parents, to the truth. Invariably the provost would suggest that Jacob soften his tone here and there, and shorten everything. Then Jacob would cross out parts, copy the good sections onto fresh sheets of paper, and send the final version on to Boxtel. But this time, the provost was out when Jacob called. Because he was in a hurry, Jacob showed the letter to Father Happaert instead, who, either less precise or less patient than the provost, changed nothing. (The provost would almost certainly have advised leaving out the slur FOY.)

All that remained was the matter of a return address. Jacob had already consulted with the provost on this, as both of them worried that Maria would reveal, or be forced to reveal, whatever address Jacob noted. Thus the provost had suggested noting the address of a woman who lived on the square where the Jesuit house stood, and Jacob could fetch any return letters there.

Hurriedly he scrawled the woman's address at the end of his letter and sent off the whole with a prayer.

Maria took that first letter in her hands some days later, but not in the joyful way that Jacob had hoped.

Instead she was distressed, and so overcome with tears that she found herself unable to respond for weeks. Her confident hope that Jacob would already have begun doubting his decision to leave home and the true faith was crushed.

At last Maria recovered enough from her disappointment to write back, on September 25. With her aging father ready to give up on Jacob, and her mother showing no sign of taking any action herself, Maria simply had to respond. She was the final hope for bringing Jacob home.

It is easy enough to picture her, in the quite empty and now somber rectory in the shadow of Boxtel's St. Peter's church, trying to find a break from her chores and the scurrying maid and even her parents in order to ponder what to write.

She probably wrote in her own room, rather than in the more public room where the now silent harpsichord stood, because it wasn't clear at all whether her parents knew that she was in touch with Jacob, or whether she wanted them to know, given all the furtive whispering and letter-passing with her secret messenger. Yet at some point, perhaps after Maria received Jacob's first letter and fell into such noticeable distress, Timothy and Catharina did find out.

If their initial reaction to her contact with Jacob was unfavorable, as she feared, it wasn't long before they thought it to be a good idea. Because of sorrow or pride, they could not get themselves to write, but they were still eager to hear about Jacob, especially about whether he regretted his conversion yet. Besides, if anyone in the family could persuade him, it was probably Maria, to whom Jacob seems to have been closest.

She might have asked her father for advice on how to go about answering her brother. But she was grounded enough in the Bible and the Reformed faith to be able to respond perfectly well on her own. Like Jacob, she had been educated by Timothy, if without the same attention and thoroughness her brother had received: she never learned Latin or Greek, for instance, or the subtleties of debate. Most fathers thought that best, as they feared that the learning of Latin, or even learning shorthand to take down sermons, would become points of pride in their daughters. But Maria's training, along with the countless sermons she had attended, and her private reading of the Bible in her little spare time made her familiar enough with at least the Dutch version of The Word, if not the Greek and Hebrew original.

In fact Maria fit the image that many foreign visitors to the Republic had of the spirituality of Dutch women: they were all theologians, said foreigners, especially the *women of the Reformed brothers*. It wasn't literally true: Maria and her sister Dutch were rarely formally trained in theology, and the foreigners' assessment simply reflected the low expectations they had of women generally in such matters. But that especially the women in preachers' families were at home in the Bible was quite right.

Just like Jacob weeks before, Maria prayed to know what she should say to convince her sibling to see the light. Then like Jeremiah she took up her pen for one long lament.

How could Jacob say that God had called him to His true church when Jacob had hardly studied the Catholic Church (she obviously didn't know about his secret meetings around Boxtel), and had hardly asked the opinions of Reformed preachers, including especially their father, about that church?

How could he write such a thing, and use that hateful word FOY against his family's faith, when he had been *nourished with the milk of your mother's breast in the true pure Reformed religion*, and when those who fear God's word, *above all else, honor their parents? For I am certain that our religion which you condemn is the true pure religion, which conforms to God's pure word, for I dare say boldly with the apostle [Paul] that neither death nor life nor angel nor power nor authority nor present things nor future things nor height nor depth nor any other creature shall be able to separate us from the love of God, which is in Christ Jesus Our Lord.*

And how could Jacob say that he loved and honored his parents when he set his heart against them, rejected their *faithful exhortations,* and entirely removed himself from their home? Surely he would bring their father's gray hairs into the grave, thanks to his constant sobbing over Jacob's departure, *May God nevertheless have mercy on you.*

Maria could only conclude that it had pleased God *to allow a cloud to descend upon your understanding.* How else to explain that Jacob could follow a religion that went outside the written word of the Bible, *which is holy and pure,* to *a word embellished and imagined by flesh and imported by the devil?* Or that Jacob could believe in the salvation-through-good-works fable taught by Catholics—*they'll have to cross out the words of the apostle [Paul again] before I can believe what they say about good works. For he says if from grace then not from works, otherwise grace isn't grace.* Or that Jacob could practice the greatest sin of all against God, idolatry, by worshiping the saints and the pope.

To Maria, Jacob's *fancy words* defending Catholicism *are but the powder and lipstick on the whore of Babylon. All that you say about her is not the truth, and I'm amazed that you've already learned to dress her up so well.* If Maria had more time, she would gladly refute, from God's word alone, all of Jacob's claims. For now she could only pray that God would preserve her in her true religion and *from the awful errors of idolatrous popery, to which you've run so horribly, so abominably, so scandalously, and so extremely lightheartedly.* She prayed as well that God would work penance within Jacob's soul, and have mercy on him, poor sinner, who had been so easily led away by *those papists* of Boxtel, most of whom, if he hadn't heard, were now in jail or missing or dead or otherwise suffering misfortune. *Thus does God punish the wicked.*

In conclusion, *I pray you my brother that you'll consider my true exhortation, offered to you with little skill but in sisterly love.* Unlike Jacob, Maria rarely bothered to edit her letters: she didn't have time. She simply wrote as she went, with almost no punctuation, and as one long stream of thought. When finished, she signed it, and sent it with the messenger.

The exchange continued in much the same manner for the next year, through September 1655.

Maria repeated often that she and her parents still constantly sobbed over Jacob. In fact, she wrote once, had she known what an abysmal end Jacob would come to, then she, despite her love for him, would have wished that he had *never seen the light of day.*

Jacob was just as dramatic in response: his family would do well to picture themselves at the judgment seat of God, being asked to explain why they had served a false religion.

Maria fired back that neither she nor their parents had any fear of standing before God, for they did not merely imagine that they served God in a true faith but were sure of it, and she was sure Jacob knew this too but would not admit it.

Jacob urged Maria not only to study Catholicism honestly and diligently but to seek the intercession of the saints, especially the holy virgin. He even wrote out a short prayer for Maria to repeat, so that she could see for herself that *this is no idolatry.*

Maria felt that she had already studied enough, and she did not need this sort of praying—she needed only the name of Christ. Jacob could claim all day long that he wasn't practicing idolatry, but that didn't make it so: *I can taste and feel that it's idolatry, and could clearly prove it, if you only had the eyes you once had. But now scales have fallen upon your eyes, from your ruined brain.*

Jacob saw in such an answer that Satan was using all of his tricks to keep Maria from learning the truth. If she really wanted to discover the truth regarding saints and good works and grace and all else, then she would have to study with an open mind rather than rely on the lies told about Catholics by the Reformed Church. Why didn't she go and talk to some Catholics themselves? *Go out among whichever Catholics you please and ask them—go from the East to the West, and I am certain that you will hear nothing other than what I have told you in all my letters.* Catholicism was not at all what she imagined.

Maria passed on their father's sorrow that Jacob had stolen the Hebrew Bible and lexicon from the library. Father had even said one night at table that when he was in Antwerp he could have had Jacob arrested right away, for theft—a claim that would have gotten the attention of authorities more easily than a charge of forced conversion. But he had refrained, in the hope that Jacob would repent.

Jacob admitted that he had indeed taken the books, but he would not call it *stealing*, for he took them only to help his schooling, and if this wounded his father then he would return them. (In fact Jacob did send back the books, which the messenger reported was a great surprise to his family.)

Maria noted how wonderfully Timothy's fellow preachers of the classis had supported him through his recent difficulties, and admonished Jacob to beware of judging them so harshly because of past mistakes: they were only human and the entire church should not be condemned because of occasional lapses by its servants.

Jacob agreed, and asked that Maria take the same forgiving view of his *fellow papists*, and stop slandering the entire Catholic religion because of a few stumbling priests: *Remember that even among the 12 apostles there was one Judas*, yet not even a thousand Judases could negate the truthfulness of the true church.

People said, wrote Maria, that the Vlierdens were behind Jacob's conversion.

But Jacob teased in response that according to the Reformed faith such a thing was impossible: faith could come only as a *pure gift* from God, not from another person. Besides, if all things were predestined by God, as the Reformed believe, then so his conversion must have been predestined as well.

And so they went.

Each letter sent caused a swell of anticipation in the sender, who was sure that the receiver would at last be persuaded by the latest counter-arguments and refutations.

Each letter received caused a collapse of sorrow in the receiver, who was dumbfounded that the other had not been convinced at all by the last message but was instead more resolute than ever.

It wasn't quite what either of them had expected.

# twenty-four

[ I'm not sure when I consciously accepted that
I was a pedigree poof. ]

Michael's hesitation to come fully to terms with his feelings began easing during the autumn of 1976, thanks in no small way to his new friend Mom J.

Although Michael had been drawing closer to his parents as he eased out of the Mormon Church, there were still subjects they didn't really like discussing as much as he did, including politics, literature, travel, and of course the church. With the urbane Mom J, however, he could talk about such things freely, as these were her favorite topics as well.

Mom J valued Michael's conversation and company as much as he valued hers. In fact even before their trip to Europe in the summer of 1976, she invited him, upon their return, to move into one of the large spare rooms in her house. She would enjoy having someone interesting around (not to mention the first-rate kitchen help), and he could save money toward another trip to Europe the following summer. A surprised Michael immediately said yes—and not only because of the savings, which would never be enough to tempt someone accustomed to total control over his living space, but because he sensed a chance to learn from this woman who might help him find the nerve he needed to move on.

It was as unofficial mentor back in Valleytown even more than as travel guide in Europe that Penelope Johnson exerted the greatest influence on Michael Sunbloom (an influence, incidentally, of which LuJean would always be slightly jealous).

This wasn't to say that he and Mom J agreed on everything, including the church. If Michael, for instance, was only gradually moving away from Mormonism during that autumn, Penelope was already absolutely hostile. In the years to come, she would tell people that she and Michael had defiantly left the church together, to which Michael would merely roll his eyes and utter his trademark *Please*. Her reasons were not his.

And despite their constant talk, they also didn't discuss everything, including the real reason why Michael was quitting the church. For the moment, her general insights into life, her experience, and her friendship were enough for him. Certainly she sensed the real issue (as her hints in Europe, and later events, showed), but she was no more accustomed than Michael to discussing such a topic and was content to let him raise it as he pleased.

It didn't please him, not for years. Talk of his social life was restricted to his lingering hopes with Susie, whom he invited to dinner at Mom J's more than once—even after he had finished counseling, even after he had met Stefan. As long as Susie did not absolutely break things off, Michael put his other feelings on hold.

Yet here too Mom J's influence was crucial. After a couple of dinners, she offered the opinion that Susie was not a good match for Michael, and that she was likely to wait for her *returning missionary* anyway rather than choose him. This came as a relief to Michael, and it helped him begin to let go—both of Susie and of his *faltering heterosexual existence*, as he later put it.

The end finally came at Thanksgiving of 1976, when Michael went to visit Susie at her distant college.

That was when she told him at last that she had decided to wait for her missionary, who would be home within months, and, if things went the way she hoped, they would marry.

Michael took on an attitude of mourning, telling friends that he didn't want to belabor his feelings about the breakup, because he wasn't yet sure of them himself, and that he was spending hours languishing on Mom J's couch, with the lights off, listening over and over to Judy Collins's *Send in the Clowns*, his favorite way of coping with difficulty. But this ending with Susie also freed him psychologically to pursue a new sort of relationship.

Stefan wasn't the first possibility who came to mind in that regard. Although they had managed to write regularly, and although Michael appreciated the feelings Stefan had stirred, he was still not convinced that a relationship was realistic, given the distance and their thin acquaintance. Over the following months Michael therefore set foot into the gay social scene closer by, starting in West Hollywood, about four hours away, and then gradually and discreetly in Valleytown itself.

During these months, unknown to Mom J and his parents, he met dozens of new people, including *assistants* of Hollywood celebrities who approached Michael to propose liaisons with their bosses, assorted young ex-Mormons who had been thrown out of their homes and one day found their belongings on the porch, *a lot of hairdressers*, and more. He was propositioned all too uncomfortably by a middle-aged Mormon man who was married with children and who sang in the choir but who led a homosexual life on the side (causing Michael to breathe a sigh of relief that he had not married Susie, which he was sure would have resulted in a similar disaster, as it did for many gay men who in the 1950s and '60s tried the *cure* of marriage).

From all these experiences—both good and bad, both disturbing and enlightening, both humorous and tragic—from plenty of mistakes along the way, and, ironically, from his Mormon background, Michael didn't take long to see the sort of life he wanted to lead: an authentic and honest life, with a long-term partner.

He understood perfectly the focus at gay parties and clubs on the sexual part of homosexuality—the exuberance, the flaunting, the casual pickups, and the *out and proud* mentality. After years of repressing an essential aspect of themselves (usually for many more years than Michael had), it was liberating to freely express that aspect.

He also understood perfectly the emergence of gay choirs, gay neighborhoods, gay churches, and more—there was a safety and comfort in associating with others who were like you in an essential way (just as any minority group, including Mormons, knew).

But if sexuality was a crucial part of his personality, to Michael it was still only one part. He wanted it to be assumed rather than the thing that he or others used to fully describe him—just as every straight person he knew wanted to be known for more than being straight.

And though he enjoyed being part of a safe community, he wanted to live in the larger world as well. He didn't want to be a gay teacher if the point was teaching—he wanted to be a teacher who happened to be gay. He was learning the importance of solidarity among gays, and of group action, but to Michael the goal of it all was to settle the sexuality question and get on with living. Now that he felt settled himself, he intended to do precisely that, and with a partner.

Two friends provided a strong example in this regard.

James and Robert were a middle-aged gay couple who each happened to have a child (from earlier marriages) in Michael's class, during the very year that Michael came out. The two men not only gave advice about the need to be discreet in Valleytown, but inspired Michael with their accomplishments (James had been an Olympic ice skater) and most of all their lasting relationship.

Michael thought that he had a possibility for such a relationship himself early in 1977, in Los Angeles. That chance fizzled after a couple of months, but it proved meaningful anyway. For it was while driving home to Valleytown up Freeway 99 after one especially happy visit that he suddenly found himself weeping in gratitude to God for having discovered the last part of the puzzle that made up Michael Sunbloom. Michael later couldn't remember whether there was a single moment at which he fully accepted that he was *a pedigree poof*, as he put it, but if there was then this was it. At that moment, he felt no doubt about who he was. Though he had made mistakes in trying to figure out what sort of relationship he wanted, he didn't feel sullied, or guilty, because of who he was—instead he felt complete and whole, as if God were saying that the way Michael was created was His doing, as if it was a part of Michael's calling.

These sentiments might have offended his Mormon friends, and other sorts of believers too, but Michael couldn't care any longer: he knew how it felt to him.

Michael certainly did still care about what certain people thought of him, including his parents, and Mom J, and me. He didn't announce the truth to any of them. Not yet.

He even continued to mislead slightly, to protect them, as he thought, and himself as well. Within weeks of that emotional drive home from Los Angeles, for instance, Michael was writing to me, his *closest male friend in the world*, that an *old flame* had come by his apartment recently and *oh the temptations she threw my way! I just kept humming "Come, Come Ye Saints,"* a favorite old Mormon hymn. He also wrote that Susie, now home from college, had invited him to a Young Adult dance, that he wished he had a date with a girl for an upcoming Valentine's Dance at church, and that a Young Adult friend who had just moved to San Francisco had no friends there to help him deal with the *temptations* and Michael was worried about the friend's spiritual state.

But he was as silent as an empty classroom on the real drama in his life at that very moment in early 1977: that his possibility in Los Angeles had ended things (which sent him scurrying for Judy Collins), and that a new and unexpected possibility had emerged in the form of the person Michael had so improbably met on his very first trip to Europe: the smiling, blinking Stefan.

In the spring of 1977, just after his breakup, Michael invited Stefan to come visit Valleytown.

They hadn't seen each other since the previous summer, and Michael still didn't think that a relationship was realistic, but they had written enough to make him believe that Stefan might be interested in visiting him and a new place.

He was right. The cosmopolitan Stefan made the necessary arrangements, and to the surprise of all who knew his tastes (a three-star hotel was camping for him) he loved Valleytown and its warm weather immediately. He stayed for a week—at Mom J's, in his own room, next to Michael's. Though sure of his sexuality by now, Michael resisted Stefan's overtures, partly because of uncertainty about any real future with him, and partly because if there could be a future then he didn't want to ruin things by rushing.

A surprising turn occurred as they sat talking with Mom J about travel plans for the coming summer. *You know*, said Stefan suddenly, in his charmingly accented English as he sat outside on a lawn chair worshiping the Valleytown sun, *if you like traveling so much you should think of becoming an airline steward*, as he called it, and as he himself was for Swiss Air.

The idea appealed immediately to Michael. But it seemed a fantasy at best: how could he give up teaching? Then it struck him: maybe that's exactly what he should do. The loss of each class every year was only getting harder to bear, and another loss was coming soon. Naturally, as every year, this class had touched him *more than any other*, which made it even worse than usual. Maybe it was time for him to end this annual torture.

Besides, the longer he stayed in Valleytown the harder it would be to keep his sexuality hidden from his parents and friends. Did he really want his parents to find out about him through gossip? He wanted to tell them before anyone else did, but not yet. And if word did spread, did he really want to put up with the common stereotype that a gay teacher wanted to either molest or convert his young students? Trying another career elsewhere, especially one that allowed him to travel, might be the graceful way to exit.

But most of all, he realized, if he started working for an international airline, there would be a genuine chance of a relationship with Stefan.

By the end of Stefan's visit to Valleytown, Michael decided (with Mom J's encouragement) that he would look seriously into becoming a flight attendant. And he had an invitation from Stefan to visit Switzerland at Christmas.

So Michael suffered through the end of another school year, enjoyed another summer trip abroad, bought a ticket for his Christmas trip to Switzerland, and began making inquiries about flying for a living.

He was interested in only one airline, Pan Am, because it was the only airline that flew exclusively to international destinations. After submitting his application, he was invited to begin interviewing in San Francisco, in September 1977. Since a new school year had begun, he took a number of personal days to make the necessary trips. He made such a positive impression that the interviewers rushed him through the usual two-month process in half the time, so that he could get working that much sooner. He was a shoo-in, they insisted.

With assurances like that, no wonder Michael was surprised when October, then November rolled by, and he heard nothing. Even as he flew to Switzerland for Christmas, there still was no word. On his lay-over in Chicago, he decided to call his interviewers in San Francisco and complain that he had not even received a courtesy letter of rejection. The surprised person on the other end said that there must have been some mistake: a package containing his hiring letter and training schedule (to begin in Hawaii in early January) had been sent six weeks before! Somehow it had never reached him.

Michael called a fellow teacher immediately and asked her to give the principal his letter of resignation (with the holiday break, the principal would have two weeks to find a replacement). Then he got on the plane to Zurich, full of anticipation—at the prospect of a new career, at seeing Stefan, and at the possibility of a serious relationship with him: the Pan Am people had already told Michael that he would likely be based in London, a short flight away from Switzerland.

The whole way across the Atlantic, Michael watched the flight attendants with new eyes.

This Christmas visit with Stefan was as moving as the last.

But it was also as platonic, because Michael wanted to be sure that Stefan was as committed to a relationship as he was.

When he returned to Valleytown, Michael had only a few days to move out of Mom J's (with many farewells and promises to visit), put surplus things in storage, sell his car, finalize the details of his resignation from teaching, say goodbye to his family and friends, and *for gosh sakes pull together a wardrobe!* His entire life was in an uproar:

moving away from the only town he'd ever lived in, leaving the only career he'd ever known, and of course pondering life with Stefan. But it was a welcome uproar.

In fact he couldn't believe how neatly everything fell into place—the car, the resignation, the wardrobe, the serendipitous move, everything. A true believer might have seen it as the hand of God. Which was precisely how Michael took it.

# twenty-five

 I have to take my leave now. I'm writing by
candlelight and am very tired.

Though all the letters between Jacob and Maria were remarkable for
their passion, and for making the big theological arguments of the day
so personal, two stood out.

Jacob's was dated November 10, 1654, still early in the correspondence.
Since he had reestablished contact with Maria, and had in hand what he
supposed were all of her objections to his conversion and flight, he was
ready to put his energy and thought into one massive, irrefutable epistle.

Over the next several weeks, he made time between classes to pray,
to marshal evidence, to organize, to draft, and of course to show a first
version to the provost. When everything was ready, in early November,
he missed an entire day of class to copy out a neat, edited version. By
the end, it covered 11 large, tightly-packed sheets—the longest and
most thorough letter he would ever write to Maria (by a few pages), the
one he counted on most to change her heart and mind, and the one
Maria kept promising to refute once she found the time.

Thanks to the more sophisticated and refined arguments he was
learning in his studies (he was after all enrolled in a class called *Controversies of Our Time*), much of the letter elaborated themes that he
had so far only introduced.

It explained more fully, for instance, why Jacob did indeed honor his
parents, despite Maria's protests to the contrary. Yes, he had sinned

heavily against his parents in the past, and was sure that he had earned *every hellish torment* imaginable because of it. But God *yanked me out of the pool of ruin*, just as he had yanked out such saints as Augustine. Thanks to his conversion, Jacob saw more clearly than ever his debt to his parents: their care and diligence had prepared him to recognize the full truth when it was finally presented to him! How could he then not love them? In fact he had no greater desire than to help his parents recognize that truth too. That's how he still honored them.

Mostly, however, the letter explained in staggering detail, with citations and references running up and down the margins and off the page, what Catholics *truly* believed about this doctrine or that. Because what the Reformed *said* Catholics believed, well *no Catholic has ever imagined such things.*

Works and Grace: The Reformed accused Catholics of not believing in grace, yet Catholics knew very well that all their good works together could not alone save them. *Even if someone had all the virtues and perfections so that he kept the word of God in every point and part, and even if he had in addition to this all the good works together ever done by any holy person, together with all the holy angels that exist or that might still be created by God, I say even if he had all these things together and even sealed all of them with his blood, they wouldn't help him one iota without the merits of Christ JESU.* The key was to *have good faith and then come to do good works, thus we come to earn the promised reward which Christ earned for us, through his bitter suffering.*

Tradition and Scripture: The Reformed claimed that Catholics practiced traditions not found in scripture, yet the Reformed did the same. They accepted the Apostles' Creed, Easter, Christmas, and more traditions never once mentioned in scripture, then neglected practices that are mentioned, such as washing of the feet during the Lord's Supper.

Saints: Catholics did not worship saints or images of them, as the Reformed claimed, but only Christ; they simply asked saints to pray for them, just as Paul asked the ancient saints to pray for him, or as Reformed preachers asked prayers for this person or that.

And so on with Confession, Fasting, the Rosary, and all the other topics that divided Catholics and Protestants. None of his answers were particularly novel; in fact they were quite formulaic, thanks to all the new handbooks. But the enthusiasm of the recent convert was clear, and he was glad to go to the trouble for his sister.

He anticipated what Maria would say: *that I'm just dressing this all up, that it's in fact not like this at all, and that I'm going against my own conscience—ah*, surely that's your good diligence speaking. He would have said much the same thing himself in years past, *even more clever things against the pope and the Holy Church; but now thanks to God's endless goodness, I see things otherwise*. He wasn't merely being hoodwinked by his new church, he wasn't ignorant of what the Catholic Church actually taught, as she claimed. Instead he saw *as clearly as the midday sun*.

And he wasn't the only one: some of her old friends, he reminded her, had seen the truth as well and converted to Catholicism, as she knew, and she could do the same if she would just *study honestly*. His own honest study made it impossible for him ever to return to the Reformed religion: *I'd rather die a thousand times than, as Holy Scripture says, return like a dog to its vomit and a swine to its slop*.

In conclusion, Jacob also reminded Maria not to be so quick to assume that the misfortunes of his Catholic friends in Boxtel were from God (for the sun shone, and rain fell, on the evil and the just, and those on whom the tower of Siloam fell were no less righteous than those whom the tower missed). He also urged her to write back with any questions she had about his religion, for he would be only too glad to explain. *May God, whom I serve, who bends all rivers, likewise bend your heart, and bring you to the true light of the Holy Gospel and His Holy Church, so that we with one heart and soul may sing with the prophet David, You Lord have broken our bands*. He assured her and *my elderly father and mother* of his unblemished love, and offered *all services* he was able.

When this letter, in all its weight and conviction, arrived at last in Boxtel in early December, it beat down his family's spirits. This was the letter that seemed to cause his parents to give up for good—to see that their son wasn't going to change. Their son whom they had raised. Their son the object of so much attention, the repository of so much hope, grandson of the great translator, to whom they had planned to leave their meager possessions and rich religious legacy.

Timothy was already low in spirits during the autumn of 1654, but around the time Jacob's letter arrived the people of Boxtel began to say that he seemed to have received a great blow to the head.

Jacob heard this too, all the way in Antwerp, and suffered for it. But it only made him more determined than ever to convert his family, for that was the only way he saw to turn their sorrow to joy.

Maria's remarkable and long-promised response came a full nine months later, in July 1655.

It took so long, she explained, because she was hindered by so many household chores, and because Jacob's letter was verbose (*you could have made it much shorter*, she complained).

Like her parents, Maria was deeply saddened upon reading Jacob's words, but unlike them she was determined to refute him, and so forcefully that he would be compelled to release his grip on the Catholic lie. After all, Jacob kept promising that if she could prove to him the truthfulness of the Reformed religion, then he would return to it, and his family. But to do so, she would have to tread on his terrain: the terrain of high theological debate.

Trading Bible texts wasn't a problem for Maria; she was ready to run more of them past Jacob than she ever had before. But *that Jesuitical sophistry* wasn't something she had learned, or cared to learn.

Her biggest problem, really, was lack of time, given her responsibilities around the house. She, her mother, and their maid did all the cooking and cleaning and organizing, which did not allow for large chunks of the day in which to write. But she did have determination—the stubborn determination that was both the blessing and curse of all the Rolanduses, it seemed, and she would compose her letter as she could, between her duties.

For eight long months, despite the cold and darkness of long winter nights, despite her weariness from long days of work, despite her broken heart, despite the knowledge that her education had been inferior to Jacob's, and despite the rumors she heard that Jacob showed her letters to the Jesuits and that they had all had a good laugh at her simple-minded ways, she girded herself to sit before a single candle almost every evening and write what she knew.

She read and reread Jacob's *overly long* letter, reviewing one part at a time and compiling contrary evidence one part at a time as well. Then at the end she wrote it all out, just as Jacob usually did, in a neat final draft.

When she sent it at last, on July 18, it still wasn't complete, but she had no more time for such things. Nevertheless, it was 13 full pages long—not as long as Jacob's, if words were counted, because she used smaller paper and a larger script, but still a monument worthy of a child and grandchild of Reformed theologians.

In fact it was the most impressive letter of the entire correspondence— not so much because of the themes, or even the specific language and charges, most of which she had stated before, but rather because in this letter all of her emotions and ideas came pouring out at heroic length and with such nerve against her better-educated brother. She gave everything she had (whereas Jacob still had numerous long letters left in him), to the point that after this she could hardly get herself to write her brother again.

She began by deriding his November letter, saying that she saw in it only *primped-up and angry words, but no proof on which the false papist religion could possibly remain standing.*

Showing that she had inherited the old Reformed (and Rolandus) prejudice against Jesuits, she added that not even *the most obstinate Jesuit there is, who knows so well with lovely appearances and shamelessness and deceit to transform and embellish lies,* would ever be able to convince her that her religion was wrong and the Catholic religion right.

She repeated that Jacob had experienced not a conversion, but a fall from the truth: he had suffered a *bewitched understanding,* the sort that the apostle Paul mentioned in his letter to the Galatians.

She reiterated the supremacy of the written word (the Bible) over the unwritten word (Catholic tradition), bolstering her claims with a flurry of texts from Proverbs, Deuteronomy, and again Galatians, which warned that even if a trumpet from heaven blew a gospel other than the true gospel already received, *do not believe it*. Christ himself said with his own mouth, *study the scriptures*, but he did not add *and any unwritten word too*.

She elaborated more than ever upon her usual theme that Jacob had not followed the biblical injunction to honor his parents, despite his protestations to the contrary, for his actions spoke louder than words, and thanks to his actions their father was suffering *a constant death*: how was that honoring his parents?

She rejected Jacob's reliance on the biblical texts about leaving father and mother for Jesus's sake because in her view these applied only in cases of compelled conscience—and this Jacob had not suffered. For the Reformed religion did not allow, and their father did not practice, violent compulsion of conscience, *as papists do*. Father had never prevented Jacob from studying true religion, and had never banished him from the home, thus Jacob's choice of scriptural texts did not hold, and *I hope with the prodigal son for your repentance and return to your father*.

She disputed Jacob's comparison of his conversion to that of Saint Augustine. *I haven't read Augustine myself*, she admitted, but she was sure that the saint could not have been as rebellious against his parents as Jacob had been, or have rejected the *lovely opportunity to gain learning and good instruction in holy truth, or have run away from his father's house by night and left his parents in the utmost sorrow* without at least repenting of such things. That Jacob did not lament or repent were signs enough that his conversion was not from God, but from the devil, *who has long tried to trap you*.

She elaborated more than ever on the weaknesses and sins of the Catholic Church, *the whore of Babylon*, and with more biblical examples than ever. Catholics were like the Pharisee in the New Testament, who knew no spiritual or internal penance but expected from his outward works to please God. Catholics eased their consciences all the time in empty works; maybe Jacob could ease his conscience for his sins against his parents simply *by confessing and reading a rosary*. Catholics were idolatrous, in Reformed eyes the most serious sin against God that there was, yet she doubted that Jacob even knew what idolatry was any more. Catholics were deceitful, especially Jesuits, and Jacob's letters displayed all the signs of the usual *shameless Jesuit brazenness* and *clever sheen and clever traps*: surely *they are your counselors*. That most of their forebears had been Catholics, as Jacob had reminded her once before, meant nothing to Maria, for they *sinned unknowingly*. More important was that later forebears saw the light, converted to the Reformed religion, and did Jacob *the favor of letting you be born into the true Gospel. But you did not love the truth, and as the apostle says in Thessalonians, those who do not love the truth fall.* Or another citation: *What you had was taken from you, for who hath shall be given, but who hath not, from him shall be taken even what he hath.*

And she defended her Reformed religion with unprecedented force, condemning Jacob's attempt at humor regarding the *predestination* of his conversion by noting that God does allow evil, and merely because something happens does not mean that it is good in God's eyes. She might have gone further and repeated John Calvin's idea that good behavior was at least presumptive proof that one was among the elect, and Jacob's behavior was not good at all.

There was a final element to Maria's letter. For all of her willingness to go beyond her usual terrain and to engage Jacob on the field of theology, her greatest concern in the end was the well-being of her brother. In fact, for all the pages she devoted to the controversies of the day, her most moving passages, like Jacob's too, were personal—which in her case meant portraying the sadness at home, or appealing to Jacob's filial duties, or lamenting his fallen state.

She regretted to the depths, for instance, that Jacob *languished in Egyptian darkness*, for despite his claims that the devil was tricking Maria, the truth was that the devil was tricking Jacob. She hoped that he could nevertheless be preserved, like King Nebuchadnezzer, from the claw of the roaring lion, for even that fallen king *was at last raised by God again, and granted his reason and judgment once more*. She promised to pray for him as long as she lived. She urged him to study harder, for her sake and his: *investigate, investigate*. She was even willing to read any *popish books* he sent her, because she loved him, but he in turn must read *our books* too, *with a proper spirit*, including the new Dutch Bible Jacob had purposely left behind in Boxtel.

Yet Maria feared that even if Jacob did study, it would do little good, as he was too easily swayed by whoever happened to be around him. *I wonder whether you might have become a Turk or a Jew, if you had happened to move with your father and mother to live among them?*

This was as far as she got. *I have to take my leave now. I'm writing by candlelight and am very tired. I pray you to let me know about your particular state, if you love me as you say you do, but do it simply and according to truth, and just tell me where you live, what you do, what you live from, and how everything is going. With this fare you well until your sincere repentance.* In other words, she didn't want to hear theology from him anymore, only his whereabouts and state of mind.

She signed it, in large letters, *Maria Rolanda*, with the feminine ending "a" rather than the usual masculine "us" of her other letters. Perhaps Maria felt that after this letter she deserved a Latin flourish of her own, like a preacher, or like her grandfather the great translator, who had Latinized the family name in the first place, if in the masculine form.

Maria's letter, for all its magnificence, no more persuaded Jacob, of course, than Jacob's persuaded Maria.

He was astonished by it, in fact—astonished that she could hold such inaccurate opinions yet still suppose that she was sound in *heart and mind*. Maria felt much the same whenever she read something from Jacob.

Maybe neither sibling made any headway because the other, as each suspected, simply misunderstood the rival religion. Both were certainly guilty of inaccuracies, probably Maria more than Jacob: he had after all been Reformed himself and knew the religion firsthand. Yet even if Maria had possessed the thorough understanding of Catholicism that Jacob hoped she would acquire, she was still not likely to have converted.

In other words, the differences between brother and sister were more than merely the result of possible distortions each made of the other's religion. Rather, their differences were the result of looking at religion through different lenses, which magnified and reduced and colored in different ways.

Jacob's *truth* about the Reformed religion was not the truth for Maria, nor for most Reformed members. Most Reformed, like most people in most religions, stayed in the faith of their birth, whatever flaws they or outsiders may have seen, because to them the benefits outweighed the flaws—they were even able to cope with the flaws in a way that made sense to them. Jacob's truth about Catholicism, even if objectively more *accurate* than Maria's, would hardly have altered the much less flattering image most Reformed held of that faith.

And the other way around too: Maria's view of Catholicism, or of the Reformed religion, was not Jacob's.

How was this to be understood?

To Jacob and Maria, and most others of their world, one of them was simply right and the other wrong. One of them was being called by Christ, and the other by the Devil. One of them saw light and the other darkness.

Some in later generations would see the situation similarly. Others, however, had other explanations.

One was that both Jacob and Maria were wrong, and that some third or fourth religion had the truth.

A second was that each of them was right. Even by the seventeenth century, some people were contending that *all can be saved*, if all lived their particular faith well. In coming centuries, the idea would be put in other terms: Jacob's and Maria's particular social station, familial context, gender, experiences, personalities, ways of feeling and thinking, and more, shaped the lens—even decided the lens—through which each perceived *truth*. In their cases, they might have grown up in the same family but there were enough other differences between them that they could look at the same practice or event or doctrine and see it quite differently from the other.

Truth for each of them, though they never would have thought of it this way, therefore didn't lie so much in the thing examined as in the lens through which they examined the thing. Jacob looked at the Catholic customs surrounding saints and images and saw a benevolent God kind enough to use special intermediaries. The lens Maria chose caused her to see any devotional practice involving a tangible image of a saint as idolatry—however clear Jacob's explanation, however pure his intent.

But again, for Maria and Jacob there was only one answer. To Maria, her lens wasn't merely *her* lens, but the *true* lens. Jacob felt the same about his. There could not be one truth for Jacob and one for Maria. There were multiple churches not because different humans needed different approaches to God, but because Satan stirred up the hearts of the weak and gullible to heresy.

Thus there could not be full reconciliation of views between brother and sister. There might be forbearance, and tolerance, and respect, and correspondence. But there could be no union of hearts, no reconciliation or acceptance, unless both of them looked through the same lens, unless one of them converted to the other's view—to *the* truth.

After her herculean letter, Maria showed signs of despairing that Jacob would ever see truth.

She didn't respond when Jacob wrote another long letter in August 1655, or yet another in September, or when he sent a few Catholic books to her and promised that if she would read these sincerely then she would at last see things clearly.

Naturally these books included a title or two by Jacob's favorite polemicist, Arnout van Geluwe. Was one the recently published *Pulled-Off Mask of the Disguised Reformed Pure Word of God*—a tract that condemned at unseemly length (some 500 pages) the new Dutch translation of the Bible rendered in part by Old Jacob Rolandus (even though Van Geluwe himself didn't read a word of Hebrew or Greek)? If so, that would have been a cruel blow for Maria indeed.

Whatever the case, Jacob still insisted that he loved his sister. After a year of passionate and sometimes hurtful correspondence, he ended his September letter softly: *Ah, Sister, do not hate me, I don't hate you.*

Maria did not hate him, but precisely because of her love she could hardly bear his strident defense of Catholicism, for it meant in her mind that her loved one was damned to hell.

She would find even harder to bear the announcement that came from Jacob in the autumn of 1655. After all of her efforts to hold onto him over the past year through her letters, she suddenly received word that he was already on his way to Rome to seek acceptance into a Catholic religious order.

# twenty-six

[ Root beer in a tall glass with lots of ice? ]

In January 1978 Michael Sunbloom fled Valleytown and began yet another life, hopeful that he would find another hundredfold of friends.

On board a lurching crew bus during his first day of training in Hawaii, he literally bumped into a person who became one of his favorites: the alliterative Bette Bouchée, from Beaverton, Oregon.

After the collision, they laughed and began a nonstop conversation. By that evening Michael was affectionately calling her *Beav* and they were already clutching each other's hands so tightly *at the intoxication and sophistication of their new world* that their circulation was nearly cut off. She already had a crush. Michael liked her too, especially her red hair and dark blue eyes and easy smile and personality. But not in the same way she liked him.

He met plenty of other interesting people as well in training, almost all of them women—so many *distinctive personalities*, observed Michael, *so much education, intelligence, and individualism*, all valued by an airline that catered to people from all over the world.

Looks still mattered too, however, as was evident enough in the appearance of those doing the training: each was a *Pegasus decked out in Edith Head attire*, thought Michael. It was evident as well the second day, when one young trainee was tactfully escorted from class (and her new career) for having failed to make weight, a less pleasant aspect of the good old days of flying. (The other trainees learned what had happened only during the next break, prompting them all to drop Snickers bars and Cheetos into the nearest trash can.)

Yet even that scare couldn't dampen Michael's spirits for long, as he thrived in training, still the kid who loved school and knew the answer to every question, though he was less obnoxious about it now. He sailed through the rigorous tests on safety, food service, first-class dining service (which included learning exactly how to carve slabs of chateaubriand and to serve up caviar), and more.

There was only one hangup: first-class bar. Michael drank alcohol before becoming Mormon, but mostly to get drunk, not as a connoisseur. Once he converted, he lost whatever familiarity with drink he had. Thus while everyone else did this test first, because they found it easiest, Michael saved it for last, and sweated. Bette quizzed him constantly and imparted all she knew about the mysteries of the martini, the brandy alexander, the gin sour, the daiquiri. But on test day Michael stumbled badly.

The imperious examiner, Ms. Torie Luke, famous for her exactness, faultless makeup, elegant string pearls with matching earrings, perfectly starched and arranged scarf, and *killer stilettos*, was baffled. Why was the bar so difficult for this bright young man? Michael gulped, fearing that his days as a flight attendant were already over: he was fine with the wine and champagne, he said, but hopeless at *long and short drinks*.

Curious, she asked with narrowed eyes, *what comes to mind when I ask you to pour a long, cool drink?*

*Root beer in a tall glass with lots of ice?* came the hopeless answer.

Fortunately for Michael, her glare melted into laughter. Out of the blue, she asked, *Are you Mormon?* Taken aback, and with no time for the long answer, he simply said, *Why yes I have been.* She stopped the exam and arranged for Michael to meet with a personal instructor, named Kalepo, whom Ms. Luke knew was a former Mormon too, and current master of the trainee bar.

Kalepo was as charismatic as Michael, and as helpful. He not only saw to it that Michael passed the test with flying colors, but became Michael's great friend. Kalepo was the happiest gay man Michael had ever met, and others would even describe him as the only gay man they'd ever known who had been happy his entire life.

Michael liked Kalepo for another reason too: he knew about Michael's relationship with Stefan, and respected it.

A couple of weeks before Michael's bar exam, Stefan had come to Hawaii for a visit, during a long layover in Asia.

Michael was happy to see him, and ready to make a commitment, given the euphoria of his training and the prospect of soon being able to move to London. From this visit on they became an official couple.

But only days after Stefan left came an unexpected disappointment from Pan Am: Michael was to be based in New York, not London. It was better than being stationed in San Francisco or Asia, but it was a lot worse than London. Michael wanted more from a relationship than a monthly visit or so.

At dusk, without his Judy Collins, he went to sit by the pool and wallow in the natural melancholy around him. The water shone, the tropical skies were clear, the scent of plumeria blossoms filled the air, and the lovely Bette Bouchée emerged from her room to comfort Michael Sunbloom. She'd noticed from her window how upset he seemed, and decided to see what she could do.

Though she had met and socialized with Stefan during his visit to Hawaii, she hadn't seen anything that made her think Michael was gay. For his part, Michael had simply assumed it must be obvious: *I mean, what could be more cliché than a gay flight attendant?*

And so Bette *got all snuggly* and told Michael how she felt about him in order to cheer him. That was when Michael realized he needed to be clear.

The news made her cry, as he had feared. But, she explained, it wasn't so much because Michael didn't like her *that way*. She could deal with that. More difficult to bear was the prospect of losing Michael as a friend: she assumed that if he preferred men, then he wouldn't want to be close with her any longer.

That alone helped Michael's mood, as he tried not to laugh: *You're kidding*, he exclaimed. Hadn't she noticed that most of his friends were women? Of course, at the training school there wasn't much other choice, so she hadn't. They ended up laughing together in what remained of the fading light, and stayed friends forever.

When training was over, Michael moved to New York with several members of his class, including Bette.

Seven of them shared an apartment in Kew Gardens, Queens, which as Michael put it was about fifty percent Orthodox Jews and fifty percent Unorthodox Flight Attendants. Most of the attendants were gone at any one time, and you were as likely to see a roommate in Tokyo as at the apartment in Queens.

Though disappointed about working out of New York, Michael tried to stay optimistic about Stefan, seeing him whenever their itineraries matched somewhere in the world. He also eased his pain with his usual Sunday phone call to his parents, and regular calls to Mom J, but especially by throwing himself into his work—in his usual creative and entertaining way, cheering himself and many of the people around him on those roomy 747s.

Before a flight he pressed and starched his uniforms and shirts, buffed his shoes to brilliance, and manicured his hands, which were *under constant scrutiny from passengers*. He did all this, of course, to the proper mood music—not Judy Collins now but Stevie Wonder's *Superstition*, Marvin Gaye's *I Heard It Through the Grapevine*, Aretha Franklin's *Respect*, or (this was, after all, Queens during the 1970s) the soundtrack from *Saturday Night Fever*.

But the best mood setter of all was putting on the famous light blue Pan Am uniform, taking the crew bus or limo to JFK, and then walking down the hallway toward the gate with the other 15 flight attendants of a 747 crew: *15 chic perfectly coifed and manicured women, in Pan Am pearls and grace, clicking along in their stilettos, always managing after only a few dozen yards unconsciously to find the same rhythm*, was how the elated Michael described it.

Like most other flight attendants, Michael preferred to work in first class, where the passengers were few, and where he found the conversations generally more interesting and less snobbish than he'd supposed.

He liked the first-class dining room in the bubble atop the 747, with its linens and silver and China and bouquets and crystal ice buckets, but he enjoyed most that people were interested in him and his colleagues beyond the food and drink they served up; some passengers offered him jobs, some sent commendation letters to Pan Am, and against the rules some stuck money in his coat pocket, which he found only when changing back at the hotel.

But Michael was even more at home in the main cabin, where his gift for dressing up the ordinary was more apparent. The breakfasts here, for instance, featured an *upscale Twinkie*, and to make them palatable Michael draped the trolley with linens, topped it with fresh flowers and silver mugs, and creatively folded the paper napkins into assorted shapes. And though there was less time for personal conversation here, he, like his mother, was a master at banter.

Michael worked the same flight with Bette only rarely during his time at Pan Am, and only one memorable time did they work together in the same part of the plane. Michael never laughed so much on a flight as on that one: *the chemistry between us and with the passengers* was so strong that people began inviting them to all sorts of parties that night. When the plane landed and the purser thanked everyone for choosing Pan Am, cheers and whistles went up from their area and people started chanting their names. And when the seat belt sign went off, people not only stood but applauded.

He laughed, embarrassed, and looked at the laughing Bette, but he was of course happy that people noticed and appreciated his efforts to make their lives a little more interesting and fun.

After almost a year of flying, Michael decided that the glamour and adventure and travel were not enough to compensate for the rarity of his visits with Stefan.

Among his newest set of friends, here was the one who mattered most, yet whom he saw least. Sometimes they just missed seeing each other in a faraway city, which only aggravated him.

Michael wanted to be transferred to London, but he didn't yet have the seniority to move. Moreover, he wondered whether a move would even make that much difference: if he flew the first half of a month, for instance, and Stefan the second, they would miss each other anyway.

And something else: though Michael loved the job, and though it was demanding when on board, he feared that by working merely 15 days a month (including layover days), and only 65 hours of that on board, he would become *indolent, selfish, and egocentric.* But maybe that's just what he told everyone who didn't know how much he missed Stefan.

Thus Michael decided that it was time to change his life again. At the end of his first year with Pan Am, he quit and moved to Switzerland to be near Stefan full-time. Ever industrious, he quickly lined up a job at the Berlitz School, teaching English, and also did some graphic design (still by hand) and modeling (*what a hoot!*) on the side. He dove into his new work, and, the better to assimilate into Swiss society, studied German seriously, and picked up some French casually.

As any immigrant, or convert, knows, assimilation is hard work. But Michael thought it was worth it, to be with Stefan at last. Or was he? Because Stefan was still gone often enough on Swiss Air that Michael began to resent it. He *didn't move to Switzerland to be alone half the month*, he said. Stefan decided to change jobs too. With his background in food, he opened a sandwich shop in 1980, right in the center of town, and was now in town full-time, just like Michael.

Only one important obstacle remained to their long-term plans in Switzerland: Michael's visa.

To live there permanently he needed the Swiss version of a green card. But the usual channels took a lot of time and trouble. Michael and Stefan turned to an increasingly popular solution among international gay couples in Switzerland, a modification of a solution used by international straight couples for centuries: namely, Michael would marry.

Not Stefan, which wasn't possible, but a Swiss woman, who would be paid a fee for her trouble. It was a formal arrangement, but the gregarious Michael couldn't help getting to know her, and they became friendly enough that when the woman later had a child with her boyfriend she named that child after Michael.

With the visa, with their new jobs going well, life seemed rosy indeed. Michael became part of Stefan's social circle, both of them made still other friends, and both maintained their favorite friends from the airlines, who often flew through and stayed the night at their apartment.

Yes, life was sunny in Switzerland, even when not literally so. There was one nagging and huge cloud, however, almost but not really forgotten in all the tumult: Michael had been with Stefan for five years, but Mike and LuJean still didn't know the truth about him.

Convenient as it had been for Michael to leave Valleytown and avoid much of the gossip spread about him, happy as he had become in his new life, if he wanted to live as authentically as he claimed then he really needed to tell a few people back home, starting with his parents.

# twenty-seven

 The longer time goes on, the more I see that
father is deceived.

The provost of the Jesuits had promised to support Jacob for one
year only.

As impressed as they were with the young man, as vigorously as they
defended him, the Jesuits did not wish to support him, or any refugee,
forever. It was expensive, and would not sufficiently test the convert's
mettle and sincerity—especially not if he was interested, as they hoped
Jacob might be, in becoming a Jesuit himself.

Jacob's support ended in September 1655, just before the next school
year was to begin. If he wanted to continue his schooling, he needed to
come up with money for tuition (not free at the advanced schools) and
living expenses. He could hope for another generous benefactor to
emerge, or he could take the initiative and find a lot of benefactors on
his own—in other words, he could go out and beg alms. Ignatius Loyola
himself, founder of the Jesuits, had spent his summers between school
years doing just that (coincidentally in Flanders), so why not Jacob?

But there was another solution too, to Jacob's economic troubles,
and this was the one he finally decided upon: to enter a religious order.
He had thought about doing so almost from the time of his conversion,
and now after more than a year in his new faith he felt ready. It would
satisfy the longings of his soul and the needs of his mortal body all
at once.

Inexplicably, however, given Jacob's debts to the Jesuits, not to mention his utterance a year earlier about wanting to become a Jesuit himself, he tried first to enter the Capuchins, an order famous for its preachers.

Or perhaps it wasn't inexplicable: this was after all the order Timothy had initially suspected Jacob of wanting to join, and in Antwerp Jacob had been impressed by the Capuchins' Thursday afternoon sermons. Did he fancy himself becoming a great preacher, like his father and grandfather, if for another faith?

Whatever his motives, the Capuchins told him no, explaining that as long as war raged in the land (this time against France) they were accepting no new entrants.

But Jacob didn't give up. Rather, he decided that he would go to the source, to Rome itself, where the headquarters of just about every Catholic order was located, and seek admission there. If there were any doubts about his sincerity, or stability, or determination, surely such a journey—more than a thousand miles made on foot and without resources and through much snow—would dispel them.

Jacob also had a backup plan in mind. If he was unsuccessful in Rome with the Capuchins, then he would try next at the headquarters of the Jesuits.

Maybe the local Jesuits in Antwerp had also told Jacob no by this time, worried that it was still too soon for the new convert to become one of them.

The Eternal City was long a popular destination before Jacob Rolandus ever set eager eyes on it—for the curious, for the well-heeled, for the seekers of social polish, and of course for the religiously devout.

Protestants saw nothing religious about the place at all. William Cecil, Lord Burghley of England, articulated the feelings of many co-religionists when he said, *Suffer not thy sons to pass the Alps, for they shall bring home nothing but pride, blasphemy, and atheism.* And Rome, obviously, was the greatest source of all three.

Jacob, however, was as rapturous as a new nun at the thought of his trip. His anticipation would carry him through the following months, when he would have no possessions except the clothes on his back and sore feet and faith that God would see him through.

He set off in early October, when the leaves were changing and winds blowing and cold rains falling. East across the Spanish Netherlands, across the southeastern tip of his native Dutch Republic, and then southeast through German towns large and small—Aachen, Königstein, Frankfurt, Asschaffenburg, and more—he progressed.

Only in late October, when he reached Catholic Würzburg, where the bishop's magnificent palace had been flattened two decades before by that scourge of Catholics, Gustavus Adolphus of Sweden, did Jacob sit down to tell his family just exactly what he was doing.

If their rebuffs, and their distress at his conversion, made him hesitate to write with the truth, they didn't stop him altogether or from waxing rhapsodically as ever once he started. He explained that the more time went on, the more he understood how *God gave himself completely for me on the cross of Calvary, so that I may attain eternal salvation.* And the more he understood that, the more Jacob wanted in return to give himself *more fully to God, as the apostle Paul counseled.*

Hearing such sentiments from their children might have pleased most Christian parents, but the Rolanduses knew that to Catholics the words *more fully* usually had a particular meaning: entering a religious order. Their fears were confirmed by Jacob's next words, which told them that he was headed to Rome, and why.

They wouldn't have cared about the rest of the letter: that he had enjoyed good health along the way, that he wanted Timothy and Catharina to study Catholicism *just once without partisanship,* and that he was sure *the longer time goes on the more I see that father is deceived.* It closed in Jacob's usual puzzling way: *Your most subject son and servant.*

But they would have seen all this only if they read on.

Jacob wrote the same news and sentiments to Maria, separately.

This letter noted as well, quite sarcastically, that while traveling through Germany he had seen both Calvinist and Lutheran towns and couldn't make up his mind which to follow. *Lutherans say they are the best, so do Calvinists, and they damn each other*. To him the answer was clear: they were both confused, like all Protestants.

He exhorted Maria not only to study harder in order to escape such confusion, but to look to the example of the most famous Catholic convert of their time, who happened like Jacob to be on the way to Rome as well, and whose path Jacob had just crossed: Christina, self-deposed queen of Sweden, and daughter of that iconic Lutheran, King Gustavus Adolphus.

Christina had rejected her religious heritage, and her crown, for the sake of the true Catholic Church, Jacob told his sister. And if such a prominent figure as Christina could give up her lofty heritage and position for the sake of the truth, then surely Maria could give up her more modest versions as well.

In fact the commonalities between Christina and Maria hardly extended beyond their gender, while those between Christina and Jacob were striking indeed. At least on the surface.

Born to famously Protestant parents in 1626, ascending to Sweden's throne in 1632 when her seemingly invincible father was killed, Christina was by 1650 weary of being queen and, like Jacob at the same date, of her birth religion as well.

Like Jacob, she first seriously discussed those doubts with Jesuits. Like Jacob, once she decided to convert she went about it cautiously, telling few people of her plans and continuing to attend Lutheran services; even when she abdicated in the great hall in Uppsala in early June 1654, only weeks after Jacob Rolandus had abdicated his position as a dominee's privileged son, she still kept quiet. And like Jacob, once she quit her position, she set out for a new land.

Though her final destination was Rome, she ended up, like Jacob, in the Spanish Netherlands. After passing through Denmark and the Dutch Republic in disguise (sporting short hair, a sword, and men's clothing, which she was said to prefer), and stopping briefly in Utrecht to meet Anna Maria van Schuurman, a woman renowned for her learning and her 15 languages (compared with Christina's mere six), the former queen reached Catholic soil at last on August 5, in Antwerp.

She stayed in the land for a little more than a year, awaiting an invitation to Rome, where she hoped for a spectacular public ceremony with all the world watching, and a new source of income as well. Part of that year she spent in Antwerp, breathing the same air as that other recent convert in town, Jacob Rolandus.

Jacob wrote in his journal that he bumped into Christina more than once during her stay.

In fact, on the very day of her arrival, she entered the Jesuit Church during High Mass, where Jacob happened to be present. Because she was still in disguise, and took an inconspicuous seat in a side chapel, most people in the church didn't recognize her. But Jacob's friends the Jesuits, Christina's confidantes, whispered to him who she was.

To the surprise of those who did know her identity, she knelt reverently during the elevation of the host—surprise because most Protestants remained standing at that moment, and were usually run out of the church for doing so. But Christina was always full of surprises, as Jacob had already heard, from the Jesuits and others.

It was said that she disbelieved not only Lutheranism, but maybe everything else too. That she was a libertine, whose sexuality was as vague as her religious beliefs. That she was not keen to marry. That she enjoyed the company of philosophers more than that of priests. That she ended most of her sentences with expletives and blasphemies. And that, despite all these objectionable traits, she somehow liked talking with Jesuits (perhaps only to bait them) and was about to convert to Catholicism.

None of this impressed the zealous convert Jacob. Neither did his second encounter with the queen, ten days later, again at the Jesuit church. This time she sat without disguise, but she also held herself *like an atheist*, or some other *abomination*.

Not even Christina's many other excursions to the church and to the Jesuits' impressive library could alter Jacob's harsh opinion. He suspected that Christina's churchgoing was a show, or motivated by artistic curiosity only. After all, the Jesuit church in Antwerp was a Baroque masterpiece, modeled after the Jesuit Il Gesu in Rome, and the first structure of its kind north of the Alps. Situated on one side of a square near the center of town (two of the other sides were occupied by the Jesuit House), it attracted crowds of people besides Christina. Even Protestants admitted that the church's splendor—its geometrically tiled floor, its wondrous barrel ceiling, its sun-bathed upper galleries, and its immortal paintings by Rubens, all guarded by four armed musketeers—was *so great that one is almost overcome. These Jesuits truly have their heaven on earth.*

A final rumor about the queen impressed Jacob even less: it was said that during any sermon (Lutheran or Catholic), Christina had a habit of stashing some classical work inside her missal and quietly reading that rather than listening to any priest.

Perhaps least impressive of all to Jacob were Christina's reasons for converting.

The strongest was supposedly the assurance of her friends that Catholicism would be more hospitable than any other religion to her wide-ranging beliefs and sentiments. In other words, if she had to belong to some church, and just about everyone at the time assumed that she did, then Catholicism would suit her best.

Here was a completely repugnant idea to young Jacob, for whom Catholicism was more than the least possible evil. And here was where some of the striking parallels between the ardent convert and the famous libertine began to diverge, dramatically. Even if there was no such thing as a pure convert, on one end of the spectrum, or a wholly cynical convert on the other, Jacob and Christina approached those ends about as closely as any converts might.

Jacob had kept his plans about his conversion quiet to avoid trouble with his parents. Christina had kept her plans quiet in order to hang onto her royal allowance as long as possible.

When Jacob fled to the Spanish Netherlands, with his father and uncles hot on his trail, he did so in obscurity, and because he wanted to live his faith. When Christina fled her homeland, she was mostly bored with Lutheranism, and though she came first in disguise she was soon saluted with torches and cannon and bells ringing in *grateful harmony*, while city gates were adorned by fireworks in the shape of two angels holding the name *Christina*, city halls were illuminated by thousands of torches, and city streets groaned from the weight of so many heavy tapestries and cheering crowds.

When Jacob made his confession of faith signaling his conversion, only the priest and perhaps one or two other people witnessed it. When Christina finally made her confession of faith, in Brussels late in 1654, the ceremony was also private, but only because of pressure from the king of Spain to keep it so; to Christina's delight, everyone knew about the ceremony anyway, and as soon as she finished swearing off her heretical faith and accepting the *One Holy, Catholic, Apostolic Roman Church and all of its teachings*, a signal went out and every gun in Brussels was fired in celebration.

After Jacob converted, he reverently swallowed the host and thanked God for His gift. After Christina converted, she shocked many around her at her first official Mass by joking about transubstantiation.

After Jacob got to Antwerp, he attended Mass and confessed as often as possible. After Christina converted, she happily exclaimed, *No more sermons for me!*

When Jacob set out for Rome in early October 1655, he did so on foot, without any money, and without knowing anyone along the way. When Christina set out for Rome, at nearly the same time as Jacob and along the same roads, she went by coach, had 221 people in her entourage, and was greeted with fanfare and the best food and lodgings at every town.

And in between these two examples were legions of other converts during the Reformation, full of an endless variety of motivations.

Some weeks after leaving Antwerp for Rome, Jacob ran into Christina again, in November 1655, this time in Innsbruck, Austria, about halfway to their common destination.

Word had come to Christina from the pope that her private conversion to Catholicism, performed in Brussels, wasn't good enough. He would not receive her in Rome unless she underwent a highly public conversion before setting foot on Italian soil.

Innsbruck was the last chance for such a ceremony, and there it occurred, on November 3, with Jacob Rolandus very possibly in attendance. Streets to the main church in the city were covered with boards to keep the mud from Christina's black silk gown and the cross of five diamonds that hung from her neck as she walked in solemn procession behind dozens of priests. Inside the church there was holy water, kissing of crystal crosses, and heavenly music, while the queen took her seat in the choir, near a chair covered in gold cloth where the officiating priest (sent from Rome) ostentatiously sat. A low stool before that chair awaited the knees of the royal convert.

Christina knelt on the stool and listened, the priest from Rome declared his business, then Christina for a second time swore off Lutheranism and swore on Catholicism, this time before an immense crowd shedding copious tears, according to chroniclers.

All this was followed by bonfires, more bells, more cannonfire, and feasting. And of course *an impious play*, which Christina would not miss.

Whatever Jacob's personal misgivings about Christina, he viewed her conversion as a great triumph for all Catholics—that was how he could hold her up as an example to his sister Maria.

A convert to one's side was a victory, an affirmation, for that side; it wasn't merely the alignment of an individual's particular spiritual sensibilities with a faith that best suited them. Christina's conversion was yet another proof, like his, of the convincing power of Catholicism.

Jacob could also honestly repeat to Maria the reports that Christina *had studied for five, maybe seven years* to know the truth of Catholicism—though he didn't repeat reports of the queen's doubts and some of the scandalous books she liked to read as well. His purpose was to get Maria to study.

Whether Christina's conversion softened Jacob's attitude toward her, he certainly recognized the logistical benefits of joining her entourage for the crossing into Italy. Surely there was a Jesuit from Antwerp somewhere in Christina's retinue who would have known Jacob, and who probably made it possible for him to travel in her train. Jacob may even have had that strategy in mind all along, for just as surely he could have learned from the Antwerp Jesuits about Christina's travel plans; his decision to leave Antwerp at around the same time as she may have been no coincidence at all.

However it was arranged, Jacob now went along with the queen. With her entourage he would be able to reach Venice more easily than if moving alone, as there were snowy passes and rivers and borders to cross and passports to be shown and porters to be paid.

Christina and Jacob and more than 200 others left Innsbruck on November 8, when the party saw a good moment to make the passage through the Alps. As she and her courtiers slowly made their way across the mountains and through the Italian north, did she notice the obscure convert walking alongside, or just behind?

Christina entered Rome six weeks later, on Christmas Eve of 1655, in a lovely blue coach provided by the pope himself, and Jacob may well have entered with her on foot.

The entry of these two converts into Rome marked the end of the often parallel paths they found themselves on during the most tumultuous year of their lives.

Christina stayed in Rome until her death in 1689, notoriously irreverent to the end, yet was laid to rest in St. Peter's anyway in honor of her conversion. Jacob stayed until late winter, when the road across the Alps again became passable, and was back in Antwerp by April 1656, as unnoticed by most of the world as ever.

# twenty-eight

[ Don't tell your parents, it will kill them. ]

Michael put off telling his parents about his sexuality for so long because he could imagine their reaction: first Mormonism, and now this!

They were happy that he had given up Mormonism, taking it as a sign that he had rejoined them (always the simplest way for religiously divided families to reconcile). But he feared they would be even more perplexed by this new revelation than they had been by his Mormonism. So he kept telling himself that he was going to have the talk soon, in keeping with his determination to live authentically—but not yet.

Moving away from Valleytown made postponing it even easier: he could live authentically in New York or Switzerland and his parents wouldn't have to know, for at such distances their social circle was in little danger of intersecting with Michael's.

His parents had met Stefan of course, and they liked him—but as Michael's friend and roommate. When Mike and LuJean started visiting Switzerland in 1979, they stayed at Michael and Stefan's lovely three-bedroom apartment, and the gracious hosts moved in advance into separate bedrooms while his parents took the third. Stefan was still the roommate.

Although slow with his parents, Michael did start telling some of his longtime friends back home about himself. It wasn't easy. Each revelation gave him a severe case of anxiety, for he never knew how even good friends might respond. And if one of them took it well, then Michael started worrying about the next.

His friend since first grade, Julie Nagata, wasn't fazed at all. But Michael thought, *It's because she's an artist.*

Joni, his first connection to the Mormon Church, also took the news in stride. But Michael decided it was only because she had quit the Mormon Church too. He doubted that his few remaining still-practicing Mormon friends would respond that way. Yet he wanted to try anyway with a couple of them, starting with Elder Jones.

Michael nervously wrote him with the news—and heard nothing. He tried again a couple of months later, explaining things as best he could and adding that if Elder Jones couldn't deal with it then he would understand, but he hoped that they could stay friends and friends had to be honest with each other. Still nothing.

Michael did his best not to fret, or to let the silence hurt him. Every change he had made in his life so far had included the loss of friends, so he knew that he might lose some now too. But he really hadn't expected to lose this one, after all their working and laughing and conversing, and after having served as Elder Jones's best man.

He decided to try one more time, and this time he got a response— from Elder Jones's wife. It politely asked that Michael not write again, and passed along the distressing news that Elder Jones had been so upset by Michael's news that he was now in counseling and that he had gone through the wedding album and torn up all of the pictures that included Michael.

This was worse than silence.

Maybe if that revelation had gone better Michael would have dared to tell me, too, his final Mormon friend, at that time. Instead he simply and gradually pulled away by writing me only occasionally and vaguely from his new home in Switzerland.

And maybe had the revelation to Elder Jones gone better, Michael would have found the courage to tell his parents sooner too. Instead he kept delaying. For five years, whether during his phone call home every Sunday, or his twice-yearly visit to Valleytown, or his parents' now annual visit to Switzerland, he never said a word.

Until one day he had no choice.

It happened like this.

Whenever Michael came home to visit, he often chatted with the woman next door, an old family friend, whom he had always liked and had once encouraged to return to college to earn a teaching credential: *you would be great at teaching*, insisted Michael.

During one of their chats while Michael was at home, the woman bluntly asked whether he was gay and whether Stefan was his partner. Michael wasn't embarrassed by the question any longer, even if he disliked it (*I mean does anyone ever ask, "Are you straight?"*). But how should he answer? The neighbor was very much inside his parents' social circle.

Believing that he had a good relationship with the woman, and that he could trust her, he finally said yes, to both questions. She responded that she suspected as much, and didn't mind herself but *whatever you do, don't tell your parents, it will kill them.*

It was just what Michael didn't want to hear. But from that statement he was at least sure that the neighbor wouldn't tell either.

Then she did anyway. In the late summer of 1983.

LuJean and Mike had just returned from their latest visit to Switzerland. One afternoon, LuJean was sitting with the neighbor at the neighbor's pool, going on about her wonderful trip, her wonderful son, and her son's wonderful roommate.

The neighbor wasn't in the mood. Her own daughter had just come out as a lesbian, and she still hadn't come to terms with it. To cope, the neighbor had started drinking more than usual, including today. After LuJean finished her travelogue, the woman apologized for her low spirits, and explained about her daughter. When LuJean tried consoling her, the neighbor could hold her tongue no longer.

*Well, your Michael isn't exactly the Golden Boy*, she blurted out. Then, just like that, *He and Stefan are gay lovers.*

LuJean almost fell out of her chair. When she was sure it wasn't a drunken joke, she marched home, went straight to the phone, and called Mom J, accusing her of having known all this time and keeping it to herself. Mom J responded that in fact she did not know, though she did have her suspicions, and that if LuJean wanted confirmation then she should call Michael himself.

When the conversation ended, Mom J called Michael to warn him: *The Vigaro has hit the Mixmaster*, she said, a favorite euphemism of hers for fertilizer hitting a machine. Michael panicked, thanked her, and promised that he would explain everything later, but for now he had to prepare for his mother.

LuJean waited a couple of hours to call Michael, taking time to compose herself and to tell the news to Mike. At last she called, but her composure disappeared when Michael answered the phone. *Is this true?!* she lashed out, skipping a greeting. *How is it possible? What about the girlfriends you had?*

Michael was relieved in a way, but also horrified at how his parents had learned the news, not to mention angry at the neighbor for intentionally causing them pain (he eventually made up with her). Still, he mostly blamed himself for not having broached the subject sooner, even as his mother's wailing reminded him of why he had not.

Thus began the Sunblooms' *year from hell*. Michael tried to explain in long letters (his first on the subject was 15 pages), and more-than-weekly phone calls, how he felt and what researchers were learning about sexuality, and more. He also ordered books and pamphlets for them regarding that research, hoping that if his parents wouldn't believe him then they might believe the experts.

But his parents never read them. And they didn't much want to talk about the subject either. Mike was willing to talk, but mostly on subjects besides homosexuality. When *that subject* came up he was silent. LuJean mostly badgered: *how could you do this to us?* she cried.

Whenever LuJean called Switzerland and Stefan answered the phone, she no longer offered a cheery greeting or even uttered his name but simply and coldly said, *This is Mrs. Sunbloom, may I speak with Michael?*

Mike and LuJean didn't want to discuss the matter because to them there was nothing to discuss. They just knew that it was *so wrong*, and *unnatural*, condemned by the Bible and by society.

During one conversation, Mike did at least broach the subject, but only in disapproval. He and his Denari 250cc belonged to a motorcycle club, and he rode often next to a man who someone learned *was homo*. When that happened, the club never saw the man again; he just disappeared. The point of the story was not that Mike had *known one*, but that the man's fast disappearance and shame made it clear he felt guilty. Hell, concluded Mike, if even the homos know they're wrong, what's to discuss?

This was when Michael started taking Valium for the only time in his life.

Mike and LuJean sought relief of their own during the year from hell.

They weren't attending a particular church at the time of the revelation, but they still held their Christian beliefs closely. They knew what the Bible said on the subject of homosexuality, but they wanted to talk to a minister anyway, so they sought out old AB at All Folks. He mostly just reviewed the biblical condemnations, which only reinforced their sentiments.

Yet after a year of mood-changing pills and increasing scripture mastery and unproductive telephone talks, there finally came a breakthrough. It happened in the late summer of 1984, during yet another long, expensive, and difficult phone conversation (made even more difficult by the usual constant static and the need to wait a second or two for words to transmit by cable across the Atlantic).

Michael was trying to explain some of the same old things in a new way. LuJean, on the line in the bedroom, was starting to badger him in the same old way. Mike, on the line in the kitchen, had finally had enough. Out of the blue he suddenly banged the table (heard all the way in Switzerland) and to everyone's astonishment shouted at LuJean in frustration, *Shut up woman or we're going to lose him!*

Michael had never heard his mild-mannered father talk like that, certainly not to his mother. The only thing close to it was when Mike had hurled the tub of cottage cheese at Michael's Mormonness.

For all his crassness, though, Mike was right about the consequences if they kept on this way: they would lose their son. They had to make a choice: either he and LuJean could stick to their convictions and keep insisting that Michael was wrong and thus drive him away, or they could find a way to live in peace and keep him coming home.

Michael saw the choice too. He didn't want to leave his parents any more than they wanted to leave him. That's why he had spent the previous year trying with every bit of energy and ingenuity he possessed to explain things in ways that they might understand, and that took into consideration their own ideals and upbringing and feelings. But he was running out of ideas and energy.

He could take their stubbornness. He could even understand how hard it was to overcome prejudice (he could remember trying to let go of some of his own, including against Mormons). And he grasped that old assumptions died hard, especially when you were 66 and 54, as his parents were. What he couldn't take any longer was their coldness and disapproval and unwillingness to treat his feelings seriously. And he was about ready to give up.

But then Mike let loose on LuJean, and Michael, though stunned, was also hopeful—for what the outburst said was that Mike wanted to keep their ties too.

The trick was how to go about it. They could all ignore Michael's sexuality by never speaking about it (but they had tried that for Mormonism and the result was constant tension). They could simply reject their own beliefs (not likely to happen). Or they could alter their beliefs by adding what social scientists would call *new cognitions*. In other words, Mike and LuJean needed to hear something new, that would help them see Michael's sexuality in a new way.

The last solution was what Mike implied he was willing to try, and it was what Michael preferred himself—but he'd been trying on the phone for a year to give them some new cognitions, without any luck. He had one more thought: he told his parents that he was going to come home, alone, for two weeks, to answer in person any and all questions they might have. But, he added, it was the last time he would come alone. Stefan was also his family now. If Stefan wasn't welcome in the future, then Michael couldn't feel welcome either and would stay away.

It was a risky suggestion, because his parents could have ended things there. But they reluctantly agreed, and Michael started making plans to go home.

For once, not one of the Sunblooms was looking forward to his visit.

# twenty-nine

 Father and mother will be very sad if you leave them for
God, but tell me, won't God be even sadder if you leave
Him for your parents?

Jacob recorded almost nothing about his thoughts or activities in Italy.

Nothing about Venice, Livorno, Calliano, Dolce, or Ferrara, through which he passed. Nothing about the ancient Christian ruins he surely went to see around Rome, or the countless and spectacular churches inside the city itself—St. Ignatius, St. Maria Sopra Minerva, or the Jesuits' Il Gesu, which looked so much like the Jesuit church in Antwerp.

Perhaps he said nothing about Rome because of his disappointment at not getting the answer he wanted from either the Capuchins or the Jesuits. For despite all the trouble he took to make that trip, neither order accepted him.

Yet if Jacob was discouraged, he didn't show it. He gave up on the idea of joining the Capuchins, but he was more determined than ever to become a Jesuit. In fact, the trip caused him to see that the Jesuits of Antwerp were not indifferent toward him at all, but simply testing him—and that they were impressed with the results. Thus his pilgrimage had not been in vain.

The Jesuits weren't the only ones able to see what such a trip said about Jacob's commitment to his new faith.

His sister Maria, who had already begun to despair that Jacob would ever return to Boxtel or the Reformed religion, gave up all hope that he would leave Catholicism. After his arrival in Antwerp, in

April 1656, Jacob wrote to her and asked which aspects of Roman Catholicism she was finding most attractive so far in the study she had surely done while he was away, but she responded in unequivocally negative terms, even stronger than in letters past. *Please tell all the details of your trip*, she wrote. *Did you get to kiss the pope's feet? Please tell me the truth, for I know that the Roman faith makes it no sin to speak untruth.*

She added her hope that Jacob had been so disgusted by Rome that he would at least give up all thoughts of entering a religious order. Besides, she warned, if he ever did enter an order, then how could she write him again (as all letters in and out of convents were read by superiors)? In that event, she wouldn't write at all.

Maria was delighted that Jacob was still alive, and she was desperate to see him in person. But she was done trying to convert him.

Jacob's testing by the Jesuits wasn't finished yet.

He had begged alms all the way to Rome and back, and he would have to beg alms all summer long to support himself, and to continue his schooling in the autumn.

It wasn't easy: he told his sister later that he struggled temporally during the entire summer after returning from Rome. But it was all part of the test. *It is no easy thing to be accepted into an order, as you all imagine*, he wrote, making unmistakably clear to her that his goal, in spite of her pleas, was still to become a Jesuit. *That's why I went to Rome and back in the winter in pure poverty, completely on foot, and mostly alone, all the way through the immense mountains of the Tirol.*

Jacob proved his mettle again during that summer of 1656, successfully gathering the alms he needed for the upcoming school year. The Jesuits had suggested that he go in the autumn to the University of Douai (farther south in the Spanish Netherlands), where he could complete the two years of philosophy required of all Jesuits. The order played leading roles at that school in both philosophy and theology, and also administered a number of scholarships for needy students. Very possibly the Jesuits granted him one of those scholarships, but certainly he paid for some of his expenses with his hard-won alms.

His latest test was, at least physically, much simpler than his recent pilgrimage to Rome had been: to continue making a good impression by excelling in his studies. He left Antwerp for Douai, yet another new home, in September 1656.

Jacob didn't hear from Maria for over a year.

He didn't write much that year either, perhaps too busy, or perhaps disillusioned that the vision of Canon van den Bosch, predicting his family's conversion, hadn't happened as scheduled. According to the canon, the happy event should have occurred no later than August 1656. But as the old saying of Dutch fishermen put it, the canon had *called Herring! before they were actually in the net.*

Jacob sent Maria and the family his usual New Year's wishes in 1657, but with a new sense of sorrow. He wanted to see Maria in person as badly as she wanted to see him: if only he could talk to her in person, surely she would be convinced! Couldn't she try to get permission during the summer to come south? Because he wasn't likely to go north now.

But Maria wasn't interested in going south, and little interested even in writing any longer. Jacob wrote her again in September 1657, pleading for a response: did she really wish *to cut off all friendship and sisterly love*, despite her past statements to the contrary? He complained that she had not even bothered to inform him that the family had moved once more, to yet another community in Brabant; other people had told him the news instead.

He sent along with his letter a short thesis, which he had recently defended at school and which he thought might interest Timothy, who had always been so concerned about Jacob's studies. At last he offered *all service* to his family, and recommended them to God *in the five holy wounds of our dear Christ Jesus.* He signed it Jacob Rolandus of Amsterdam, a place that to him was as psychologically distant as China by now.

Maria wrote to Jacob during that same month of September 1657, but for the last time.

She may not have meant it to be her final letter, but it proved to be so—and it even had something of the tone of a farewell. She repeated her usual regrets: *it is a great sorrow and persistent ache that I notice no sobering up in you from the wine of the glass of the great whore, which has made you drunk, and touched your mind, taken your reason, and even blown out the light of natural love.*

And: how could Jacob say that he offered *all service* to his family, when he knew perfectly well that by staying away he *can't do the least bit of service for us?*

Finally, what was this odd manner of recommending us in the five holy wounds? But she had no more energy to dispute such matters. She closed with the last words she would ever send him, and that summed up all else she had said since his flight from home: father and mother were *reasonably healthy, but your absence, plus your conversion to that abominable popedom, are perpetual wounds.*

When Maria didn't write during his second year at Douai, Jacob could at least take comfort in one thought: his studies had gone so well that the Jesuits told him he could enter their order at last.

This was to occur at the beginning of the next school year, in September 1658. Maybe the Jesuits made Jacob wait this long not only to test him, but because they wanted him to reach his majority, which he did in January of that year: then there could be no dispute at all about whether he was acting of his own accord.

Jacob was in ecstasy at the news of his acceptance. But that ecstasy also meant another dose of sorrow as well: his entry into the Jesuits meant the end of all contact with his sister Maria, and thus with his entire family. For his remaining 26 years—more than half of his entire life—he would never hear from any of them again.

He understood perfectly well that the news of his entry would upset everyone at home. He couldn't even summon the nerve to convey the news himself, and instead asked his only Reformed friend from home, the schoolmaster Gerard van Hogerlinden, to do so. He lived near the Rolanduses and was taking Latin lessons from Timothy at the time.

Gerard reported to Jacob that he had indeed passed along the news, and that though no one in his family wished to send any letters, Maria still wished to see him *like a fish desires water*. Could Jacob not come to Boxtel before he entered the Jesuits' novice house at the end of the month? Gerard would see to all the arrangements, including a secret meeting place. (That Gerard considered such a place necessary suggested that Jacob's parents weren't exactly eager to have Maria in touch with her brother any longer.)

But Jacob had no time at the moment for such a journey. He set out for the novice house, located in Mechelen, on September 26, *to serve God and to win souls*. Still, he let Gerard know that both he and Maria were free to visit him there: he was not dead to the world yet. He also pleaded with Gerard exactly as he had with Maria: *Please don't hate me. I don't hate you.*

What thoughts and emotions careened around inside Jacob that first night in the novice house?

Did he, like the famous Flemish Jesuit Jan Berchmans, cry tears of joy? Or was he simply nervous? He certainly wasn't alone. Eight other novices had entered that day as well, two of them from the Dutch Republic. And one of the teachers at the novice house was named Vlierden, just like his old friends in Boxtel.

The main purposes of the novitiate were to test the strength of an individual's vocation, and to learn what it meant to be a Jesuit—not only through schooling but through care of the sick and poor, and going into the countryside to teach the catechism to peasant children. Jacob passed every test once more, and after the usual two years was allowed in September 1660 to take the traditional three religious vows of poverty, chastity, and obedience, marking him as a member of the order. Jesuits also took a special fourth vow, of absolute obedience to the pope, but that required another dozen or so years of training to achieve.

Jacob began his training right away, by moving once again—to Kortrijk, in western Flanders, where he would study the year of letters required of all Jesuits, and where he taught Latin and Greek to boys at the Jesuit secondary school, just as his father had taught him and his grandfather had taught Timothy. Jacob also set himself to learning Spanish there (he already knew German, thanks to his father, and in Douai was no doubt improving his French).

After another year of teaching at the Jesuit college in Aalst, Jacob moved in 1662 to the University of Leuven, to start his four years of training in theology (the year he had taken in Antwerp wasn't counted). It would be the last place he lived in Europe.

Even after becoming a Jesuit, even when he received no letters in return, Jacob kept writing to his family.

He still sent New Year's greetings, and always lamented that they never wrote back. Was his conversion to Catholicism, he asked his father, really something *through which I've earned the right never to see you again, either in person or through letters?* His parents' continued silence, and now Maria's too, was a more articulate answer than any letter would have offered.

Their silence was surely reinforced by Jacob's continued habit of expressing love for his new religion and disdain for his old—his family's. He was, he wrote, *prepared to give my life a thousand times for the preaching of the One Holy Roman Catholic and Apostolic Church, even in the middle of pagans, in the flames of fire.* Or, he exclaimed, *how the devil has learned to blow into the ears of you Reformed!* He prayed, *May God give you light to see the difference between the Holy Roman Church and a heretical church.* He asked, how could his father *cling to that doctrine, and be grounded upon such infernal and untrue principles?* And he urged them all to awake from the *death of a God-denying heresy.*

Jacob repeatedly failed to understand how deeply such words wounded his family, or that they were as convinced of their own faith as he was of his. In a letter from 1662, he in all seriousness asked Maria to run away to Antwerp and join him in the true Catholic faith, for this would surely inspire their dear parents to follow. He had it all worked out: she could live at the widow's house where he had long lived, and earn her living by doing needlework, as all the ladies of that house did. It was sad to think about leaving their father and mother, he knew from experience and from our *natural inclinations*; but *won't God be even sadder* if she left Him for their parents? As if Maria, after five years of silence, would now suddenly find his latest plea attractive.

In another letter the following year Jacob even more naively asked his father to write back in Greek, for Jacob was trying to improve himself in that language. As if this would somehow make Timothy, who had never written, suddenly write, and suddenly forget the real issue: that his only son had been gone for nine years, his now thirty-year-old, Jesuit son.

Most naive of all was Jacob's recounting to his father of the conversion to Catholicism of Mathias Zelhorst—like Timothy, a Dutch Reformed preacher, who despite his position and a large family to support gave it all up for the truth. And he was just about Timothy's age! As if Timothy, despite all his woes as a preacher, had ever pondered leaving his church.

Jacob mourned his family's great silence toward him, and considered it a sign of their little affection. But did he share no blame?

It was true that his sister was the one who stopped writing, and that his parents never wrote. But did he not contribute as well to their silence with his repeated condemnation of Reformed beliefs and repeated adoration of Catholicism? Or when he soon decided to write directly to his father's classis in Den Bosch (he might have picked a theological fight with any classis in the Dutch Republic, but he chose his father's) and challenged them to explain how the church that Christ founded could possibly have been the Reformed Church. Was that letter read aloud to all the classis, while Timothy listened stone-faced? Or did the brothers keep it secret and whisper about it among themselves?

In short, Jacob so thoroughly offended his family with his letters and behavior that they could no longer bear to read his words, and would rather hear and say nothing at all.

He pleaded with Maria always to stay in contact—*let us keep friendship as long as we live*. But then he would poison such a sentiment by adding another venomous statement against her faith. In that sense, Jacob too helped to break relations with his family.

Maybe the very silence from his family sparked Jacob's desire to move even farther away from home, to the strangest new world he would ever know.

Most Jesuits labored in Europe, but some went abroad as missionaries, often to the great distress of their families. Jacob could not distress his family any more than he already had, so what did he have to lose?

So even before completing his studies in Leuven, Jacob put himself forward to be a missionary in *the Indies* (which in the usage of the time could mean either Asia or the Americas) and spend the rest of his life converting the heathen.

He wanted to be a missionary, just like his father, but for another side.

# thirty

[ I put it all in a shoebox and put the shoebox in the closet. ]

In the early autumn of 1984, 34-year-old Michael Sunbloom went home to the winding streets and modest ranch houses of Hillcrest Estates to have a talk with Mom and Dad.

No one was really in the mood. Mike was glad that his son at least wanted to keep a close relationship, which he knew didn't always happen when grown children had a rift with parents—but he really didn't know how to talk about this subject with Michael or what to expect.

LuJean was still fuming about everything, including Mike's hurtful outburst.

Michael, though dreading the visit, was relieved his parents had said they were willing to talk, which they had never said about his Mormonism.

A week went by. Mike, now retired from his job as a gardener, puttered in the yard at home. LuJean busied herself around the house when not brightening the counter at McDonald's. Michael read and visited friends and his brother David (who had already figured out Michael's secret and wasn't troubled by it). The only talk around the Sunbloom house was small.

Still more days went by, until Michael, his trip nearly over, finally suggested early one morning that it was time to sit down. Mike agreed. Michael chose one of the two sofas in the living room. His father, who usually sat on the other sofa, this time chose the big chair directly across from Michael. This alone was a sign of how serious things were: today he wanted to look Michael right in the eye. LuJean couldn't sit at all. She just kept pacing, in and out of the room, across the linoleum floor in the kitchen, over the shag carpet in the family room, around the floral couches, and past the new painting of a French garden scene (a purchase inspired by their recent trips to Europe), blurting something here or there.

Michael had come home to answer questions rather than to ask them, but he began the conversation with one anyway: had they read any of the material he sent?

LuJean responded that they had not: instead, she explained, she had stashed every book and article away in a shoebox, put the lid on it, and secreted the whole thing away in a closet, out of sight, so that none of the grandchildren would accidentally stumble upon it.

You couldn't make up a metaphor like that in a novel, not without being accused of inelegance or cliché or lack of imagination. But this was real life, so it was fine.

LuJean went and found the box, then carried it to the table as if it bore germs and set it down in irritation. It sat there throughout the conversation.

Mike was willing to get things rolling with a few questions of his own. All of them came down to one thing: did Michael *choose to be homo?* He found it hard to believe that a person didn't choose, but if there was a chance Michael hadn't, well, that might make a difference.

Michael had tried to explain himself on this, and much else, for months, but he was willing to try again—because this time he was no mere voice on the phone interrupted by echo and static but instead their son in the flesh whom they loved, and because he understood that as far as Mike and LuJean were concerned the burden of proof still lay upon him.

Especially Mike was listening hard to his son, desperate to hear something that would make it possible for him to accept his namesake, for whom his hopes had always been so high.

• • •

For the rest of that heartstopping morning, Michael recounted in a long stream of consciousness what he had learned from his own experiences and from the latest findings in psychology, biology, anthropology, sociology, and history regarding human sexuality.

Sort of the 95 Theses of Michael Sunbloom (though he had only about 50).

Most of his theses would be almost commonplace a couple of decades later, if not universally accepted.* But to Mike and LuJean in 1984 they might as well have come from outer space.

Years later, Michael couldn't remember exactly how the discussion had gone: it seemed almost surreal, and outside of time, something you weren't sure was actually happening. Moreover, there were plenty of interruptions from both sides. But he remembered well enough the points he tried to make, even if they came out much less tidily than a simple summary might suggest. Such as:

That sexuality in general wasn't as clear-cut as assumed, because though in all known times and places most people were born obviously male or female, some were more male or female than others, a few were born looking like one gender but feeling like the other, and another few were born both male and female at once.

That sexual attraction wasn't so clear-cut either, but ran along a spectrum: most people were mostly or completely attracted to the opposite sex, some (maybe one to four percent) were mostly or completely attracted to the same gender, and some were in the middle of the spectrum and attracted to both.

That though you certainly could choose how to *behave* sexually, and though you might be physically capable of any sort of sexual behavior, there was much less choice about your basic attraction—which would not change just because you changed your behavior.

That the reasons for a person's attraction were still not completely clear, but it appeared that biology, genetics, and events in the womb mattered more than socialization or conscious choice. (*I'm sure I didn't*

---

* A Pew Survey in 2009 showed that 49 percent of Americans still thought homosexuality to be morally wrong, though the percentage varied dramatically according to age.

*choose to be homosexual any more than you chose to be heterosexual*, was how he summed the matter up for his father.)

That the favorite old explanation for homosexuality (absent father and domineering mother) couldn't explain how so many more straight people emerged from such parenting, or how so many gay people emerged from more balanced parenting.

That if given a choice about his sexuality, he would not have chosen to be gay, because it was simply too much trouble.

That the trouble included ridicule and formal punishment and informal threats of violence and even subjection to the favorite desperate remedy for socially undesirable traits, electric shock therapy.

That despite all these troubles gay people kept appearing anyway, telling you how difficult or impossible it was to change your basic attraction.

That the difficulty was also apparent in the attempts of doctors during the 1950s (when many thought sexuality could simply be socialized) to raise as girls those children who were born as hermaphrodites, or those boys who had suffered botched circumcisions—but after years of heavy socialization many such children still felt like boys anyway.

That because of this difficulty it was no more fair to ask a gay man to change his attraction than it was to ask a straight man. (*Could you make yourself suddenly like men, Dad?*)

That it was more helpful to view homosexual attraction not as the result of some social or physical trauma or as a biological or moral defect but as something neutral, neither good nor bad by itself—just like heterosexual attraction or hair color or eye color.

That the morality of sexuality lay not in which attraction you happened to have but in how you acted upon it. (*Exactly!* exclaimed Mike, who supposed that sexual morality for a gay man would simply mean never acting on the attraction.)

That it wasn't any more fair (said Michael in response) to expect a gay man never to act on his attraction than it was to expect the same of a straight man; if someone chose to lead a celibate life, that was one thing, but to expect it of someone was another.

That the morality of sexual actions should be judged not by how a person had sex but by whether sex occurred in a loving, committed relationship that helped each person progress toward full potential.

That homosexual couples were certainly capable of loving, committed relationships and of achieving full potential together, contrary to the old assumption that homosexuals were inherently perverted or emotionally stunted and therefore incapable of real and lasting love.

That psychologists had long believed homosexuals were incapable of healthy relationships and emotional maturity because the only homosexuals they saw were all emotionally troubled—and their sexuality was assumed to be the cause.

That this would be like drawing conclusions about the emotional health of all heterosexuals based on the challenges of a few.

That when some psychologists in the 1950s realized this flaw and at last went out and found some healthy and happy homosexuals (including couples) and compared them with happy heterosexuals, they saw no difference in the level of emotional health.

That because of such findings (and not mostly for political reasons, as rumor had it) the American Psychological Association removed homosexuality from its list of mental illnesses in 1973, and the number of therapists trying to change homosexuals had been in decline ever since.

That old notions about homosexual relations being *unnatural* and perverted were based on the assumption that what felt *natural* to the vast majority must be natural for all, rather than merely natural for most.

That it felt just as *unnatural* for Michael to have sex with a woman as it would for Mike to have sex with a man (which made LuJean cry out, right on cue, *but you did have sex with women!*).

That precisely because of this Michael thought he could speak with some authority about what felt natural, as could those many gay men who had married and fathered children, often with disastrous results; physically, sex with a woman was doable but emotionally it felt wrong.

That what societies have considered *natural* and *normal* (in regard to sex and much else) was not fixed but changed often over the centuries, and was more likely *conventional* rather than *natural*.

That maybe the simplest and least threatening example of changing views of *nature* was left-handedness, no longer regarded as either good or bad in itself, but for centuries seen by right-handers (some 90 percent of the population) as not merely inherently unnatural but deviant and even evil—thus the Latin word for *left* was *sinister*, in Hebrew the left hand was the shaming hand, and the word for *right* in many languages referred not only to direction but to morality.

That for centuries in the West left-handers were beaten into using their right hand (even if they still felt left-handed), as right-handers insisted that changing was a matter of will and habit; only recently was left-handedness accepted as another sort of *natural*—as in natural for those who are left-handed—and only recently were the unique qualities that might come with left-handedness valued rather than condemned or feared.

That whatever the *cure rate* for left-handers may have been over the centuries, it was worse for homosexuals; the rates were never high, and they measured only changed behavior, not changed attraction, and they didn't measure how long any change lasted.

That accepting left-handedness and no longer trying to cure it hadn't increased the percentage of left-handers in the population but simply made their lives a little easier and their particular gifts more appreciated.

That it seemed especially immoral to Michael to try to cure homosexuals through such treatments as electric shock therapy, because this approach could ruin a person in an effort to change the sexual orientation that was a key part of that person.

That homosexuality was not simply about sex, no more than heterosexuality was, but was a whole way of being and expression and seeing.

That there seemed little point in trying to change homosexuals when they had a lot to offer society just as they were; of course they weren't all the same, no more than any other group was, but in general they had, for instance, a keen sense of empathy, which led them to such service-oriented fields as teaching, nursing, and counseling (or of course the travel industry).

And more. But these were the topics Michael remembered best. Most of all, he tried to convey that he really did feel the way he said:

it wasn't an excuse, or a deception. *Maybe some people do choose to be homosexual, but I don't know anyone like that, and I'm sure that I didn't,* he repeated several times—adding at last that although he had usually managed to be happy during his life he had been even happier since accepting his feelings instead of wishing he was otherwise.

It was an overwhelming torrent of ideas and information for Mike and LuJean, who were inclined to be suspicious of it all, and to regard it as a lot of propaganda.

How could something be considered wrong for so long and now all of a sudden be right, they wondered? Was it just because a few people wanted it to be right and so those few changed the rules?

Michael knew that just because there was a new way to look at something didn't necessarily make it good or right. Science was never exact, and psychology and history were even less so, but you could at least check the evidence for all of these conclusions and you couldn't simply dismiss them because they disagreed with your beliefs.

As for things changing, it was true that if you never wanted to see something differently then you never would. A thing usually changes (Michael had read a little Kant, the eighteenth-century philosopher despised by so many undergraduates) not because the thing itself is transformed but because people look at the thing in a new way, thanks to new information and perspectives. People with Down syndrome were now living longer, not because their condition had changed but because how they were viewed and treated changed. Or when Galileo said the sun was at the center of the universe it wasn't because the sun and planets had suddenly changed positions; it was because he looked at them in a new way. He didn't look at the universe differently just because he wanted it to be a certain way but because he thought a new way of looking might make more sense than the old, even though the old way was based on such authorities as the Bible.

The same with homosexuality: looking at it in the old way—as an illness and as something chosen—couldn't explain all the emotionally healthy homosexual people running around or the inability of psychologists to *cure* homosexuality. But looking at it as something natural for the small minority of people shaped that way—just as left-handedness or red hair was natural for those small minorities of people—explained things better.

LuJean and Mike didn't much hear this last example, because their minds had seized upon the word they had been waiting for, the word that had been pushed to the background this entire discussion but that now marched onto center stage: the word *Bible*.

In all of Michael's talk they had strained to hear what explanations, what new ways of thinking, he might have for what the Bible said about homosexuality.

When they now pressed him on this, Michael didn't have any new ideas. Seeing their chance, LuJean and Mike started in. *Scripture clearly and harshly condemns homosexuality*, they insisted, citing the famous texts in Leviticus: *You shall not lie with a male as with a woman. It is an abomination.* An abomination!

At last Michael was silent, bludgeoned by the Leviticus texts, which he already knew. He didn't have a Galileo-like reinterpretation for these. And his parents hadn't accepted his analogies with left-handedness because this was homosexuality they were talking about, not which hand you used to eat or throw! No one cared about that!

As much as he had read, as much as he had visited churches during his youth, Michael had no answers for the Bible's passages on homosexuality. Like many in his position, he had mostly ignored those words and listened to science and personal experience.

That might have been enough for his parents too, had they been unbelievers: but they weren't. He knew that all the scientific evidence in the world wouldn't satisfy them if it couldn't be squared with the Bible. If it came down to God or Michael, God would win, Michael had no doubt.

Thus he simply said that he didn't know what to say, and the long conversation at last fizzled out.

LuJean gathered up the box, in a huff, and put it back in the closet, safely out of sight.

If little was resolved, at least talking in person had helped.

His parents had even seemed interested in some of the explanations he offered. And his dad had always been a pragmatic soul, which gave Michael hope. But he also knew LuJean's stubbornness, from long experience, and because he had inherited a good dose of it himself.

Michael was scheduled to go back to Switzerland just a couple of days after the big talk. The heavy tension that lingered until his departure made him glad that he had waited as long as he had to start the conversation. Yet on his last day at home, his father surprised him by hovering about, just to be near him—he certainly didn't want to talk any more about homosexuality. Did he worry that Michael would never come back? His mother surprised him as well by practically disappearing.

Just before leaving, Michael urged his parents again to have a look at the literature he had sent. Yet he knew from their reluctant noises that they never would. They didn't *want* to see things differently, because it was too threatening to how they understood the world, and God.

As they said goodbyes at the airport, Michael felt a little relieved that it was over, because it had been so exhausting. But he also felt a little sad as he wondered whether he would ever see his parents again. Both of them seemed to wonder the same thing about their son, for as they walked Michael to his gate (which you could still do in those days) they were crying even before the final hugs and kisses.

As Michael left them outside the gate and was about to walk through the door, Mike called him back for one more hug and one more kiss on the mouth. Then he said, *You take care of yourself, son.* It sounded all too final to Michael.

# thirty-one

 And that Jacob obeyed his father and his mother.
—*Genesis* 28:7

The Rolanduses of Boxtel did what they could to cope with the loss of their son and brother, and the vicissitudes of living in Brabant.

Timothy recovered enough from his blow-to-the-head state to pick up his full duties again in early 1655, even to begin serving the classis as an inspector of other parishes. But life was still hard for him.

There was almost certainly a formal excommunication of Jacob by the classis, a ritual that was supposed to occur whenever a Reformed member converted to another faith.

There was still a chronic lack of income, as Timothy complained in 1655 that his salary was now 18 months in arrears.

There were the same trouble-making Catholics in Boxtel, who if they felt any sympathy for Timothy soon lost it as he angrily blamed them for Jacob's flight.

There was his continuing feud with the Reformed sheriff, because Timothy had blamed him too for Jacob's escape.

And of course there was Timothy's eternal feud with the Reformed schoolmaster, which after a brief pause was all stirred up again.

The wretched barn that divided their properties was still at the center of the dispute. Timothy had supposed when the schoolmaster tore up all the legal documents and reconciled with his preacher, in the autumn of 1654, that the man also meant to say he was ceding his claims on the barn. But not so. The schoolmaster was simply saying that he was sorry for misunderstandings, and could they not solve their disagreement as reasonable men and colleagues in private, rather than as antagonists in court?

When Timothy realized that the schoolmaster wasn't actually yielding, he went on the attack again, more aggressively than ever, as if the barn had become the repository for all his frustration over Jacob's departure and the role the schoolmaster might have played in it. The most tangible evidence of this was his decision to transform part of the barn into a privy for his own household, though he made sure that its contents emptied out into the schoolmaster's yard.

Psychohistorians in future centuries could not have imagined a more suitable metaphor for Timothy's state of mind.

The court overseeing the dispute between the two men sent more delegates to Boxtel in July 1656 and ruled for the second or third time in the schoolmaster's favor: the preacher was to restore the barn to its former state, construct his privy in some other place on his own property and at his own cost, and pay for the damage he'd caused to the barn.

By October Timothy still had not obeyed the decree, and this time the court wielded a heavier hammer. It instructed the steward of ecclesiastical goods to withhold Timothy's salary until he complied. Since Timothy claimed to rarely receive that salary anyway, it must not have seemed like much of a threat.

In November 1656 Timothy even used his favorite old preacherly trick of withholding communion from those he considered unworthy of it, including the schoolmaster, the custodian, and now the organist— about half the Reformed leadership in town. Needless to say, this hardly eased the discord in the community.

As for the privy, the steward of ecclesiastical goods had to step in himself and remake it.

In short, although Timothy eventually overcame his low spirits after Jacob left home, he also became crankier than ever. It didn't help his mood when he decided to cut off all contact with his departed son.

Here was a drastic and depressing choice, indeed, for any parent. Parents might threaten to cut off children, even to disinherit them, for any number of reasons, but following through on such a threat was another thing—as numerous spectacularly disobedient but still-inheriting children could attest. And parents might ask a rebellious child to leave home, but many of them tried to keep in contact anyway.

Not Timothy and Catharina. They weren't indifferent to Jacob. They mourned and wept regularly over his absence, for several years they hungered after news of him, and Timothy was apparently willing to let Jacob remain Catholic if he would only return home. But when Jacob wouldn't return, Timothy gave up for good.

If Timothy really was willing to tolerate his son's Catholicism as long as he returned home, then it would seem that Jacob's leaving and his staying away were even more painful to his parents than his conversion had been—which explained their silence best of all. Jacob's outbursts of Catholic joy were painful to read, but his refusal to return home was like a death blow. This was why they wouldn't write back, and thus left him as much as he'd left them.

There was scriptural justification for leaving the unrighteous, of course, including the texts about Jesus's word dividing rather than bringing peace, or his metaphors about separating sheep from goats and wheat from tares, or of course the verse that Jacob used to justify his own leaving: not only he who loved father and mother more than Jesus was unworthy of him, but he who loved *son or daughter* more.

Timothy could also look to the Jacob of the Old Testament, who *obeyed his parents*, and who as a grown man said to his own upstart son, *Shall I and thy mother and thy brethren indeed come to bow down ourselves of thee to the earth?* He could further rely on the Old Testament words, *Whoso curseth his father or his mother* (which Jacob had done by his actions), *his lamp shall be put out in obscure darkness.* Or, *The eye that mocketh at his father, and despiseth to obey his mother, the ravens of the valley shall pick it out.*

Timothy could even have echoed the words of the French Catholic parent Guichard Coton, furious at his minor son Pierre for running off to join the Jesuits: *Is this how you promise to obey and serve me and lighten the burden of my old age? Do you wish to make your mother and me die of melancholy? Do you wish to shorten our days? Are you of age to make a choice against our will? Do you prefer to serve strangers instead of living with your parents?*

Parenthood did not require parents to endure every behavior of their children, concluded Timothy. If one had to choose between righteousness and a wayward child, the choice was clear.

Did Catharina feel the same? Or did she merely go along with her husband to keep peace?

She had additional scriptural reasons to be displeased with her son, including one from Proverbs: *Hearken unto thy father that begat thee, and despise not thy mother when she is old.* But even if she had wanted to write Jacob, would her husband have opposed it?

Surely it pained both of them further to watch the continued development of their nephew, the other Jacob Rolandus, son of Timothy's brother Daniel, who not only became a dominee in the year that Jacob fled but started fathering a huge brood of Reformed children too (18 eventually). This was not to mention two of Daniel's other boys, also preachers by now, and eventually fathers and grandfathers of still more Reformed preachers.

Through other branches of the family would go the Rolandus name, and the legacy of preaching.

By 1657 Timothy decided that he had had enough heartache in Boxtel, and that he wanted a change of scenery.

Despairing that Timothy would ever repair the breach with his community, the classis of Den Bosch agreed to let him go. Timothy found a new calling quickly, in the smaller and more desperate community of Helvoirt, some 10 miles to the northwest and numbering only 120 households (thus reducing the chances for arguments).

He accepted the position on March 1, but didn't actually move until autumn—naturally because of an argument. Specifically, Timothy refused to budge from Boxtel until he received all of his back pay. When he finally did move (still not fully paid), he declared that he deserved as well the income owed to the preacher of Helvoirt since the time that he had accepted the position in March. Probably to ensure that his claims regarding his salary in Boxtel didn't die, he also took with him all of the church's account books from that village (just as he had upon departing Ouderkerk), for Boxtel's surviving account books begin only right after he left.

Still, perhaps the troubles in Boxtel weren't completely Timothy's fault. It was a difficult place for anyone. His predecessor had been shot at, his successor stayed a mere six months, and in 1679 the latest Reformed schoolmaster was stabbed in the head on a warm July evening and the son of the preacher was shot at in broad daylight.

The church building of Boxtel soon had problems as well, as part of the roof over the nave, and part of a wall of the nave, collapsed. No doubt local Catholics saw this as a judgment of God, for the Reformed had stored animals and other goods in the nave, as if the church were an ordinary barn. With no money to rebuild it, the Reformed simply left the church in partial ruin for decades. It was restored only in the early nineteenth century, when the great Reformed experiment in Brabant was finally given up: Catholicism was at last made legal in the Dutch Republic, and all the old Catholic churches confiscated by the Reformed were given back, including Boxtel's, which is still Catholic today.

Except for the school that in the twentieth century was named after Jacob and the tiny chapel that was conceded to the Reformed (and which seemed more a monument to failure than anything else), it was as if the Rolanduses and the Reformed had never been in Boxtel at all.

Timothy spent the last ten years of his life in Helvoirt, where things were, as he had hoped, a little calmer than in Boxtel.

He and Catharina knew here some of the chronic problems they had known elsewhere, such as trying to get work done on their unfinished rectory. They also suffered the pains of aging, as Timothy turned 63 in 1657 and Catharina was just a few years behind him.

And they had to scuttle any cherished images they might have entertained of what their old age would look like—such as being happily surrounded by friends and children, telling favorite old stories, admiring the newest grandchildren, and watching them all age and laugh and play. Their son and heir was a Jesuit, and their daughter still lived at home in 1662, perhaps 32 years of age.

But, again, at least life was calm in Helvoirt, if a little dull. Unlike in Boxtel or Ouderkerk, Timothy's name rarely appeared in civic or church records, which was surely a good thing for all.

The rectory, in all its inglorious rectangularity, reflected that dullness. The only thing of note about it lay two centuries in the future, when it was occupied by a Dominee van Gogh and his family, who also had a troubled son leave home. That dominee donated his old Dutch Bible to the church, and it still graces the pulpit.

The church itself, though much smaller than Boxtel's, was the best thing in town. Its smallness made the Sunday services tolerable, it boasted a fine wooden ceiling, and it received good care from Timothy—regular whitewashing, a new pulpit, the installation of pews (still a novel idea), a board for the day's psalm numbers, a stove in the pulpit during winter, and more.

That Timothy and Catharina stayed in Helvoirt until the end says something about his contentment: ten years was far longer than the tenure of most preachers in Brabant. After Timothy died, Helvoirt went through three preachers in three years.

His demise came at last in 1667, when Timothy was 73. The death notice was signed on August 2, in Amsterdam, for he wanted to be buried there, in the New Church, near his father, and not in Brabant, where he had suffered so sorely. Perhaps he was laid near his father's portrait, beneath which Timothy had composed 13 lines of pious verse in honor of Old Jacob, making clear to all that Timothy was his son and an Amsterdammer and preacher too.

No trace remained of Catharina. Certainly she was still alive at Timothy's death, for as was the custom when a preacher died, she, as his widow, received his income for a year, the so-called grace year, while neighboring preachers took turns each Sunday filling in for the deceased.

But after that, where? Very possibly she went to live with Maria, who according to a family genealogy compiled in the nineteenth century finally married, though she bore no children. If Catharina did live with her daughter, then she was luckier than many preachers' widows, who were supposed to be taken care of by the community but who often lived in poverty anyway.

At least the Rolandus women had a chance at a bit of extra income thanks to Timothy's unusually rich library, which they sold soon after his death, as he did not have a son to whom he might bequeath it. A newspaper ad in the *Oprechte Haerlemse Courant* announced that the sale would occur in Leiden, the university town, where it was supposed that interest would be greatest and prices highest; the library included many rare books in Hebrew, Greek, and Latin, items one hardly expected to find in such abundance in the library of a country preacher.

Surely Timothy owned such a library because he had inherited the books, and the languages, from his father, Old Jacob, the great translator, then had taught those same languages to his son Jacob, the Jesuit, who was using them still—plus many others his progenitors had never dreamed of.

For the last 21 years of his life, Jacob the Jesuit got his wish to be a missionary in distant lands, putting him farther from his family than ever.

He was lucky to get the chance, because the Jesuits of Flanders had no distant mission of their own. But in early 1663 the Portuguese Jesuits in Brazil asked their confreres in Flanders for help; many local Jesuits put themselves forward, and the gifted Jacob was the only one chosen.

Was this the moment, in the spring of 1663, that Jacob gave his papers, including his journal and the letters from his sister, to the order? Or did he give them first to his good friend and fellow Jesuit, Philip van Straeten, who added some letters of his own to the stack and then deposited the whole into the order's *archive*, such as it was? For Jacob also asked Van Straeten to serve as liaison with his family: would his friend please write the Rolanduses in Helvoirt and tell them the happy news that Jacob was headed to Brazil? And would Van Straeten please watch for any news from them, and forward it to Jacob across the Atlantic? Van Straeten did write the news to Timothy, exclaiming *happy is the father of such a son!* Timothy surely read this with the same numbness that overcame his soul when reading letters that arrived in Jacob's own hand.

Besides putting his papers in order that spring, Jacob was also ordained a priest, after only one year at Leuven (ordination usually occurred after at least three years of theology, but Jacob was able and leaving soon on a mission). Then in June he set out for Brazil. After various misadventures along the ocean way, including being taken hostage by pirates and set on an English beach, Jacob finally landed at Salvador da Bahia, the mission's headquarters, in January 1664.

Despite his separation from his family, Jacob proved as a missionary to be a Rolandus through and through. He learned a wide array of languages (Latin, Greek, Hebrew, Spanish, and German before arriving, Portuguese and two or three Indian languages after), and he showed the same streak of self-assured stubbornness that ran through his father and grandfather.

Both traits led Jacob to the novel idea of wanting to work among Brazilian Indians where they were, in the interior, rather than bringing them to the coast, where the Jesuits and Portuguese settlers were. Even after the provincial (the mission leader) approved Jacob's plan, and even after reports of his phenomenal success reached mission headquarters, many of the local Jesuits criticized the approach as against custom.

Jacob never understood this criticism, nor did he ever fully understand Portuguese Catholicism, among either his fellow Jesuits or the settlers. In fact he found himself struggling against his co-religionists as regularly as his father had once contended with his own Reformed flocks.

Neither did Jacob ever quite find the satisfaction he sought from his mission, at least for long: in 1669, after he had heroically baptized five villages of Indians, slave traders came through and flattened them all, including small churches and crosses and holy objects, breaking Jacob's heart, and prompting him to plead with the Jesuit General in Rome to send no more missionaries to Brazil lest their hearts be broken too, and to please transfer him—to the Congo, the Philippines, Japan, China, anywhere but Brazil.

Maybe that transfer came: from 1670 to 1672, Jacob's name disappeared from the mission's rolls. But by 1672 it was there again, and he was moving into the interior once more; in 1675 he even took his special fourth Jesuit vow.

His superiors in Brazil recognized his talents and shortcomings alike. In a report from 1677 sent to Rome, the provincial mentioned Jacob among 17 members of the mission (out of some 190) whose virtues stood out. He was, said the report, always ready to undertake a difficult mission. True, he didn't *gladly bear supervision*, and *his ardor may lack a bridle*, but in the end he did seem to do *all things for the glory of God and the salvation of his soul*.

The annual assessment of each Jesuit's talents recorded a similar verdict. Jacob's *intelligence* was always described as *optimum*, the highest possible rating, and his gift for languages was widely known. But his *judgment* was often described as merely *good*, and his *prudence* as plain old *mediocre*. Perhaps that reflected his changing temperament: when he entered the order, at age 25, he was described as *melancholic*, but by around 50 he was said to be *choleric*—a temper quick to boil. Maybe watching villages burn down did that. Or maybe such was the natural progression of a melancholic disposition as it reached middle age.

Whatever the case, none of these descriptions were far from fitting his father or grandfather as well.

Toward the end of his mission, Jacob had one last controversy in him— over slavery, the thing that had destroyed his villages.

Though not wholly opposed to slavery, the Jesuits opposed it more than most settlers, and they even denied the sacraments to anyone who enslaved Indians outside the rules. But for a variety of reasons Jacob concluded that rule-breaking slave traders in the volatile town of São Paolo should be allowed to receive the sacraments—then he said so on paper.

His superiors weren't happy, especially because Jacob had just been elevated to the office of provincial secretary. Although the mission would one day adopt the policy he advocated, he was soon reassigned to the distant island of São Tomé, off the coast of Africa.

Maybe the transfer was Jacob's idea. According to reports, after the bishop of São Tomé requested two missionaries, Jacob pleaded to go— perhaps because he was weary of Brazil, or eager for a new challenge. São Tomé was an unusual place featuring such phenomena as racial mixing and black priests, rarities in the Catholic world. It might have been a happy spot for Jacob, and he might have reached a ripe old age there, something like the 70-plus of his father and grandfather. But he didn't get to find out, because three weeks after landing he contracted one of the island's *noxious diseases*, probably malaria, and, with *great pain in all his senses*, died—among strangers, far from his roots in Amsterdam and the Reformed Church, far from his birth family, far from his adopted home in Antwerp, and even far from his home among the Tapuya Indians of Brazil. He was 51 years old.

It's easy to wonder whether Jacob, during those hours of misery before his lonely death, thought of his parents and sister.

Surely he regretted his alienation from them, but only in the way he understood it: that his family had not followed him in the true religion. Jacob would have agreed with a Spanish ambassador to Switzerland who said to Catholics there that they should feel more kinship to a Catholic Indian or African than they did to their heretical Protestant countrymen—even if those countrymen were family.

It's also easy to wonder whether his sister Maria, if she was still alive, ever received word of his death. Certainly Jacob's fellow Jesuits in Brazil and Flanders did, because they were soon writing tributes about him. The provincial of Brazil, Alexander Gusmao, told Rome of the province's sorrow over Jacob's demise but *at least there remains the unerasable memory of his glorious virtue*. And a Portuguese Jesuit named Angelus do Reys, who owed his vocation to Jacob, wrote from Brazil to Rome in 1704 to ask the general to include Jacob Rolandus in the order's special *Memory Book*, which noted the anniversary of the death of all notable Jesuits around the world.

But nothing ever came of that request, no doubt thanks to Jacob's tendency to go his own way—the tendency that had allowed him to become Catholic in the first place, then a Jesuit, then a missionary in the Brazilian interior. The tendency that he had inherited from his late, estranged, Reformed father, and from the famous grandfather he never knew.

# thirty-two

[
And he shall turn the heart of the fathers to the children,
and the heart of the children to the fathers, lest I come and
smite the earth with a curse.
—*Malachi 4:6*
]

Before the exhausting talk with his parents on that long autumn day in 1984, or before quitting organized religion altogether, Michael would have found it helpful to know that a few believers were in fact already beginning to incorporate the latest understanding of sexuality into their reading of the Bible and their religious traditions.

They were hardly the first to try something of the sort. Over the centuries, countless other believers had, thanks to new ways of seeing, likewise rethought a variety of other matters also long held to be condemned by the Bible, such as usury, racial mixing, women speaking in church, a sun-centered universe, and more.

But again, by Michael's time the number of Bible believers trying to rethink homosexuality was small, in just about any religious tradition, and certainly in the Mormon and Evangelical traditions he knew best. In fact he knew no churchgoing homosexuals at all. They were there (emerging studies would conclude that gay people as a group were particularly spiritual, and that many found ways to stay in their churches), but most were still quiet about their sexuality or about how they reconciled it with a specific religious tradition. Those willing to speak out were clearly not enough of a chorus for the usually keen-eared Michael to hear. Without guides or role models, he simply assumed that there wasn't to be any reconciling, and that his only choice was, again, either to be openly homosexual or a churchgoer. Not both.

Among the strongest of the scattered voices trying to suggest otherwise was a Catholic priest (a Jesuit at that), psychologist, and moral theologian named John McNeill, whose book *The Church and the Homosexual* appeared in 1976, the year of Michael Sunbloom's great crisis. McNeill concluded that homosexuality per se was not intrinsically sinful, and that in some circumstances homosexual relationships could be moral, even in the eyes of the church—and he based those conclusions not only on his work as a counselor and psychologist but on the latest biblical research as well.

That's what would have most surprised Michael. He knew from other sources many of the psychological and scientific findings cited by McNeill, but he had no idea about the biblical ones.

The research McNeill cited in that regard took an approach favored by many Bible scholars during the previous couple of centuries, but not by Evangelicals like Mike Senior and LuJean. This approach basically tried to find the meaning of a biblical text by studying the circumstances in which the passage was written, rather than assuming that its meaning would be obvious to a reader living 2,000 or so years later, in quite other circumstances.

Such an approach wasn't saying that the Bible contained no lasting truths. Rather, it was saying that identifying a lasting truth wasn't always so simple and straightforward as a plain reading of a passage might suggest. For instance, if every passage was held to be lasting, applicable at all times and places, then believers today would still have to take literally passages that put the earth and not the sun at the center of the universe, that forbid lending money at interest, or that legitimize slavery. To find the lasting truths, you first had to make sense of the often puzzling language and customs and assumptions and forms in which they were wrapped at a given moment, and then translate or convert those truths into forms that could apply to your own language and customs and assumptions.

Precisely what you must do for any past from which you want to learn.

Thus, had Michael known about McNeill's book, he would have read that Leviticus's penalty for homosexuality (death) was not something extraordinary but rather quite in keeping with other punishments of the time; neighboring passages in Leviticus also condemned to death people who ate shellfish, lit fires on the Sabbath, allowed their offspring to marry people of other faiths, and cursed their parents—none of them capital crimes to Bible-believing Christians of the 1970s.

He would have read that the word *abomination*, so often paired with homosexuality, did not have in Leviticus the connotation of eternal hellfire that it came to have in later English: the word simply meant *ritually impure*, as in not able to participate in religious rites. Other abominations included eating pork or shrimp, mixing crops, and blending linen and wool in the same garment—hardly serious offenses for the omnivorous, polyester-cotton wearing crowd in a typical Christian church of Michael's day. That Leviticus's condemnations of homosexuality survived in modern Christian churches while its condemnations of other abominations did not could be taken to mean that homosexuality was more inherently sinful; but it could also be taken to mean that understanding of homosexuality simply changed more slowly, and that people took longer to ask new questions about it.

He would have read further that also behind the Old Testament's prohibitions on homosexuality was the chronic fear of underpopulation among the Israelites, their tendency to measure God's favor by the number of their offspring, and thus their stress on marriage and fertility and the preciousness of human sperm (which also explained the related condemnations of *spilled seed*). In the New Testament, in contrast, marriage, fertility, posterity, and even blood relationships declined in importance, as ascetics, celibates, and *eunuchs for the kingdom of heaven's sake* appeared on the religious scene, and as one's familial or tribal identity was based on a new standard: *Whosoever shall do the will of my Father which is in heaven, the same is my brother, and sister, and mother,* said Jesus in Matthew and Mark.

And finally Michael would have read that even though several New Testament texts continued the Old Testament's condemnations of homosexuality, as in Paul's lament in Romans about men leaving the *natural use of the woman,* these later condemnations too were wrapped up in assumptions and understanding of the time. Unlike later understanding of nature, for instance, Paul assumed that *nature* included cultural as well as biological influences: thus, a person was Jewish *by nature* and long hair on a man was against nature rather than against custom. He also assumed that celibacy was superior to marriage, and that marriage was a way to avoid *burning*—not exactly the exalted image of marriage promoted in the Christian churches Michael knew. Moreover, every condemnation Paul made of homosexuality included aggravating circumstances that seemed to bother him more, such as prostitution around pagan cults or unequal homosexual relationships between Greek men and boys, so that it was not clear whether he was condemning all homosexuality or specific forms of it.

Clearly the Bible condemned homosexuality in six or seven places. The question raised by McNeill's approach was whether the condemnations applied to all homosexual acts or merely certain ones, and whether the condemnations still held or were based on assumptions that might not be considered valid in another place and time (like Joshua's understanding that the sun went around the earth, and longstanding notions of what constituted pure food and clothing and *nature*), or that at least needed adaptation—conversion—to a new context.*

For McNeill, the answer was clear: understanding of sexuality and relationships in the time of the Bible was dramatically different from understanding in his own time. And the new understanding required new parameters and mores for sexuality in general and homosexuality in particular. The still novel idea that marriage should be founded on love and commitment rather than familial interests was one such

---

* The principle of adaptation was not new, of course, as Paul himself famously adapted Christianity to new contexts. But it was perhaps articulated most clearly by the first Reform rabbi of Berlin, Samuel Holdheim, in 1845: *A law, even though divine, is potent only so long as the conditions and circumstances of life, to meet which it was enacted, continue; when these change, however, the law also must be abrogated, even though it have God for its author. For God himself has shown indubitably that with the change of the circumstances and conditions of life for which He once gave those laws, the laws themselves cease to be operative, that they shall be observed no longer because they can be observed no longer.*

adjustment based on more recent understanding, for instance. And there could be others for homosexual relationships.

In short, if Paul himself (who certainly condemned at least some forms of homosexuality but who was also flexible in his adaptation of the Christian message to all sorts of people) had lived in 1980 and thus had a different understanding than he possessed in A.D. 50, would he have amended his famous passages in Galatians and Colossians to read that *in Christ Jesus* there was not only neither Jew nor Greek, neither bond nor free, neither male nor female, neither circumcised nor uncircumcised, and neither barbarian nor Scythian, but also neither homosexual nor heterosexual?

Perhaps most interesting of all to Michael would have been to read in McNeill that the Sodom and Gomorrah story—arguably the single most important image in the minds of those believers who condemned homosexuality—was probably not about homosexuality in the first place.

The sin of Sodom and Gomorrah, concluded McNeill (and others before him), was their lack of hospitality to strangers. This wasn't hospitality in the Miss Manners sense, as in some breach of etiquette, but in the sense of indifference and hostility to other human beings: the men of Sodom who gathered outside Lot's doors and demanded that his guests come out so that they might *know* them had in mind not sex, but rape.

A low-lying city such as Sodom, on the flat plains of southern Israel, was nervous about security and thus wary of strangers, such as Lot's guests. Moreover, Lot was a resident alien in Sodom, and possibly abused his status by hosting these strangers. The suspicious neighbors who approached his residence therefore felt justified in treating the strangers harshly, and the harshest and most humiliating treatment they could imagine was rape—especially the rape of a male by another male.

It was the insult a medieval or modern English-speaking male intended when he yelled *f—— you* at another male, or the same insult certain closed male societies might actually impose on new or code-breaking members. It didn't mean that the insulter preferred male sex (in most cases he probably did not) but rather that he wanted to degrade another male in the worst way he understood: by treating them, as they saw it, like a woman.

Inhospitality of any sort was no trivial matter—in many societies it was at the heart of religion and human relationships. And rape was as inhospitable as it got. Ancient cultures, and not only the Israelites but such cultures as Rome too, were filled with warning stories of cities punished by the gods for refusing hospitality to strangers, or abusing them. Often in these stories, if the stranger did receive hospitality it was from some other outcast, such as Lot, for the outcast knew all too well how it felt to be excluded. It was also often the outcast who helped strangers to escape from what was sure to be the violent destruction of a guilty city by gods who were displeased at such absence of affection.

That Lot readily offered his daughters to the men of Sodom was a measure of how desperate he was to treat his guests well, even at the expense of his daughters' own humiliation and suffering (reflecting assumptions about women that were also different from modern sensibilities, but that's another topic).

The main point was that this famous story, for centuries held over the heads of homosexuals, wasn't about a city rampant with male sex; rather it was about a city that treated strangers horrifically. Yet eventually the homosexual aspect of the attempted rape came to overshadow the rape aspect, Sodom and Gomorrah came to be synonymous with homosexuality, sodomy became the legal and criminal name for homosexual acts, and Sodom came to be held up by believers as the prime example of what happened to cities that tolerated homosexuality.

McNeill explained how this happened too. For centuries after the final editing of the Old Testament (which occurred around the sixth century B.C.), homosexuality was not the meaning of the Sodom story. The city was referred to throughout the Old Testament as a symbol of sin—but sexual sin wasn't mentioned. Ezekiel 16 blamed Sodom's *pride, plenty, and thoughtless ease* and *abominations* (of which there were, again, many sorts), Isaiah its lack of justice, Proverbs 19 its inhospitality, Deuteronomy its pride and inhospitality, and so on. Malachi spoke similarly about divine destruction: the earth would be cursed if parents and children (understood literally or figuratively) failed to turn their hearts toward each other. None of these texts, nor Leviticus's condemnations of homosexuality, singled out homosexuality as a reason for divine destruction: instead they emphasized lack of affection toward others, especially toward strangers.

This all changed beginning in the second century B.C., when Jews living in the eastern Mediterranean (Paul's place of origin) were shocked at the homosexual relationships of Hellenistic Greeks around them, especially those between men and boys (viewed by some Greeks as a higher form of love than a relationship with any inherently inferior woman). Not coincidentally, this was when the apocryphal Jewish book of Jubilees first suggested that the biggest sin of Sodom and Gomorrah must have been homosexuality. The book of the Secrets of Enoch, around 50 B.C., was explicit: the sin of Sodom was most definitely homosexuality.

By the second half of the first century A.D., when the New Testament was being composed, all Gentile wickedness, and especially homosexuality, was symbolized for both Jews and Jewish Christians by Sodom and Gomorrah. References to Sodom's sexual sin in two late New Testament books, 2 Peter and Jude, emerged from that development (though the passage in 2 Peter seems most offended by the desire of the men of Sodom to trespass the boundary that existed between humans and angels, which Lot's guests were).

All the classic stereotypes of homosexuality were already present by then too: that homosexuals could never really love each other, that they were always child abusers, that a male who was passive in the sex act was shamelessly behaving like a woman, and of course that when God destroyed cities it was because of homosexuality.

All endured through the ancient Christian period, then were reinforced and elaborated during the medieval and modern eras too—even though the Sodom and Gomorrah story was most probably meant to emphasize the virtue of hospitality to outsiders, who so often over the centuries have, ironically, included homosexuals.

Not everyone agreed with John McNeill when his book appeared, starting with his own Catholic Church.

Although originally granting ecclesiastical permission for publication (the *imprimatur*), the church withdrew that permission after the book was published, and by the early 1980s it had also ordered McNeill to stop speaking or even privately counseling on the subject of homosexuality. In 1985, feeling he could no longer live under those restrictions, McNeill resigned from the Jesuits and the priesthood.

That wouldn't have kept Michael from finding McNeill's book helpful. But even had he known about it at the time he talked to his parents in 1984, they wouldn't have been persuaded much anyway.

For John McNeill was a *papist*, after all, and a Jesuit at that. He was also a psychologist, another group Mike and LuJean didn't exactly trust. And most of all McNeill was gay. How could they believe anything he said on the subject?

Another potentially helpful book to Michael, which would have been closer to his orbit had he still been living in the United States, appeared in 1983 from the author Carol Lynn Pearson. It not only told the moving story of her experiences with her gay husband but, like McNeill, reflected on the religious implications of new findings about sexuality and homosexuality. Yet this would have done no more to convince Michael's parents, for Pearson was Mormon.

Although Mike and LuJean were not likely to be impressed by McNeill's conclusions about homosexuality and the Bible, it was ultimately the Bible that helped them to accept their homosexual son.

In essence, they did this by deciding to prefer one part of the Bible over another. They didn't really want to do so, no more than many other Christians did. Like others, they feared that picking and choosing among God's words could threaten the integrity of the Bible every bit as much as did the high-flung approach advocated by the likes of John McNeill. But they picked and chose anyway, just as legions of Christians had done before them, such as Martin Luther, who favored whole books of the Bible above others, or Christian abolitionists, who decided to favor the Bible's passages on love over those that sanctioned slavery (even though no Bible verses condemned slavery).

The Sunblooms, who had studied the Bible for decades, now did much the same. They weren't likely to change their minds about homosexuality based on evidence such as McNeill's, which to them seemed to contradict the Bible, but they just might reconsider if one Bible verse could rise in their minds to a position of superiority above some other. During their months of uncertainty and thought, the Bible's passages about love came to matter more to them than all its words about homosexuality, or about hating father and mother and son and daughter, or about Jesus's message dividing people like a sword.

LuJean and Mike didn't need the love passages to persuade them to love their son, but the passages did help to legitimize their love, rather than make them feel that in order to love their son they had to reject the Bible, or that to love the Bible they had to condemn their son and lose him.

Michael never learned exactly how this process played out between his parents, since he was in Switzerland when it occurred and they never really talked about it afterward. Mike didn't exactly remember himself. But it certainly involved reading familiar old passages with fresh eyes.

He and LuJean were motivated to do so, of course, because Michael was their son. But you would have had a hard time convincing them that their conclusions were therefore wrong, or that the main point of the New Testament was to drive people, especially families, apart—not with all the passages about Jesus's love for his disciples, and his disciples' love for him, and his love for Mary and Martha, and his crying over the death of his friend Lazarus, and his comments about laying down your life for your friends; and not with Paul's famous chapter in I Corinthians about love mattering more than even spiritual gifts or prophecies or other favorite signs of religiosity.

There was also Jesus's saying that the two greatest commandments were to love God and to love your neighbor, and that those two things weren't actually separate. You didn't choose between God and your neighbor, because they were joined—at least that's what Michael's favorite verse in I John said: that he who hates his brother can't love God and he who loves God then necessarily loves his brother.

The best way to show your love to God was to love your brother, concluded Mike, and in this case his brother just happened to be his son.

But what about those verses that said you had to leave your loved ones to follow Jesus? Here things went a bit in circles. Because the next thing you knew Jesus was saying again that the best way to follow him was to love others; but wouldn't *others* also include anyone you might have just left? So maybe leaving didn't really mean leaving.

Other verses helped to explain it: Jesus also said to leave your father and mother in order to marry, but he didn't mean to leave them forever or completely, because all over the New Testament he kept saying to honor your parents, your whole life long. Even hanging there on the cross, he made sure that his mother was cared for.

So, leaving your father or mother or brother or sister for Jesus's sake meant something other than abandoning them. It meant something more like leaving the small way you usually loved—your father and mother and brother and sister and friends and those who do things the way you do—for the way Jesus loved, which as far as Mike and LuJean could tell was to love everyone. Including, again, their son. Maybe they could feel the same sort of love for anyone that they felt for Michael, if they went to the trouble to get to know that anyone the same way they knew Michael. Maybe that was Jesus's big message. Maybe that's what he meant by the new sort of family he kept talking about, and how he could say to John from the cross that Mary was John's new mother, or why he said to the multitude when his mother and siblings came looking for him that everyone who followed him was his brother and sister and mother and father. He didn't mean to quit loving your family, or that you should love others more than you love your family, but that you could love others the same way you loved family, and make them family too.

As for hating, it turned out not to mean the same thing it had come to mean in modern English: it simply meant loving someone less than you loved another. (This kind of fancy Bible-reading they could accept, since it simply involved the translation of a word.) You weren't really to *hate* anyone, especially not when you remembered that Jesus said to love your enemies, and do good to those who hate you.

One way or another, Mike and LuJean realized that they didn't have to leave their son, or hate him, in order to follow Jesus. They just had to love him. And they were going to do so, by God. They didn't have to choose between their faith and their love for their son, because the best version of their faith was to love their son, and everyone else, and to make everything else secondary—even the things they didn't get. Or as Mike later summed it up to Michael, *I don't understand homosexuality, but I love my son.*

They hadn't thought about things like that when Michael was a Mormon. But maybe they would have if his Mormonism had pushed things to the edge the way his homosexuality did—if it had come to the point of possibly losing him.

During this process Mike played something like the role of Peter, who had a vision that caused him to see strangers differently.

In that famous vision, in Acts, Peter saw descending from heaven a lot of beasts that he had never dared to eat, because God had said they were unclean. But suddenly there came a voice that seemed like God's telling Peter to kill and eat the beasts anyway. How could that be? Peter refused, saying *I have never eaten anything that is common and unclean.* But the voice spoke again, and said, *What God hath cleansed, that call not thou common.*

The idea was still so new to Peter that he had to be told three times to eat up.

When he awoke, he understood what the dream meant. It wasn't so much about food, but about seeing those outside his own tribe, those he'd assumed were unclean because of their eating habits and sexual habits and more, as not so outside or unclean after all. God had *put no difference between us and them,* he saw.

Soon after the dream some of those outsiders started coming to Peter to hear his message. He told one of them, Cornelius, that although it had long been unlawful for him to keep company *or come unto one of another nation,* God had revealed that *I should not call any man common or unclean.*

That's how Mike felt about Michael too. His homosexuality didn't matter any more than Cornelius's Gentileness had. It was a difference that didn't make a difference.

LuJean soon felt the same. There was no chance she could call Michael unclean when she considered the delightful child he had been, or how much he had loved his students, or how routinely he made life enjoyable for people around him, or even how much he loved Stefan.

In fact, if Mike was the Peter of the relationship, LuJean was the Paul, because like Paul she proved to be more exuberant about declaring to the world the new vision of the stranger. She became a champion of gays (mostly through informal conversation) more than her husband ever would. And, perhaps because she was more outgoing than her husband, she was the one who first reached out in reconciliation to Michael.

A few months after the big talk, as the earliest flowers of spring 1985 pushed up through the ground in Zurich, LuJean gave Michael a call one Saturday, when she knew he wasn't working.

Answering the phone, Michael heard only a new song playing that he knew his mother liked. It was Stevie Wonder singing through the static, *I Just Called to Say I Love You*. When it ended, LuJean's cheery voice came on the line to say the same thing, and to add that she loved Stefan too and that both of them were welcome to visit. Corny as the gesture was, Michael appreciated what it meant, and they had a happy, reconciling sort of chat.

The next summer, Michael and Stefan visited Valleytown for the first time as a couple and stayed in the family home together. LuJean soon became the family expert on homosexuality. As she told her relatives about Michael, she was surprised to see how many gay cousins and nephews—all along the West Coast, from southern California to Washington state—started emerging to seek her advice. (This pattern fits recent studies suggesting that homosexuality in a male comes mostly from his mother's biological influences.)

Michael and Stefan continued over the years to visit Valleytown, twice a year, and LuJean and Mike resumed visiting every year in Europe. Mike, a bit hesitant like the biblical Peter, still occasionally needed to be reassured that a person didn't choose to be gay (*Are you* sure, *son?*). He also needed to repeat regularly that he didn't understand homosexuality but he loved his son and that's what mattered most.

He and LuJean felt so energized by the experience of reconciling with Michael that after a period of absence from church they decided to find a new one. They went back to All Folks temporarily, but finally found what they were looking for at an Assembly of God church, more conservative and charismatic than their last and where the topic of homosexuality came up sometimes and not in a pleasant way; still, they felt at home there, and reminded themselves that it had taken time for them to see another point of view, too.

Ironically, standing up for their beliefs, for *the truth*—the posture that they had always assumed was the best way to show religiosity—during that year from hell hadn't made them feel like going back to church at all. Only the new posture, of sitting down and reconciling, for the big truth of love, had made them want to do that.

## thirty-three

If one of my children were tainted with [heresy], I would myself offer them in sacrifice.
—*King Francis I of France*

I wondered often while putting together the Rolanduses' story whether they could have done things any differently.

Whether they could have found a solution like the Sunblooms', for instance.

Was there no other possibility for mixed families of the Reformation than total alienation? Especially in the Dutch Republic, where people of various faiths famously lived side by side in remarkable peace? Didn't neighborhood peace translate into domestic peace as well?

I found no precise answer. No one could say (and no one may ever be able to say) just exactly how many mixed families there were in Reformation Europe, much less just exactly how many such families behaved in this way or that when someone converted. But as I made my way through thousands of fragmented documents and caught glimpses of hundreds of other mixed families around Europe, I did indeed see other solutions than the drastic one the Rolanduses chose.

Yes, other families too cut off converting children and siblings and cousins. Some even expressed willingness to kill offenders, as heard from the Most Catholic King of France, or the Netherlandish Catholic father who threatened to bash in his son's head if that son converted to one of the new faiths. If few parents actually carried out such a threat, many shared its basic sentiment: toleration of religious deviance was not a virtue. Luther could not *conceive of any reason by which tolera-tion could be justified before God*, while Calvin urged the execution of heretics and blasphemers and insisted that those who would spare such offenders offended God. To tolerate evil in the community, to leave sinners unpunished, was to condone their sin and even to be complicit in it, which only invited God's wrath.

Yet despite such rhetoric it also seemed to me that the most common solution of mixed families was not outright rejection but rather some form of tolerance anyway. Not, again, that any of these tolerating families really liked tolerance: in fact, as an ideal, it was regarded as infinitely inferior to order, conformity, and unity, both in church and society. But for most mixed families it was at least better than banishing or killing a deviant son or daughter or sibling or spouse. And it gave you time to change the deviant's mind until he or she saw the light.

The forms of tolerance evident in these families were as varied as the ships in Amsterdam's ever-busy harbor. Some families barely spoke to each other, others muddled along through constant tension, and still others interacted peacefully. But what all tolerant families had in com-mon was that they kept some degree of contact, and they looked at the deviant with some degree of regret: after all, the meaning of the Latin verb *tolerare* was *to bear, to endure*.

Tolerance, even in its most peaceful form, was always about put-ting up with someone's unfortunate choice, or undesirable condition, or inferior religion. Deep inside, or right out loud, you wished that the offender would have chosen as you did. In other words, tolerance was also inherently intolerant. You tolerated something you didn't like, or accept. You didn't kill or banish, but you still might punish or despise (however kindly), and you still regarded the deviant as inferior rather than as an equal who made a choice as legitimate as your own.

Even the famously large-minded Dutchman Dirck Coornhert, one of the few people in the sixteenth century to praise tolerance, took it only so far. Other-believers should be drawn out of darkness with light rather than violence, and should have their sins washed with mod-erate streams rather than floods, but they still needed enlightening and washing and still had to be endured. He also reserved the right (like almost all tolerant people) to be rudely intolerant to select groups who truly deserved it, such as Anabaptists: Coornhert simply had fewer groups than most on his list of undesirables.

Some families, I saw as well, seemed to go beyond tolerance and to achieve a genuine acceptance of other-believers.

Sometimes it happened the simple way: a family followed the convert, or the convert returned to the family's religion. But it happened as well, and most impressively, the hard way: when members of rival churches stayed in their rival faiths but loved each other nonetheless.

Here was a final sort of conversion, or turning—not merely rejoining those you have left or who have left you, but turning back toward those who *won't* join you. This wasn't about grudging or even peaceful coexistence with inferiors, or about hoping that others would change, but rather about mutual respect and understanding among equals.

This lofty sentiment wasn't easy to distinguish from the most peaceful sort of tolerance, of course, because who can read precisely the hearts of the people involved? But certainly such a sentiment was present in the Reformation, long before the Sunbloom family practiced it.

There was the Amsterdam magistrate and poet C. P. Hooft, a contemporary of Old Jacob Rolandus, who in the 1590s urged his fellow Reformed to walk more peaceably with those of other faiths rather than regard them as inferior: he knew from watching his own wife that she was just as edified by her Mennonite sermons as he was by his Reformed.

There were also those mixed couples, already mentioned, who willingly alternated the baptizing of their children, or had the boys follow the father's religion while the girls followed the mother's.

There was Michel L'Hôpital, a famous Catholic councilor to French kings, who was so devoted to his Protestant wife and daughter that fellow Catholics suspected him of being Protestant himself: no true believer would accept an other-believer so equally.

And more. These families weren't abundant by any means, but they showed that in the Reformation too some people required more from relationships than mere tolerance.

●　●　●

And so I saw under the Reformation sun that there was indeed a variety of choices for mixed families, just as for families of later centuries. But I wanted to see most of all *how* they did it—how families ended up with the relationships they did.

I was sure that this was just as complicated a matter as conversion itself, affected by all the usual suspects: social status, gender, personality, occupation, geography, chronology, theology, and more. A preacher's family, for instance, probably found it a lot harder to accept the conversion of a family member than, say, a noble family, which tended to draw its primary identity from its name, not its religion. A family living after 1650, when religious lines were drawn more firmly than ever, probably found it harder to accept religious deviance than did a family who lived in earlier decades. And a family living in Brabant probably had a harder time with conversion—whether Catholic or Protestant—than one in Amsterdam. But whatever the precise and complicated mix of influences on a family's decision, what struck me most in general was this: those who rejected or tolerated could not see other-believers as quite like themselves, while those who accepted could.

I saw that to the rejecters and also to the tolerant, deviants were not merely different but were dangerously different, so that whatever derogatory slurs-of-the-moment they might have suffered individually (heretics, sodomites, lepers, Christ-killers), they all in truth had only one name: Other.

Just about any society allowed some level of difference in people's tastes, of course, but the Other went beyond *ordinary* difference. Other was strange and foreign, rather than normal and regular. As the Irish first put it, Other was *beyond the pale*—outside the boundary of legitimate human behavior or thought, and thus you probably not only treated the Other poorly but felt perfectly justified in doing so.* You had to keep your word to most around you, but not to heretics. You didn't cast stones and mud and slurs at fellow Christians, but in Rome during the annual race for Jews you certainly could.

---

* *Pale*, an old word for stake, indicated boundaries, referring specifically to a large area around Dublin; anything outside that area's boundary was beyond the Pale.

You also tended to build your identity against the Other. Being Reformed meant in large part *not* being Catholic (papist), or Lutheran (heretic), or Mennonite (itself a derogatory term). The Dutch Reformed preacher Olivier van Hattem was one of many reprimanded by his local church council for failing to rant sufficiently against *papists* in his sermons, and for seeking common ground with them rather than separating from them. Being Dutch long meant mostly being against evil Spain; whenever truce talks between the warring countries threatened to break out, numerous Dutch patriots angrily opposed them on the grounds that unity and identity might be lost in peace. In England, the *orthodox* labeled anyone who thought otherwise with the convenient and clearly inferior name of *dissenter*. And the Catholic kingdom of France tolerated members of the Reformed Church from 1598 to 1685 but referred to them (and required the Reformed to refer to themselves as well) as the *so-called Reformed Church*—not quite equal, not quite legitimate.

You made sure as well to tell awful stories about the Other, full of the most gruesome and incredible details—and the stories could be believed, because of their subject. Christians of the Reformation knew perfectly well the tales that pagan Romans told of early Christians (that they were criminals, and atheists, enemies of public morals, that they ate small children, practiced incest, and so on), and deplored them as the worst lies, but most Reformed or Catholics of the seventeenth century would hardly think themselves guilty of the same unfounded lies: *their* stories were true, and *their* enemies were genuinely evil.

And of course to keep Others other you avoided familiarity with them, lest you be contaminated or, worse, begin to believe that they weren't so other. It was easier to keep people other if you knew them as part of an easily definable group, not as complicated individuals. Anglican authorities in England feared that one Anglican father might not object to his daughter's Catholic suitor because the father had been friends with the suitor's family for so long. French Catholic and Reformed leaders knew that the unflattering images they held up of the rival faith would fall apart when rival believers interacted with each other daily. Reformed authorities in the Dutch Republic did not like people to visit their Catholic relatives in the Spanish Netherlands, as too often the visitors realized that these relatives weren't so different after all. A Dutch pamphlet of 1579 summed up the sentiment early on: *We have been told that these people are monsters. We have been sent after them as after dogs. Yet if we consider them, they are men of the same nature and condition as ourselves . . . children of the same father.*

The zealous believed that the tolerant were as dangerous to the church as were outside rivals of that church. Such fears were of course right: familiarity could cause one to lose zeal against rivals. The question was whether that was desirable.

Finally I saw that those who managed to accept family members of rival faiths emphasized what they had in common rather than what they did not.

The family connection alone would seem to make obvious what they had in common, but not necessarily—a family member who took an unexpected action, such as converting to an *apostate* faith, could suddenly seem an even greater stranger than an ordinary stranger. But accepting families never lost sight of their intimate connection, or they were motivated to rediscover it.

In the Reformation, mixed families might do this the same way Mike Sunbloom Senior did: by preferring the Bible's passages on love to the passages on division. But there were other ways to think about the process too, including in terms not used by families of the distant past.

One way that people of the Reformation knew well was the ancient principle of hospitality—if not so much from the frightful example of the Sodom and Gomorrah story then from the positive example of the Good Samaritan. The Samaritan didn't wonder about whom he was obligated to treat well, but simply took the initiative and treated a stranger well—even a stranger who himself ordinarily looked down on Samaritans.

At any period in history hospitality is obviously risky, as the scholar Martin Marty has noted: to regard the stranger as *worthy of equal, dignified treatment*, especially if you didn't know him or her at all, made you vulnerable. The stranger might take advantage of you, pretend to be someone he or she is not, and so on. *Strangers so often appear to be menaces, and sometimes they may be.* But for there to be a possibility of real fellowship, of finding out that the stranger is not really a stranger after all, of amending your view of the group to which the stranger belongs, of sparking in the stranger a sense of gratitude and hospitality in return, the risk has to be taken.

To those who extend hospitality, reconciling matters more than separating. The religious moment, or impulse, lies not in the drawing of lines or in the defending of a position but in crossing lines and inviting the Other to meet on common ground; it lies not in being right about this issue or that, but in being right with others. For some, hospitality, or reconciliation, *is* holiness—it's not simply a platitude, not a desirable extra, not something secondary to a faith's rituals, but the supreme religious act, the one that gives all the rituals their highest meaning.

More modern ways to think about dispelling Otherness and finding acceptance were especially abundant, I noticed, whether buried in scholarly journals or shining brightly among the *New Arrivals* at bookstores.

Among the useful scholarly approaches was the sociological concept of *multiple reference groups*, which suggests that rather than limiting your identity to a single group you see yourself belonging to many: the more groups you belong to, the more likely it is that you'll intersect with other people who may not share every reference group with you but with whom you'll at least have something in common.

Most useful of all to me as a way to reconciliation was another sociological concept, called *master status*. This says that one of your reference groups, or identifiers, shapes you more than all others you may have. Thus you might be, all at once, female, American, Catholic, teacher, white, sibling, child, spouse, heterosexual, and a lot more. But you tend to identify yourself, and others tend to identify you, by only one of these: the master status.

The master status affects not only our personal identity but our relationships. We tend to identify most, and get along best, with those who share our master status, even if our secondary identifiers differ. And we tend to get along less well with those of another master status, even if we share all sorts of secondary identifiers. In other words, we don't have to agree on everything to have a strong and equal relationship with someone; but we do have to agree on what matters most.

It seemed to me that master status, or *what matters most*, can be fluid, changing according to context and need. Thus we don't have to seek relationships merely among People Already Like Us, or rigidly stay with just a single identity. Rather, we can play an active and creative role in the process. We may not have control over the master status others assign to us, but we do control the status we assign to ourselves, and to others—and we can use that control to find a master status we agree on even with those not apparently like us.

This is what reconcilers, or accepters, of any era are able to do, even if they don't use these terms. They don't have to give up their secondary identifiers, which also matter to them. But they do give up their old master status in exchange for a new one that they think works better with others. This is more than compromise, which suggests that no one is satisfied or standards are lowered. Instead it's finding a status that those involved value more than the old one.

A famous example of this from the Reformation were the *politiques* of France, who concluded that the only way to end religious wars between two sides equally convinced of being God's true religion was to find some other meaningful common identifier: namely, a peaceful France. But the politiques were not universally loved for their efforts (as many reconcilers are not): many on both of the warring sides refused to relinquish their primary identity as either Reformed or Catholic, thinking it a violation of their faith, even a denial of their faith. Thus they kept fighting. To the politiques (who also were believers), however, the most religious act was to find peace, even if it meant rendering as secondary the questions of whether the wafer and wine turned to Christ's flesh and blood, or how one attained salvation. A believer could still hold convictions on such matters, but not at the expense of peace.

A similar process could occur, of course, in a family. It didn't occur in the Rolandus family, because they could not give up their separate primary identities for a new one they shared, such as *loved family member*. To himself and to his family, Jacob was Catholic more than he was brother or son or family member, while his parents and his sister were above all else Reformed. The family relationship, their love for one another, certainly mattered, but it was not paramount.

In the Sunbloom family, in contrast, Michael was no longer primarily *gay* to his parents, but a *loved one*—which was how Michael primarily regarded his parents as well.

Certainly some don't mind being at odds with others, and prefer to have a competing master status; they may even revel in it, proud of their separation from the unclean—just as the Rolanduses were. Some may also refuse to engage with you in the search for a common master status: it can be threatening, even frightening, to let an old one go. And perhaps some relationships are beyond reconciliation. But maybe much of the time we're simply not willing to work as hard as the rabbi, the sheik, and the minister (this isn't a joke) in Seattle who meet together often to seek mutual understanding. They discuss texts they find offensive in the others' scriptures, they declare what they value most in their own tradition, and they name what they see as *untruths* of their own tradition. It takes a lot of time and effort, but it helps them to find commonality and respect, to correct misconceptions, and to soften disagreement. The process hasn't caused them to leave their traditions, but to leave a particular version of their tradition, and of other traditions.

But maybe master status isn't such a new idea after all. What else did Paul mean with all his words about no longer male or female, no longer Jew or Gentile, and so on, than that once divided people had found another common identity to unite them? Or when he said that holders of this new identity were no more strangers to each other?

The Rolanduses had Paul's ideas available to them, but they read them in a way that allowed for reconciliation only through joining the other's particular view of things, not through subordinating that view to something they might have valued even more, such as their relationship. To them, their relationship had meaning only within a particular religious identity. Thus they remained Jew and Gentile, Protestant and Catholic, heretic and true believer, rather than simply Rolanduses. And they mourned for each other the rest of their lives.

# thirty-four

[ It's to be near my dad, and my brother's family. ]

*Recently*. Taking the Number 11 tram from central station, I step off at Bellevue, on the edge of Lake Zurich, and walk a scant ten meters to reach the best sandwich shop in the city.

The line is long, as usual at lunch (and breakfast), but Stefan, still trim at 60-something and affable as ever at the window, handles the crowd with ease and charm, for he knows many of them by name and also their lunchtime preferences. Currently the shop rotates 42 sorts of sandwiches (15 or so every day), many of American inspiration but all assigned suitably Swiss-German names. Only one sandwich bears an untranslated name, and it's for sale every day because it's by far the most popular: *Mom Sunbloom's Tunafish*.

I hear her son Michael in the back, chopping things and emitting a steady stream of chatter to his employees. Some days he humorously sings a few lines of the old Mormon hymn *Put Your Shoulder to the Wheel* to get them going, but I don't hear it today. Though he has the genes and skills to work the window, Michael is jumpier than Stefan, and more worried about getting things right than about chatting graciously with customers or subtly moving them along. Besides, he says, Stefan *would let the workers walk all over him.* So Stefan calmly sees to the public relations while Michael nervously runs the kitchen, making sure that even during peak times there is no drop in standards.

And what standards they are. The sandwiches are striking for not only their imaginative combinations but their appearance and flavor. Traditional favorites have a little extra touch to make them interesting, new favorites are surprising (brie, fig, and apricot on multi-grain triangolo bread), and every one, of whatever sort, is neatly cut in half, wrapped in clear plastic without a crease, then slapped with one of Michael's neatly designed but now computer-generated labels, ready to be carried away.

The tuna includes finely chopped pickles, onions, and celery, a little sugar to bring out the pickle, and *the best* mayonnaise, while the tuna itself is first pressed in a juicer to squeeze out every drop of water—then the mix is spread evenly on whole wheat bread. Twelve different types of bread are available, but Michael, not you, chooses which one best matches which filling.

Curry egg is another favorite, but I order (after being heckled from the back by Michael, who has noticed my arrival and tells Stefan to charge me double) a modified Caprese sandwich. Michael leaves the kitchen to bring it out, along with my favorite sort of juice, setting both on the small table before me, under the trees. He's eager to hear what I think about it, but has to rush back inside. The sandwich tastes even better than it looks, I have to admit. I've never really been one to get excited about sandwiches, yet I do now, just like all the regular customers of the Bellevue Deli.

Not a day goes by but someone walks past the window after eating and says to Stefan (who always gets the credit), *This is the best sandwich I've ever tasted*, and Michael proudly overhears it from the back.

There's one more thing available here too, which Michael prepares every morning starting at four o'clock in his own kitchen and which sells out every day despite its exorbitant price: *Mom Sunbloom's Blonde Brownies*.

If Michael's fingerprints are all over the deli, then so are LuJean's. And I can't help but wonder as I sit there eating whether that would have been the case, and whether Michael would be as exuberant as he is today, had his relationship with his parents gone the way of the Rolanduses. Because it certainly could have. Just as there were more choices in the Rolanduses' world than alienation, so there were more choices in the Sunblooms' world—our world—than reconciliation.

When I finish the sandwich, Michael comes back outside and I pay my compliments. Then I ask, since he's in the mood for waiting tables would he be so kind as to fetch me a brownie, my little Mormon indulgence to compensate for no wine with lunch?

He rolls his eyes, then limps away to get my order. Immediately, a nearby pigeon starts limping right behind him, even favoring the same leg as Michael. I point out that he's got an admirer. But he's already seen the bird and now starts talking to it.

Returning with the brownie, he explains that the pigeon had been around for months, and that at first he hated it—partly because he hated all pigeons and partly because he irrationally felt that it was mocking him. Every time Michael came outside, the bird would swoop down and limp alongside. Then somehow, after a while, the limp became their bond. *Now we're pals*, he concludes.

I laugh and say, *that's actually really good, even better than your big gay Mormon story.*

*You're such a Waste*, he replies, using his favorite nickname for me as he sets down the brownie, sure that I'll like it, too.

After several years at Berlitz and then a decade as a copy writer, Michael joined Stefan at the sandwich shop in the early 1990s.

His touch was soon evident, including in the new name, the Bellevue Deli, which became an even bigger success than its predecessor. The business has allowed Michael and Stefan to rent a comfortable flat in Zurich, and buy a small seventeenth-century stone home near Lugano, where Michael has created a colorful flower garden in the narrow, stone-walled backyard. He owes that particular skill in large part to his other parent, Mike Senior, who has admired the garden often through the years.

Recently, the weekend getaways to Lugano have become increasingly rare, as work and stress have piled up. Like most couples, Michael and Stefan have had their difficult moments, but they recently celebrated 32 years together and are making plans to retire—more a doddering middle-aged couple now than the jetsetters they once were.

In fact, anyone who wants to experience the delights of the deli should do so soon, because Michael and Stefan will in the next few years retire not only from working (Michael just turned 60) but from Switzerland too, at least for half the year. They plan to spend the other half in Valleytown—far more time than the usual three or four trips Michael currently takes home each year. Stefan is thrilled at the prospect of basking in the sun almost daily, a passion he shares with legions of cloud-covered northern Europeans (though Michael has made him start wearing a hat outside after a second cancerous mole was removed).

Michael's limp is getting worse, but would be worse still if not for a successful operation on his back in 1996; being on his feet every weekday from four in the morning until two in the afternoon doesn't help his condition. He now regularly loses feeling in one or both feet, which has led to several falls and broken ribs, but he keeps pushing himself and you won't hear him *whining*, which he loathes. Thanks to his reduced mobility, and pain, and love of good food, his middle is spreading; his hair, in contrast, is not, because he finally cut it several years ago, revealing his ears at last to the world. He's also picked up (of all things) a liking for baseball caps bearing the names of various American universities.

He loves Switzerland still, but is weary of being the eternal outsider, no matter how long he lives there, no matter how good his Swiss-German. Still, I am surprised that he wants to spend so much time back in Valleytown.

*It's to be near my dad, and my brother's family*, he explains. But it all depends on Stefan's health, especially some heart trouble, which may necessitate longer stays in Switzerland than they've planned. Still, Michael wants to somehow be around even more than usual for Mike's final years. LuJean, alas, died in March 2009, coincidentally during one of Michael's trips home. They had assumed that Mike, 12 years older and now 91, would go first, but instead it was the fit LuJean who one night suddenly fell ill and died in minutes.

Michael was glad he was there when it happened, and she would have been glad too. A stalwart at her Assembly of God Church since

1985, she regularly and publicly declared her *love for Michael and Stefan* in the same breath that she declared her *love for the Lord*. Michael and his brother David organized her funeral, arranging music, invitations, flowers, speakers, and food, and snuffing out a plan by some of LuJean's *people* to have an open microphone during the service (a disaster waiting to happen, insisted Michael).

During the service, he sat up front with Stefan, imagining that people were probably looking at him and whispering, *There's her gay son and that must be* . . . But he *got over it*, because the pastor turned out to be *a great guy*, because the reason people knew about Michael and Stefan was that LuJean had been so open about them, and because of what Michael noticed in the newspaper obituary written by Mike Senior (included in the printed program for everyone to see).

Not the part of the obituary that gave LuJean's occupation as *homemaker* (she had also worked outside her home her entire life; at least it mentioned Hollywood Hats and *McDonald's Restaurant*, where she was known for her *friendliness and genuine concern for customers*).

Not the part that called her a *devoted wife and mother*, or said that she never met a stranger, or mentioned her extensive travels in Europe with her son Michael, or remarked that the church would mourn the empty space where she proudly sat each Sunday, or recounted her famous turkey and dressing or her apple and pumpkin pies (no mention of the tuna), or told how she loved to *cuddle up* with her great-granddaughter, or said that her *devoted husband* would miss LuJean's smile and caring, or expressed confidence that she *went to be with the Lord peacefully*.

No, the part Michael noticed was at the end, where it listed her survivors, including *son David Sunbloom and his wife Kim of Valleytown, and son Michael Sunbloom Jr. and his companion Stefan Keller of Zurich, Switzerland*.

The mention of Stefan didn't surprise Michael, not after so many years of good relations with his parents, but he had had his doubts: Mike and LuJean never had put up a picture of Michael and Stefan in the house, as they had of David and Kim. It wasn't because of shame, they said, but because it would take too much explaining to friends. Michael wasn't sure he bought it: maybe acceptance of others can run only so deep. But this last public acknowledgment in the obituary was gratifying: he knew more than anyone how different things could have been.

More surprising to Michael than LuJean's obituary were some of the people who showed up at the funeral.

He lost track of how many cousins were there, including one gay cousin who handed Michael a note saying how much he had appreciated being able to talk to LuJean during his own sexual crisis years before, and how accepting she had been of him.

The principal of the school where Michael last taught, 31 years earlier, was there, as were several old teaching friends—including his favorite co-teacher, Kathy, whom he had baptized into the Mormon Church. She and her husband later invited Michael and Stefan to their home, and over dinner they thanked Michael for *changing their lives*, and that of others too, because now her sister and some friends had become Mormon. Flustered, Michael could only say, *Please pass the potatoes*.

Michael's old Mormon girlfriend Susie, whom he hadn't seen in thirty years, was also there, as she had noticed the obituary and decided to attend even though she never did properly meet LuJean. Susie even hoped that on one of Michael's future visits she, her husband (the missionary she had waited for), Michael, and Stefan could all get together for dinner.

Finally there was Joni, plus several other formerly Mormon friends, with whom Michael had been in contact for some years.

All these friends together in one place made Michael feel that he would have even more company than he'd expected for his return to Valleytown, and the next stage of his life.

One old friend was absent from the funeral: Mom J, who died in 2003. Michael missed her deeply, despite their occasional clashes over race (she had prejudices that Michael couldn't bear). Those prejudices didn't extend to homosexuals, and when they at last got around to talking about Michael's news, back in 1983, she readily accepted it— she had always suspected that her husband was gay and because she knew him so long and so well she completely believed that such an orientation was natural. When Michael visited Valleytown, he made a point to eat lunch with her every other day (to LuJean's slight irritation), and she visited Michael and Stefan in Switzerland several times. When she died, her friends from her new church, Northwest Baptist, plus Michael, held a memorial service, quite against her wishes, replete with her favorite dishes and a fittingly odd combination of tributes.

Still, what struck Michael most was the reemergence of his Mormon friends.

Michael didn't mind, not at all. He had always remembered his experience in the church with fondness, had always been amazed that, even though he had left the church years before, *its relevance in my life is still so palpable that I still hold great respect for it*, and had always written, whenever some Swiss form asked for his religious affiliation, *Mormon* in the blank space next to *Other*.

He had even often defended the religion to surprised friends and acquaintances, especially in Europe, where almost no one actually knew any Mormons or much about them, except rumors of the worst sort. The pattern was always the same: at a party or dinner it would somehow come up that Michael had been Mormon, people would look in amazement and start denouncing the religion because they expected him to do likewise, Michael would respond to the contrary that his experience had been *overwhelmingly positive*, and it would escalate at last to greater disbelief or even full-blown fireworks. How could he have allowed himself to have been brainwashed by a cult? people would ask. Then came the wild claims, such as that the church owned most of the porn industry, as well as Coca-Cola. Or that perhaps Michael didn't know what the church really believed after all, while the accuser, who had read a whole unsympathetic book about Mormons, really did.

Michael was in the classic squeeze of the leaver: those he left didn't want to hear his reasons why, and those he joined wanted to hear only condemnation of the group he was leaving.

There were things in Mormonism that Michael did indeed find objectionable, or perfectly debatable, and he would have been happy to discuss those. But he wanted people to get their information right first.

It surprised him more when he encountered such attitudes in the United States, as during a recent presidential election when one poll showed that 43 percent of Americans would not vote for a Mormon as president (another poll put it at only 24 percent). The extent of frank bias alarmed him. Maybe it shouldn't have: even in the United States only 45 percent of the population knew a practicing Mormon in 2010, which went far toward explaining why in one poll 49 percent of Americans had an unfavorable view of Mormons (coincidentally, this was exactly the same percentage of Americans who had an unfavorable view of homosexuals; not coincidentally, only 40 percent of the population knew someone who was openly homosexual).

Michael wasn't sure how he ended up being the church's defender in Switzerland; he suspected it had to do with his general dislike, learned through hard experience as both a Mormon and a gay man, of the pain and inevitable inadequacy of stereotypes—the least desirable form of master status that someone could put on you.

But his days as a defender of the faith ended in 2008, when Proposition 8 (banning gay marriage) hit California, with the support of the Mormon Church. For the first time, Michael was deeply upset with the church; for the first time since leaving it, he realized how much he still cared about its actions; and for the first time he decided to have his name formally removed from its rolls.

Over the years, he had watched with interest the church's evolving views of homosexuality. They had gone from suggesting that homosexuality was evil and the parents' fault (1974), to urging compassion and stating that causes were unknown but evidence pointed to biological factors (1992), to admitting that it was unlikely gays chose their attraction. Moreover, gays had gone from being outcasts in the church, or people of vague status, to being accorded full fellowship, at least if they remained celibate. It still wasn't quite where Michael hoped it would be, but he was happy to see things evolve and he thought them likely to evolve further, given past trends. Then came Proposition 8.

The church's active support of it felt to Michael—even though the church hadn't intended it that way, even though Michael hadn't participated as a Mormon in 30 years—like a personal slap in the face, as if the woes of the American family were to blame on homosexuals, as if homosexuals again had something physically and emotionally wrong that made them inferior. Where at least, he wondered, was the church's sense of irony? In the nineteenth century, good medical opinion declared that people who converted to Mormonism were probably mentally ill, a conclusion that only deepened existing prejudice against them. At about the same time Mormon polygamy was condemned as the major threat to traditional marriage and families, which Mormons thought ridiculous, given their tiny place in American society: the real threat, they responded, lay in the vast number of Americans who neglected their families. Michael would have said the same about gays.

When the church more recently launched an ad campaign featuring ordinary Mormons, because research showed that *long-held myths about Mormons were usually dispelled when other Americans got to know them personally*, Michael thought again that the same would be true of gays (along with Jehovah's Witnesses, Mormons bring up the rear among American religions in favorable attitudes toward homosexuals).

By then Michael had read the work of Carol Lynn Pearson, and he preferred the attitude she urged on her fellow Mormons: *We can be polite to our homosexual brothers and sisters, but we are not being "kind" unless we acknowledge them as "kin," not as "the other," but as our very own kind.*

Many Mormons would have lamented Michael's alienation from the church, would have regretted that he had missed out all these years.

But it was equally possible that the church had missed out on Michael, too. After all, I teased him, he could also have been the greatest Homemaking Leader in church history.

I was glad that I was around to tease Michael, that I was one of the other Mormons he'd found again, even before his mother's funeral. After a decade of sporadic and mostly superficial correspondence following his move from Valleytown, we met once more in person in 1988, when I started traveling to Europe as a historian in search of fantastic documents and asked Michael whether he would like to get together for a visit. He and Stefan and their friend Elena took the trouble to fly to Belgium to see me, and we laughed a lot over a long weekend, like old times. Elena's presence confused for me the issue of who was with whom, but I didn't think too hard about it. Some months later, however, Michael decided to clarify things for me, in a letter.

Our visit, he said, made him realize that he wanted to remain friends, but friends had to be honest. And so he at last explained to me at length what he'd been through—the emergence of his feelings, his decision to follow them and to leave the church, the pain he experienced with his parents. He summed it all up with a badly mixed metaphor: *the chromosomal dice had been cast, and I had to play the hand dealt me.*

I was probably more surprised by his mixing of metaphors than by his news, despite my naïveté regarding homosexuality. Though at the time I still didn't know any gay people—or didn't know that I knew any—even I wasn't completely blind to the possibility that he and Stefan were partners. Still, for an instant after reading the letter I was alarmed: did this mean that Michael had always had a crush on me?! Or that I'd somehow had one on him?!

Yet in the next instant it hit me: it didn't really matter whether Michael had had a crush on me (he would of course later taunt me that he never had), because he had been a great friend and wanted to be so again, and also because I realized, for the first time in a conscious way that nevertheless came from deep in the marrow, that I could never have a crush on him, or any man. That was when I also realized he could never have a crush on any woman.

He accepted me the way I was, and trusted that I was living the best I knew how, including in my choice of religion. How could I not do the same for him?

Yet it was probably good that Michael hadn't told me from the start, in 1980 or so, because I might have reacted as frostily as some others before me.

By the time of his letter in 1990, however, I had been studying history for ten years and was no longer surprised by much, including cultural change. I could by then name dozens of values and practices that for centuries or even millennia were assumed to have been chiseled in stone and yet they changed anyway—if usually too slowly for the non-historically inclined to see. Not only racial mixing, and a sun-centered universe, and women studying and voting and speaking, and left-handedness, but also polyphonic music and vaccination were all long denounced in the West as immoral, if not unbiblical, hard as it may be to imagine today. But each began to be seen in new ways as people asked new questions and learned new information, until each also became widely acceptable. And of course there was usury: for more than a millennium Christians condemned it, and Dante placed money lenders in the same corner of Hell as, ironically, *sodomites*. Yet churches today are full of respectable bankers, blissfully unaware of their former damnation or of who their neighbors were supposed to be—because people like John Calvin started rethinking how lending money could be moral after all. Even Mormons themselves, in their brief history, had undergone monumental changes, including in such once seemingly immutable matters as polygamy, or the Negro Policy, as people began to understand marriage and race in new ways.

Thus in historical perspective it didn't seem terribly surprising that long-standing attitudes toward homosexuality might one day be questioned too, as new understanding emerged: debate over the issue might prove to be another latest crisis of the moment, which, if one day resolved and widely accepted, would, like previous crises, cause later generations to wonder what all the fuss was about, if they are even aware that a fuss occurred.

Yet more important than big patterns of history in influencing my reaction to Michael's letter were various painful memories of a personal sort, recently risen to the surface, of moments when I had treated others poorly or been treated poorly myself—because of who I imagined others to be, or others imagined me to be. The excruciating thought of the one-time friend who my friends and I alienated for the whole of eighth and ninth grades because someone said he was *a fag*, the memory of being reduced myself to a *damn Mormon*, the incredulity of some new acquaintances when it comes up that I am Mormon (*are you serious?*), all pierced me any time I found myself about to alienate someone. I wasn't going to do so now to Michael, or even merely be tolerant of him, which he wouldn't, well, tolerate.

But most important of all as I read Michael's letter was the same feeling that Mike Senior had had when he decided he wanted to keep his son: because he liked him. I was pretty sure that I liked Michael because he had liked me first, the same way Jesus's disciples said that they *loved Him because He first loved us.*

I thought about the big surprise party he threw for me before I left on a mission, a party so big and memorable and well-choreographed that my vaudeville-loving grandmother was still talking about it years later as one of the most hilarious events of her life, while my sister, who paints, still regards it as one of the defining moments in her life for impressing upon her the importance of detail. I thought of how Michael gave me the nerve to quit law school and start studying what I really wanted to study, history, because as he put it in a rare letter at the time, we ought to *love life, every minute of it,* rather than wait to be happy in the future or only in (he used Mormon jargon here) *the post-mortal life.*

I didn't engage in any conscious process of seeking a common master status with him. In fact I no longer really thought of Michael as gay, or Mormon, or ex-Mormon, or a teacher, or a fabulous cook, but simply as Michael. Come to think of it, maybe someone's name is the best master status you can give, as it's simply another word for *highly complex individual,* just like you.

All these thoughts and feelings made it easy for me to respond positively to his letter. Still, it took me a month to write—maybe too long for Michael. It wasn't because I hesitated, as Michael still insists, but because two of my kids were sick for the month after I got his letter, because my wife was just finishing a graduate program, because I was teaching a new class that took all of my remaining time to prepare, and because I wanted to compose a thoughtful letter. Yet had I known by then about the stress he had suffered over earlier revelations he had made, I would have written at least a short note sooner.

He had told me in the letter that if I couldn't accept him then that was okay—but it wasn't really. Stefan later told me that Michael fretted for weeks when he didn't hear anything. At last I wrote, however, and said that I was fine with his news. I had only one concern, I said: since teasing had been such a major component of our past friendship, was it okay to joke about this new subject too, as he still joked about my Mormonism? I mean, family could tell family jokes, right?

About ten days later, I received Michael's response in the form of a card. On the front was a disturbingly hairy man dressed in a floral dress, big thick-framed glasses, an awful wig, and a cigar in his mouth, saying *Write Soon* (open card) *Or I'll Come Visit*. Now we were friends for life again.

We visited regularly in Europe after that.

On one trip I told him that our Swedish ancestors had lived in villages only 30 miles apart before immigrating to America—a distance easily within the movable world of preindustrial laborers. We could be fifth or sixth cousins, I teased.

On another, Michael and Stefan drove me to a village near Bern so that I could find another set of my great-grandparents. Johannes Krebs and his wife Louise Mueller converted to Mormonism in that village, around 1890, then emigrated to Utah, where one of their many daughters married one of Carl and Mathilda Harline's many sons. While we were there, Stefan even offered to call some of the Krebs families he found listed in the local phone book, but I was still recovering from the last flood of cousins in Sweden, and was content merely to take in the lovely scenery.

Getting to know Michael's full story during all those visits helped me better understand what the Rolanduses were going through when I found their documents later. Because of Michael, I understood more profoundly than otherwise what was at stake in that family, and how hard and creative reconciliation was, and how real Timothy and Catharina and Maria and Jacob were, rather than merely names on an old page.

I was glad for these insights, but more glad that Michael and I remained friends. He and Stefan soon met my wife and three children, and stayed with us a few times on their way back and forth between

Valleytown and Switzerland. They are even planning a short trip to buy lunch for our daughter, who is on a Mormon mission in France.

I was also glad that people at the deli could benefit from Michael's gifts, that he was still making life better for many around him, and that he was again seeing friends from all stages of his life—his school days, his Mormon days, his flight-attendant days, and his Swiss days. He's also begun mentoring a gay, ex-Mormon young man, urging him, among other things, to stay close to his still-Mormon parents; and though praising the young man for his virtues and talents, Michael also laments to me the lack of *morals and responsibility* in young people today, sounding like the very best of old fogeys.

But I was especially glad that Michael had known, except for one year from hell, an entire lifetime of happiness with his parents and brother, and half a lifetime with Stefan.

Michael's still weekly phone conversation with his 91-year-old father goes something like this.

*Hey Senior, Junior here.*

*And don't you ever forget that.*

Then Mike, unhampered by the phone static of past years, clearly describes life—chuckling that he's already forgotten what he ate for breakfast, that it's 100 degrees outside but he's still wearing a flannel shirt because *the darn air-conditioning works too good*, that he's gained eight pounds in recent weeks thanks to his daughter-in-law's peach cobbler, that he wonders about Michael's weekend place whatever-Italian-name-you-call-it, that *if it wasn't for you boys why we never would have seen the world like we did*, and that he *went to that Mormon eye doctor of mine, and that Mormon eye doctor couldn't do a thing, and that Mormon . . .*

Michael chuckles at this: Mike has mostly gotten over his prejudice toward Catholics, but he can't quite let go of his old sentiments about Mormons. Still, reflects Michael, at least he has a Mormon eye doctor, and at least Michael, when at home, can now talk about his Mormon friends without worrying that some dairy product might be thrown his way.

Then Michael responds with observations and news of his own, but mostly he listens.

Finally the conversation ends, as it has for the past thirty years, with Mike saying, *Hear ya next week*, a phrase that means more and more to Michael as he faces the difficult truth that soon his elderly father really will leave him, at last.

# Postscript

When a historian enters into metaphysics he has gone to a far country from whose bourne he will never return a historian.

*—Shailer Mathews*

After finding the fantastic documents about the Rolanduses, after putting their story on paper, after thinking about the connection their story had to my own world—in other words, after going through the usual process of writing a history book—I started getting an urge that wasn't usual at all: to put Michael Sunbloom's story on paper too, right alongside theirs.

I'd never had that sort of urge before, for any book I'd written. Certainly I'd felt connections to other books, but I'd never said much about them. I planned not to say much in this book either, but to proceed as I always had: tell a Reformation story in the most accessible way possible, and keep to myself any thoughts on how that story might connect to me and my world.

There were a lot of good reasons to keep my connections to myself, beyond the reason of difficulty mentioned earlier.

I worried that fellow historians might think it nuts to be explicit about *the relation between the hours of our life and the centuries of time* (Emerson), or to stress the psychological sameness of the past rather than its otherness.

I worried that abandoning the favorite old pose of authorial absence might come across as self-absorbed (that's all we need, another self-absorbed book).

I worried that fellow Mormons (perhaps unaware that the church's own position had softened over the years) and various others might dislike my sympathetic treatment of homosexuality, while critics of Mormonism might dislike my sympathetic treatment of Mormons.

I worried that gays would wonder what in the world a straight middle-aged Mormon man was doing writing about a subject they had already treated themselves with greater authority and insight.

I worried less that Protestants might be offended by my sympathetic treatment of Catholics, or Catholics by my sympathetic treatment of Protestants, but had I been writing fifty years ago I would have worried more about that.

And fittingly, given the theme of this book, I worried that my parents might find such a detailed look into the mind of one of their precious offspring to be more than a little unsettling.

But then I considered that it was fellow historians who had taught me the importance of imagination in trying to grasp the past, and telling Michael's story alongside a Reformation story was just another way of trying to exercise some.

I considered as well my growing conviction that to care deeply about the past you *have* to be a little self-absorbed: you have to find your story in someone else's story, if it's to have any meaning for you. The process doesn't have to be narcissistic, but it has to be personal—and in the best possible world, a personal story should have some universal quality to it anyway.

I considered that it was from my Mormon teachers and texts, not from training as a historian, that I'd learned the ideals of viewing others not as Other but as yourself, and of trying to understand them on their own terms—ideals urged both by Michael's favorite Bible verses in I John and by such uniquely Mormon texts as Alma 7, in the *Book of Mormon*.

I considered that perhaps gay people might find it interesting that a straight middle-aged Mormon male had written such a story at all.

And I considered at last that much of what has always gone on in my mind is the fault of my parents themselves, as they taught me better and longer than anyone else, through how they lived, to put myself in the shoes of others and to include the outcast. The concrete forms they gave to these ideals stayed with me forever, even when I failed miserably to live up to them: my father as a young teenager in Los Angeles lamenting the sending of his Japanese friends to internment camps, or befriending a kid (whom I saw in class pictures) everyone else called Fish Eyes; my father as an adult making sure that every new kid who wanted to play in whatever game he had organized got to play, even though I wailed that it would mess up the game; my mother telling me how as a young teen she had brushed up against her black lockermate and in that very instant realized, quite against what she had heard from others, that this girl was just like her. And much more. Their examples caused me to see Michael's story as just another version of the same thing, in a more updated form, and to be just as worthy of telling.

After considering all this, I decided, despite the very real difficulties and worries, to follow my urge, and to write Michael's story too rather than merely to ponder it. Just this once, I thought, I wanted to show explicitly how the distant past could possibly have meaning in the present, and vice versa.

Or as Einstein put it, to show that *the distinction between past, present, and future is only a stubbornly persistent illusion.*

I was weary, I admit, of comments like the one from the corporate executive who upon learning my field of study just shook his head and exclaimed, *You people who study the past.* Or of people supposing that a historian's value lay in prowess at Jeopardy or other parlor games, or in serving as *an ornament of discourse* in conversation (in the words of Francis Bacon), rather than in offering genuine insight into life.

Too often the distant past is seen as something mostly suitable for school, or hobbyists, something to be discussed recreationally among those who organize a club around it, rather than as something that might inform present experience.

Too often the distant past is treated like the decorative family Bible on the living room coffee table: an heirloom, a relic, something to be admired and fetishized, something you like to know is there, but not necessarily something you draw upon for wisdom.

And too often, if the distant past isn't vital or connected to life today, then it's the fault of historians ourselves, at least when we act like high priests of history, keeping the sacred places for a chosen few, rather than as evangelists, taking the message to the world.

I know hundreds of historians of the distant past who have important things to say about life right now, but readers don't always know it. Not only because we sometimes write only for each other, in our special language, but also because we (including I) choose to write about subjects that are not exactly obvious in their relevance, and then, even though we see that relevance ourselves, we don't bother to spell out it for those outside the clubhouse.

Setting the Rolanduses and Sunblooms next to each other could be a way to combat that, I thought. Not only would it emphasize the parallel lines of their stories, but the physical proximity on the page would suggest the relationship of distant past and close present a little more forcefully than usual.

My desire to try increased when I started noticing all around me countless other parallels in today's world to the Rolanduses, convincing me more than ever of the timeliness of their story.

I read about Noah Feldman attending his tenth yeshiva reunion with a non-Orthodox fiancée, only for both of them to be erased from the group picture because of her non-Orthodox standing; and even though he sends updates every year about himself and his (now) wife and children, these are never included in the newsletter.

I learned of a Mormon girl who quit a relationship with a Catholic boy solely because of his faith.

I knew a man who left his childhood faith and grew alienated from his sister because he felt that she wanted him to *come back to the Church in order to be happy* rather than simply to *be happy*, which made him feel unequal; she in turn felt that he looked down on her decision to stay in the faith, which made her feel unequal.

I read an article from *Harper's* in the 1970s (cited by John McNeill) in which the author stated that he had a liberal attitude toward gays but then compared them to the lepers of the Bible and said that he'd rather have his son be a dope addict or murderer than a homosexual.

And I read a memoir by James Carroll, an antiwar activist, about his never resolved conflict with his father, a leading military officer, over the Vietnam War.

Especially this last example convinced me that Michael's story wasn't merely a gay or Mormon story, and the Rolanduses not merely a Protestant or Catholic story, but they were part of a bigger story about anyone seen as Not The Same, even by their own family. As the medieval historian R. I. Moore concluded, in *The Formation of a Persecuting Society*, it's pointless to study separately the hostility directed against various undesirable groups in the Middle Ages, including Jews, lepers, heretics, and homosexuals, because they were all the victims of a single persecuting impulse that society had developed toward its chosen set of deviants: all were *the monster by which their adversaries believed themselves to be threatened.* The same impulse simply finds different combinations and labels in other times and places.

Yet also motivating me to tell Michael's story were positive examples of families who had reconciled, such as his. I read of a Jewish man in New York who was ostracized by his parents when he became Mormon, to the point that when his parents saw him coming the other way on the street they would cross to the opposite side. But eventually the father took a risk and restored the relationship with his son, concluding that Mormonism had helped make his son a better Jew.

I heard a radio program called *Adventures with Extremists* tell of another Jewish man who went out and met with anti-Semites because he wanted to see whether he could look the most frightening person he could imagine in the face and still see their common humanity (he did).

I read of couples who kept their relationships strong even after one of them left their common church, because they accepted that the other's leaving or staying was what felt right for him or her.

And then I met a final example in person. One night leaving a restaurant in a town where I used to live, I saw a couple I knew and admired. They were obviously subdued. When I went over to ask how they were, they related with difficulty that their gifted college-going son had just quit his scholarship and their faith and their faith-sponsored school, all at once. I fumbled around for something to say, knowing perfectly well that I had nothing to teach them about parenting and not wanting to make them feel worse. I decided simply to listen, but they weren't much in the mood for talking. Then quite out of the blue, and quite against my usual inclination in social settings, I began to tell what I'd been learning from my recent research—about mixed families who rejected, and mixed families who muddled, and mixed families who accepted and reconciled. Unbelievably to me, who in 25 years as a historian had never had much of anything practical to tell anyone, a light went on in their heads: they realized that they had been muddling but that they could see a way to get beyond that. I was as surprised as they were about the whole thing.

This example more than any other made me decide to include Michael's story. I wasn't sure that I had the best possible comparison in Michael and the Rolanduses. I wasn't sure either that I had the best possible details, or even that the side-by-side technique of going back and forth in time between two stories was necessarily the best way to link the flesh and blood and gristle of past and present—especially after one recent critic called the back-and-forth technique the *blight of so much contemporary fiction* (at least she didn't say nonfiction). But I wanted to try anyway.

And so I picked up the phone and called Michael, to tell him what I was thinking. And to say that if he agreed, then I needed to come visit again in person, soon, to learn from him even more details than I already knew about his story. He couldn't imagine that anyone would find his *boring life* interesting, he said, but after some hesitation he agreed to try.

As I sat on the plane, I thought about the reluctance in his voice, and wondered whether he would really go through with it—whether it would be too much for him to live it all again. But if he couldn't, well, there would at least be the Bellevue Deli as consolation, which was sure to be nearly as fantastic as a hot archive.

# Bibliographical Essay

To keep the text unencumbered by notes and numbers, to keep the book trim, and to avoid the complications of footnoting "Michael's" story, I offer here simply a general discussion of sources, organized by story and subdivided (mostly) into primary and secondary materials.

## Jacob Rolandus

The chief *Primary Sources* were Jacob's journal for 1654 (perhaps the only journal he ever kept and certainly the only one that survived), letters to and from his family between 1654 and 1663, documents about the Jesuits in Flanders after Jacob entered the order in 1658, documents from Jacob's years as a missionary in Brazil (1663–84), and documents about the Rolandus family—mostly in the records of the Dutch Reformed Church from the 1580s to the 1660s.

### Jacob's Journal and Correspondence with His Family

Jacob's journal and letters ended up in the archives of the Jesuits, which then ended up in the National Archive of Belgium—and they're still moving. When I found the documents, they were in the National Archive (Algemeen Rijksarchief) in Brussels, Fonds Jezuieten, Vlaamse Provincie, 1436. But Jesuit materials in Brussels were recently moved to the Provincial Archive in Antwerp and merged into the large

Jesuit collection already there, making them into one new collection, which was then recatalogued and renumbered. Thus the new and correct citation for Jacob's papers is Rijksarchief in de Provincie Antwerpen, Archief van de Nederduitse Provincie der Jezuïeten, 3477.

## Documents of the Jesuits in the Province of Flanders

Jesuit documents used in this study were (in the Antwerp collection just cited) numbers 6 (annual reports of the Flemish Province, sent to Rome), 9 (annual histories of the Aalst House), 10 (annual histories of the Antwerp College), 11 (annual histories of the Antwerp House), 21 (annual histories of the Kortrijk House), 25 (annual histories of the Mechelen House), 38–43 (annually compiled lists of Jesuits in the province, including basic biographical data, studies completed, positions held, and talents), 1472 (results of theology exams taken by Jesuits), 2023 (alms given to the Antwerp House), 2049 (lawsuit for libel brought by the Jesuits against the lawyer Tongerloo), 2827 (annual histories of the Holland Mission), and 3428 (list of Jesuits who put themselves forward for the Indies). Helpful basic published sources were A. Poncelet, *Nécrologe des jésuites de la province Flandro-Belge* (Wetteren, 1931), and W. Audenaert, *Prosopographia Iesuitica Belgica Antiqua: A Bibliographical Dictionary of the Jesuits in the Low Countries, 1542–1773*, 4 vols. (Leuven, 2000), plus such anti-Jesuit pamphlets as *Dialogus oft Tzamensprekinge ghemaect op den Vredehandel* (n.p., 1608), and a more colorfully titled tract (translated here) *A New Song of Several Falsely Virtuous Jesuits, Who with This Truce or Treaty Come Here in Holland, to Deceive the Simple and with Lovely Appearing Words Try to Mislead Tried and Sincere Catholics* (n.p., [1607]).

## Documents from Jacob's Mission to Brazil

Documents about Jacob's mission are in the Jesuit Archive of Rome, Provincia Brasiliensis et Maragnonensis, 1 (Letters from Rome, 1678–1759), 3 (II) (Letters from Brazil to Rome, 1661–95), 5 (I–II) (Triennial catalogues of Jesuits in the mission; volumes that survived from Jacob's time were made in 1667, 1670, 1679, 1683), 9 (Histories, 1651–1702). Jacob's letters are mostly in volume 3 (II), with entries by or about him dated (1667) August 11; (1668) January 25 and August 14; (1669) February 7, June 29, August 7, August 12, September 7, September 11; (1677), August 21; (1684) June 20, June 25, July 27.

## Documents About the Rolandus family

These are scattered around various Dutch archives, but are most dense in the records kept by the three levels of the Reformed Church: the provincial synod, the regional classis, and the local church council (kerkenraad). The proceedings or *Acta* of many synods around the Republic have been published, starting with the general work of J. Reitsma, S. D. van Veen, *Acta der provinciale en particuliere synoden, gehouden in de Noordelijke Nederlanden gedurende de jaren 1572–1620*, 3 vols. (Groningen, 1892–99). The Acta of the synod of South Holland in particular are continued in W. P. C. Knuttel, *Acta der Particuliere Synoden van Zuid-Holland, 1621–1700*, 6 vols. (The Hague, 1908–16). Numerous passages involving Jacob the Older and Timothy are referenced in the indices of both publications. But the Rolandus men show up most often in classis and church-council records, which are almost always still in manuscript and poorly indexed, and must therefore be patiently worked. Records for the classis of Amsterdam, to which both Jacob the Older and Timothy belonged, are located in the Municipal Archive (Gemeente Archief) of Amsterdam, Archief van de Classis Amsterdam, Acta 1–5 (1582–1656); records of Amsterdam's church council, to which only Jacob the Older belonged, are in the Gemeente Archief as well, in the collection Archief van de Hervormde Gemeente, Kerkenraad, especially Acta 1–8 (1578–1653). (Other Rolandus men who became preachers can also be found in both printed and manuscript volumes of the Acta, such as Timothy's brother Daniel, Daniel's son Jacob, and that Jacob's preacher-son Daniel, and so on.) See also in the Gemeente Archief Amsterdam the registers for Baptism (Doop), Marriage (Ondertrouw), and Death (Sterf), where relationships among the many Roladuses can be traced (such as in Ondertrouw, 2702, 2710, and Doopboeken, 1558). Jacob the Younger is mentioned in Arnout Van Geluwe's *Veerthien Stercke Beweegh-Redenen vanden Godt-saligen uytganck, van ses-en-vijftich Gereformeerde, Godt minnende herten, uyt het nieuwe Gereformeerde*

*Babylon: Die haer tot de Heylighe, Roomsche, Apostolijcke, Alghemeyne Kercke, nu cortelinghe begheven hebben* (Antwerp, 1657). Jacob the Older's manuscript translation of the new Dutch Bible is in the National Archive (Algemene Rijksarchief) in The Hague, Tweede Afdeling, Collectie 497, Rolandus.

Records of Timothy's life in Brabant are thickest in the Provincial Archive (Rijksarchief) Den Bosch. The proceedings of the Great Church Meeting held in that city after the Treaty of Munster in 1648 have been published, thanks to P. H. A. M. Abels, A. P. F. Wouters, *Acta conventus sylvae-ducensis extraordinarii 1648* (The Hague, 1986). Timothy doesn't show up there, because he wasn't yet in Brabant in 1648, but the context from that meeting is crucial to understanding the world he was entering and the expectations held by Reformed preachers for the area. The communities Timothy served in Brabant belonged to the provincial synod of Gelderland and the regional classis of Den Bosch; records of both institutions are also in the Rijksarchief Den Bosch. Timothy shows up occasionally in the Acta of the synod, and far more often in the records of the classis, especially Acta, vol. 1, which runs from 1647 to 1654. Unfortunately the volume from 1654 to 1669, when Timothy was in Boxtel and Helvoirt, did not survive; the next volume commences only in 1670, after his death. But these missing years can be supplemented with other records from the classis, including number 10 (Correspondence), 309 (Various Accounts and Incomes), and 310 (Chapters of Canons, Plus Altars and Church Fabric). Other useful collections in the Rijksarchief Den Bosch were Ontvangers der Belastingen en Domeinen (Receivers of Taxes and Domains), numbers 211 and 225, and Raad van Brabant (788.174, a lawsuit that among other things includes the only surviving letter by Catharina Rolandus). Crucial for the dispute between Timothy and the schoolmaster of Boxtel were records in the National Archive in The Hague, Raad van State, 1819, Tiende Verpachting (or Tithing Leases and Accounts), between 1653 and 1658, because the Raad van State was, under the direction of the States General, in charge of financial affairs in the newly won lands of Brabant. There are no Acta for local church councils in St. Michielsgestel, Boxtel, or Helvoirt, during Timothy's years, though there are a few other sorts of documents for those communities, most of which are now in the Rijksarchief Den Bosch, including the Nederlandse Hervormde Gemeente St. Michielsgestel en Schijndel, the Nederlandse Hervormde Gemeente of Boxtel, and the Streekarchief Langs Aa en Dommel, Haeren (Helvoirt), especially Dorpsbestuur Helvoirt, 1340–1813, number 547, plus the church accounts between 1661 and 1672. A few relevant records were in the small community archive of Boxtel, E255A, Rekeningen 1653. The inventories for each collection in the Rijksarchief Den Bosch include helpful introductions and context.

The most important *Secondary Sources* for the Rolanduses' story may be organized around a number of large topics, starting with the Rolanduses themselves.

### The Rolandus Family

Two articles about Jacob were long ago published in a local Catholic journal by W. van Nieuwenhoff, "Eene zeventiend'-eeuwsche bekeeringsgeschiedenis," *Studien: Godsdienst, Wetenschap, Letteren* 65 (1905): 1–54, and 127–57. Anton van Duinkerken wrote a serialized novel, "Rolandus' Bedevaart," published in *De Gemeenschap: Maandschrift voor katholieke reconstructie* (1932–33). Some material about Jacob in Brazil is included in S. Leite, *Historia da Companhia de Jesus no Brasil*, 5 vols. (Rio de Janeiro, 1948) (my thanks to Jonathan Harline and Kendall Brown for help with the Portuguese), and E. Op De Beeck, "A Liberdade dos Indios: De Braziliaanse indianen in de spiegel van de Westerse Christenheid, 1549–1683" (Licentiate thesis, Katholieke Universiteit Leuven, 1997). A genealogical study of the family, based on an eighteenth-century family genealogy, was published by J. D. M. de Klerk in the *Nederlandsche Leeuw* 1 (1883): 65–66, 74–75. Jacob the Older is also in the *Nieuw Nederlandsch Biografisch Woordenboek*, vol. 3 (Leiden, 1914), col. 1088 (Jacob the Younger in col. 1158), and in various parts of *De Statenvertaling, 1637–1937* (Haarlem, 1937), C. C. De Bruin, *De Statenbijbel en zijn voorgangers* (Leiden, 1937), and W. van 't Spijker, et al., *De Synode van Dordrecht in 1618 en*

*1619* (Houten, Netherlands, 1987). See further two genealogical studies about the Rolandus family, by E. Post, "Jacobus Roelandus de jongere, boekverkoper," http://cf.hum.uva.nl/bookmaster/fransz/archivalia_roelandus.htm, and H. Meuleman, "Een domineesdochter en een banket-bakker," http://cf.hum.uva.nl/bookmaster/fransz/archivalia_triumphe.htm. Yet another Internet source, dedicated to Netherlandish preachers who studied in Geneva and Heidelberg, contains educational information about Jacob the Older and Timothy Rolandus as well: www.dbnl.org/tekst/_jaa002186501_01/_jaa002186501_01_0015.htm.

## Conversion

On the general concept of conversion, see as well the works mentioned below with Michael Sunbloom's story. Helpful studies of ancient and medieval conversion were M. O. H. Carver, ed., *The Cross Goes North: Processes of Conversion in Northern Europe, A.D. 300–1300* (York, 2002); R. Fletcher, *The Barbarian Conversion: From Paganism to Christianity* (New York, 1998); A. Haverkamp, "Baptised Jews in German Lands During the Twelfth Century," in *Jews and Christians in Twelfth-Century Europe*, ed. M. Signer, J. Van Engen (Notre Dame, 2001), 255–310; J. N. Hillgarth, *Christianity and Paganism, 350–750: The Conversion of Western Europe* (Philadelphia, 1969); K. Mills, A. Grafton, eds., *Conversion in Late Antiquity and the Early Middle Ages: Seeing and Believing* (Rochester, 2003); K. Morrison, *Understanding Conversion* (Charlottesville, 1992); J. Muldoon, *Varieties of Religious Conversion in the Middle Ages* (Gainesville, 1997); and E. Pagels, *Beyond Belief* (New York, 2003).

Useful starting places for early modern conversion, which often include some mention of family struggles, were numerous articles in *La conversion au XVIIe siècle: Actes du XIIe Colloque de Marseille, janvier 1982* (Marseille, 1983), and E. Andor, I. G. Tóth, eds., *Frontiers of Faith: Religious Exchange and the Constitution of Religious Identities, 1400–1750* (Budapest, 2001). Also H. J. Allard, "Bekeerlingen onder de geestelijkheid van 't Haarlemsche bisdom," *Bijdragen voor de geschiedenis van het Bisdom van Haarlem* 2 (1874): 276–301, 3 (1875): 89–96, and 5 (1877): 179–92; B. Bradshaw, "Sword, Word, and

Strategy in the Reformation in Ireland," *Historical Journal* 21 (1978); E. Carlebach, *Divided Souls: Converts from Judaism in Germany, 1500–1750* (New Haven, 2001); J. Demos, *The Unredeemed Captive* (New York, 1994); J. Friedman, "Jewish Conversion and the Spanish Pure Blood Laws: A Revisionist View of Racial Antisemitism," *Sixteenth Century Journal* 18 (1987): 4–29; M. J. Harran, *Luther on Conversion: The Early Years* (Ithaca, N.Y., 1983); C. Kooi, "Converts and Apostates: The Competition for Souls in Early Modern Holland," *Archiv für Reformationsgeschichte* 92 (2001): 195–214; E. Labrousse, "La conversion d'un huguenot au catholicisme en 1665," *Revue d'Histoire de l'Eglise de France* 64 (1978); K. Luria, "The Politics of Protestant Conversion to Catholicism in Seventeenth-Century France," in *Conversion to Modernities: The Globalization of Christianity*, ed. P. van der Veer (New York, 1996), 23–46, and "Rituals of Conversion: Catholics and Protestants in Seventeenth-Century Poitou," in *Culture and Identity in Early Modern Europe, 1500–1800*, ed. B. Diefendorf, C. Hesse (Ann Arbor, 1993), 65–81; K. Mills, A. Grafton, eds., *Conversion: Old Worlds and New* (Rochester, 2003); A. Pettegree, *Reformation and the Culture of Persuasion* (Cambridge, 2005); J. Pollmann, "A Different Road to God: The Protestant Experience of Conversion in the Sixteenth Century," in *Conversion to Modernities: The Globalization of Christianity*, ed. P. van der Veer (New York, 1996), 47–64; R. Tielemans, "Dolende Herders: De overgang tot het katholicisme van vijf gereformeerden in de zeventiende eeuw" (Licentiate thesis, University of Rotterdam, 1995); M. Questier, *Conversion, Politics, and Religion in England, 1580–1625* (Cambridge, 1996), and "John Gee, Archbishop Abbot, and the Use of Converts from Rome in Jacobean Anti-Catholicism," *Recusant History* 21 (1993): 347–60.

Helpful studies of individual converts, starting with Queen Christina, were S. Akerman, *Queen Christina of Sweden and Her Circle: The Transformation of a Seventeenth-Century Philosophical Libertine* (Cologne, 1991); V. Buckley, *Christina, Queen of Sweden: The Restless Life of a European Eccentric* (New York, 2004); P. Lewis, *Queen of Caprice: A Biography of Kristina of Sweden* (New York, 1962); B. Quillet, *Christina van Zweden: Een uitzonderlijk vorst* (Baarn, 1982);

S. Stolpe, *Christina of Sweden* (New York, 1966); parts of R. Pintard, *Le libertinage érudit* (Geneva, 1983); and the printed source G. Gualdo Priorato, *The History of the Sacred and Royal Majesty of Christina Alessandra, Queen of Swedland* (London, 1658), which includes an account of her trip to Rome. A few other helpful studies of converts famous and otherwise were (Dutch examples) H. J. Allard, *Petrus Bertius, Hoogleraar aan de Leidsche Academie* (Den Bosch, 1870), and *Matthias Zelhorst, Predikant te Hengelo* (Den Bosch, 1875); A. Nijland, *Joost van den Vondel, 1587–1679* (Amsterdam, 1949); J. Pollmann, *Religious Choice in the Dutch Republic: The Reformation of Arnoldus Buchelius, 1565–1641* (Manchester, 1999); (French examples) C. Desplat, "La religion d'Henri IV," in *Henri IV, le roi et la reconstruction du royaume: Volumes des actes du colloque Pau-Nérac, 14–17 septembre 1989* (Paris, 1990), 223–67; E. Labrousse, *Bayle* (Oxford, 1983); and M. Wolfe, *The Conversion of Henri IV: Politics, Power, and Religious Belief in Early Modern France* (Cambridge, Mass., 1993).

Useful conversion accounts from the time included Mathias Zelhorst, *Den Catolijck-Gereformeerde Predicant Verthoont de onweder-standelijcke redenen die hem ghenootsaeckt hebben, te keeren totten H. Roomschen Catholijcken Gheloove* (Antwerp, 1649); *Bekeeringe van P. de la Faille, predikant te Koudekerk, uyt de Calvinissche ketterye, tot het H. Katholyk geloof, der H. Katholyke Roomsche Kerke, door het lesen der Oud-vaders* (Antwerp, 1644); A. van Geluwe, *Belydenisse van Rebecca Broeckaers uyt 's Gravenhaegh, huys-vrouwe van den eersamen Martinus de Baets dewelcke sy is af-sweerende alle oude ende nieuwe ketterijen* (Antwerp, 1650), and *Kort verhael van een achthienjarighe Hollantsche reyse, ghewandelt van een vlaemschboer* (Antwerp, 1650). A modern edition of a convert's story is A. Le Blond, ed., *The Autobiography of Charlotte Amélie, Princess of Aldenburg, née Princess de la Trémoille, 1652–1732* (London, 1913).

## Tolerance and Religious Mixing

The most helpful recent studies were B. Kaplan's consistently insightful *Divided by Faith: Religious Conflict and the Practice of Toleration in Early Modern Europe* (Cambridge, Mass., 2007); supplemented by

B. Gregory, *Salvation at Stake: Christian Martyrdom in Early Modern Europe* (Cambridge, Mass., 1999), which among much else defines the absolute limits of tolerance; S. Schwartz, *All Can Be Saved: Religious Toleration and Salvation in the Iberian Atlantic World* (New Haven, 2008); and A. Walsham, *Charitable Hatred: Tolerance and Intolerance in England, 1500–1700* (Manchester, 2006).

For the general concept and theory of tolerance, which was long the only way to study the subject, I consulted N. Fornerod, "L'édit de Nantes et la problème de la coexistence confessionnelle dans la pensée de Philippe Duplessis-Mornay," in M. Grandjean, et al., *Coexister dans l'intolérance: L'édit de Nantes, 1598* (Geneva, 1991), 135–52; D. Heyd, ed., *Toleration: An Elusive Virtue* (Princeton, 1996); J. C. Laursen, C. J. Nederman, eds., *Beyond the Persecuting Society: Religious Toleration Before the Enlightenment* (Philadelphia, 1997); S. Mendus, ed., *Justifying Toleration: Conceptual and Historical Perspectives* (Cambridge, 1988); R. Murray, *Erasmus and Luther: Their Attitude to Toleration* (New York, 1972); C. Nederman, J. C. Laursen, eds., *Difference and Dissent: Theories of Toleration in Medieval and Early Modern Europe* (Lanham, Md., 1996); G. Remer, *Humanism and the Rhetoric of Toleration* (University Park, 1996); M. Smith, *Montaigne and Religious Freedom: The Dawn of Pluralism* (Geneva, 1991); and P. Zagorin, *How the Idea of Religious Toleration Came to the West* (Princeton, 2003).

On medieval tolerance, I read M. Gervers, J. Powell, eds., *Tolerance and Intolerance: Social Conflict in the Age of the Crusades* (Syracuse, 2001); R. I. Moore, *The Formation of a Persecuting Society: Power and Deviance in Western Europe, 950–1250* (Oxford, 1987); C. J. Nederman, *Worlds of Difference: European Discourses of Toleration, c. 1100–c. 1550* (University Park, 2000); D. Nirenberg, *Communities of Violence: Persecution of Minorities in the Middle Ages* (Princeton, 1996).

Studies of early modern tolerance and intolerance in practice, or what can also be called religious mixing, are now legion; beyond Kaplan, Gregory, Schwartz, and Walsham, I found also useful (General Studies) J. Delumeau, ed., *L'acceptation de l'autre: De l'édit de Nantes à nos jours* (Paris, 2000); O. Grell, B. Scribner, eds., *Tolerance and Intolerance in the European Reformation* (Cambridge, 1996); W. J. Sheils, ed., *Persecution and Toleration* (Oxford, 1984); (France) P. Benedict, *The Huguenot Population of France, 1600–1685: The Demographic Fate and Customs of a Religious Minority* (Philadelphia, 1991); R. Briggs, *Communities of Belief: Cultural and Social Tension in Early Modern France* (Oxford, 1989); B. Diefendorf, *Beneath the Cross* (Paris, 1991); D. Leonardo, " 'Cut Off This Rotten Member': The Rhetoric of Heresy, Sin, and Disease in the Ideology of the French Catholic League," *Catholic Historical Review* 88/2 (April 2002): 247–62; K. Long, *Religious Differences in France: Past and Present* (Kirksville, Mo., 2006); K. Luria, *Sacred Boundaries: Religious Coexistence and Conflict in Early Modern France* (Washington, 2005), and *Territories of Grace: Cultural Change in the Seventeenth-Century Diocese of Grenoble* (Berkeley, 1991); R. Mentzer, A. Spicer, eds., *Society and Culture in the Huguenot World, 1559–1685* (Cambridge, 2002); L. Racaut, *Hatred in Print* (Aldershot, 2002); L. Racaut, A. Ryrie, eds., *Moderate Voices in the European Reformation* (Aldershot, 2005); G. Saupin, ed., *La Tolerance* (Rennes, 1999); M. Turchetti, "Religious Tolerance and Political Concord in Sixteenth- and Seventeenth-Century France," *Sixteenth Century Journal* 22 (1991): 15–25; (England) J. Bossy, *The English Catholic Community, 1570–1850* (New York, 1976); P. Caraman, ed., *The Other Face: Catholic Life Under Elizabeth I* (London, 1960); P. Collinson, "The Cohabitation of the Faithful with the Unfaithful," in *From Persecution to Toleration: The Glorious Revolution and Religion in England*, ed. O. Grell, J. Israel, N. Tyacke (Oxford, 1991), 51–76; T. A. Davies, *The Quakers in English Society, 1655–1725* (Oxford, 2000); P. Lake, M. Questier, eds., *Conformity and Orthodoxy in the English Church, c. 1560–1660* (Rochester, 2000); P. Lake, *The Antichrist's Lewd Hat: Protestants, Papists, and Players in Post-Reformation England* (New Haven, 2002); (Ireland) V. P. Carey, U. Lotz-Heumann, *Taking Sides? Colonial and Confessional Mentalités in Early Modern Ireland* (Dublin, 2003); (Spain) D. Coleman, *Creating Christian Granada: Society and Religious Culture in an Old-World Frontier City, 1492–1600* (Ithaca,

2003); M. Perry, *The Handless Maiden: Moriscos and the Politics of Religion in Early Modern Spain* (Princeton, 2005); (Eastern Europe) M. Craciun, O. Gitta, G. Murdock, eds., *Confessional Identity in East-Central Europe* (Aldershot, 2002); (Germany) T. Brady, *German Histories in the Age of Reformations, 1400–1650* (Cambridge, 2009); M. Forster, *Catholic Revival in the Age of the Baroque: Religious Identity in Southwest Germany, 1550–1750* (Cambridge, 2001); (Judaism) J. Edwards, *The Jews in Christian Europe, 1400–1700* (Abingdon, 1988); A. Foa, *The Jews of Europe After the Black Death* (Berkeley, 2000).

For tolerance and mixing specifically about the early modern Dutch Republic I began with R. Po-chia Hsia, H. van Nierop, eds., *Calvinism and Religious Toleration in the Dutch Golden Age* (Cambridge, 2002), and C. Berkvens-Stevelinck, J. I. Israel, G. H. M. Posthumus Meyjes, eds., *The Emergence of Tolerance in the Dutch Republic* (Leiden, 1997). A helpful reference was H. Knippenberg, *De religieuze kaart van Nederland* (Assen, 1992). More specific studies included W. Bergsma, "Religious Diversity in the Netherlands of the Sixteenth Century: The Impressions of a Northern Dutch Land-owner," in *Anabaptistes et dissidents au XVIe siècle*, ed. J.-G. Rott, S. L. Verheus (Baden-Baden Bouxwiller, 1987), 215–32; J. Briels, *Zuid-Nederlanders in de Republiek, 1572–1630* (St. Niklaas, 1985); A. Th. van Deursen, *Plain Lives in a Golden Age* (Cambridge, 1991); H. A. Enno van Gelder, *Getemperde Vrijheid* (Groningen, 1972); W. Frijhoff, "La coexistence confessionnelle: Complicités, méfiances, et ruptures aux Provinces-Unies," in *Histoire vécue du peuple chrétien*, ed. J. Delumeau (Toulouse, 1979), 229–57; S. Groenveld, *Huisgenoten des geloofs: Was de samenleving in de Republiek der Verenigde Nederlanden verzuild?* (Hilversum, 1995); 35–53; B. Kaplan, *Calvinists and Libertines: Confession and Community in Utrecht* (Oxford, 1995); D. Nobbs, *Theocracy and Toleration* (Cambridge, 1938); J. Pollmann, *Religious Choice in the Dutch Republic: The Reformation of Arnoldus Buchelius, 1565–1641* (Manchester, 1999), "From Freedom of Conscience to Confessional Segregation? Religious Choice and Toleration in the Dutch Republic, 1580–1750," in *Persecution and Pluralism: Calvinists and Religious Minorities in Early Modern Europe*, ed.

R. Bonney, D. Trim (Bern, forthcoming), and "Women and Religion in the Dutch Golden Age," *Dutch Crossing* 24 (2000): 162–82; R. Rommes, "Lutherse immigranten in Utrecht tijdens de Republiek," in *Nieuwe Nederlanders: Vestiging van migranten door de eeuwen heen*, ed. M. 't Hart, J. Lucassen, H. Schmal (Amsterdam, 1996); H. Schilling, "Religion and Society in the Northern Netherlands," in *Religion, Political Culture, and the Emergence of Early Modern Society: Essays in German and Dutch History* (Leiden, 1992); J. Spaans, *Haarlem na de Reformatie* (The Hague, 1989); and G. Voogt, *Constraint on Trial: Dirck Volckertsz Coornhert and Religious Thought* (Kirksville, Mo., 2000).

For early modern tolerance in specific communities I read D. Beaver, *Parish Communities and Religious Conflict in the Vale of Gloucester, 1590–1690* (Cambridge, 1998); E. Dursteler, "Education and Identity in Constantinople's Latin Rite Community, c. 1600," *Society for Renaissance Studies* 18/2 (2004): 287–303; E. François, *Protestants et catholiques en Allemagne: Identités et pluralisme, Augsbourg, 1648–1806* (Paris, 1993); G. Hanlon, *Confession and Community in Seventeenth-Century France: Catholic and Protestant Coexistence in Aquitaine* (Philadelphia, 1993); P.-O. Léchot, *De l'intolérance au compromis: La question d'une coexistence confessionnelle, Le Landeron, XVIe–XVIIIe siècle* (Sierre, 2003); P. Wallace, *Communities and Conflict in Early Modern Colmar, 1575–1730* (Atlantic Highlands, N.J., 1995); J. Whaley, *Religious Toleration and Social Change in Hamburg, 1529–1819* (Cambridge, 1985).

Some useful studies of families (or individuals) and religious mixing specifically included the two largest studies of the subject, R. Mentzer, *Blood and Belief: Family Survival and Confessional Identity Among the Provincial Huguenot Nobility* (West Lafayette, Ind., 1994), and J. Rosenthal, "The Sword that Divides and Ties that Bind: Faith and Family in the French Wars of Religion" (Doctoral thesis, University of Arizona, 2005). Also valuable were H. M. Baird, *Theodore Beza: The Counsellor of the French Reformation, 1519–1605* (New York, 1899); S. Manetsch, *Theodore Beza and the Quest for Peace in France, 1572–1598* (Leiden, 2000); M. Chrisman, "Family and Religion in

Two Noble Families: French Catholic and English Puritan," *Journal of Family History* 8 (1983): 190–210; B. Diefendorf, "Houses Divided: Religious Schism in Sixteenth-Century Parisian Families," in *Urban Life in the Renaissance*, ed. S. Zimmerman, R. F. Weissman (Newark, 1989), 80–99, and "Give Us Back Our Children," *Journal of Modern History* (1996), 1–43, which though focused on the problem of Catholic children who entered convents without the permission of their Catholic parents involved many of the same dynamics that were present in families that knew conversion; S. A. C. Dudok van Heel, "De familie van de schilder Pieter Lastman, 1583–1633," *Jaarboek van het Centraal Bureau voor Genealogie* 45 (1991): 111–32, the account of a painter in a wildly mixed family; D. Kelley, *François Hotman: A Revolutionary's Ordeal* (Princeton, 1973); L. Martz, *A Network of Converso Families in Early Modern Toledo* (Ann Arbor, 2003); J. Grieser, "The Household Divided Against Itself: Anabaptists and Their Families in Tyrol, 1536–1560," in *Piety and Family in Early Modern Europe*, ed. M. Forster, B. Kaplan (Aldershot, 2005), 134–51; and in the same volume L. G. Lazar, "Negotiating Conversions: Catechumens and the Family in Early Modern Italy," 152–77; E. Dursteler, *Renegade Women* (forthcoming, Johns Hopkins University Press); and most recently, two articles in S. Dixon, D. Freist, M. Greengrass, eds., *Living with Religious Diversity in Early-Modern Europe* (Aldershot, 2009), namely B. Kaplan, "Intimate Negotiations: Husbands and Wives of Opposing Faiths in Eighteenth-Century Holland," and B. Forclaz, "The Emergence of Confessional Identities: Family Relationships and Religious Coexistence in Seventeenth-Century Utrecht."

An excellent introduction to the related subject of early modern intermarriage is B. Kaplan, " 'For They Will Turn Away Thy Sons': The Practice and Perils of Mixed Marriage in the Dutch Golden Age," in *Piety and Family in Early Modern Europe*, ed. M. Forster, B. Kaplan (Aldershot, 2005), 115–33; see also G. Audisio, "Se marier en Luberon: catholiques et protestants vers 1630," in *Histoire sociale, sensibilités collectives et mentalités: Mélanges Robert Mandrou* (Paris, 1985), 231–45; E. Labrousse, "Les mariages bigarrés: Unions mixtes en france au XVIIIe siècle," in *Le Couple interdit: Entretiens sur le racisme, la dialectique de l'altérité socio-culturelle et la sexualité*, ed. L. Poliakov (Paris, 1977), 159–76; H. F. W. D. Fischer, "De gemengde huwelijken tussen katholieken en protestanten in de Nederlanden van de XVIe tot de XVIIIe eeuw," *Tijdschrift voor Rechtsgeschiedenis* 31 (1963): 463–85; B. van Leeuwen, *Het gemengde huwelijk: Pastoraal-sociografisch onderzoek naar de huwelijken van katholieken met niet-katholieken in Nederland* (Assen, 1959).

### Family Life, Including Religious Life and Tolerance

P. A. Barentsen, "Het gezinsleven in het oosten van Noord-Brabant," in G. M. van den Brink et al., *Werk, Kerk, en Bed in Brabant* (Den Bosch, 1989); L. Coon, K. Haldane, E. Sommer, eds., *That Gentle Strength: Historical Perspectives on Women in Christianity* (Charlottesville, 1990); N. Davis, "Ghosts, Kin, and Progeny: Some Features of Family Life in Early Modern France," *Daedalus* 106 (1977): 87–114; J. Delumeau, *La religion de ma mère: Le rôle des femmes dans la transmission de la foi* (Paris, 1992); K. Eisenbichler, ed., *The Premodern Teenager: Youth in Society, 1150–1650* (Toronto, 2002); M. Forster, B. Kaplan, eds., *Piety and Family in Early Modern Europe: Essays in Honour of Steven Ozment* (Aldershot, 2005); D. Haks, *Huwelijk en gezin in Holland in de 17de en 18de eeuw* (Utrecht, 1985); B. Hanawalt, *Growing Up in Medieval London: The Experience of Childhood in History* (Oxford, 1993); J. Harrington, *Reordering Marriage and Society in Reformation Germany* (Cambridge, 1995); G. A. Kooy, ed., *Gezinsgeschiedenis: Vier eeuwen gezin in Nederland* (Assen, 1985); K. A. Lynch, "The Family and the History of Public Life," *Journal of Interdisciplinary History* (1994): 665–84; S. Ozment, *Ancestors: The Loving Family in Old Europe* (Cambridge, Mass., 2001); S. Ozment, "The Private Life of an Early Modern Teenager: A Nuremberg Lutheran Visits Catholic Louvain, 1577," *Journal of Family History* 21/1 (1996): 22–43, and S. Ozment, *When Fathers Ruled* (Cambridge, 1983); L. Pollock, *A Lasting Relationship: Parents and Children Over Three Centuries* (London, 1987); L. Pollock, *Forgotten Children: Parent-Child Relations from 1500 to 1900* (Cambridge, 1983); B. Roberts, *Through the Keyhole* (Hilversum,

1998); A. Schuurman, P. Spierenburg, eds., *Private Domain, Public Inquiry: Families and Lifestyles in the Netherlands and Europe, 1550 to the Present* (Hilversum, 1996); an excellent contemporary comportment book for girls was *Duyfkens en Willemijnkens Pelgrimagie tot haren Beminden Binnen Jerusalem, Haer-lieder teghenspoet belet en eynde* (Amsterdam, 1627), which comments on all sorts of morals and virtues and lack of them.

For preachers and their families in particular I read T. Clemens, "Searching for the Good Shepherd," *Dutch Review of Church History* 83 (2003): 11–54; C. S. Dixon, L. Schorn-Schütte, eds., *The Protestant Clergy of Early Modern Europe* (London, 2003); I. Dobbe, "The Theological Education at the University of Franeker," unpublished paper; N. Enssle, "Patterns of Godly Life: The Ideal Parish Minister in Sixteenth- and Seventeenth-Century English Thought," *Sixteenth Century Journal* 28 (Spring 1997): 3–28; G. Groenhuis, *De Predikanten: De sociale positie van de gereformeerde predikanten in de Republiek der Verenigde Nederlanden* (Groningen, 1977); W. Janse, ed., *The Formation of Clerical and Confessional Identities in Early Modern Europe* (Leiden, 2005); W. Janse, T. Clemens, eds., *The Pastor Bonus* (Leiden, 2004); S. Karant-Nunn, *Luther's Pastors: The Reformation in the Ernestine Countryside* (Philadelphia, 1979); K. Maag, "Called to Be a Pastor: Issues of Vocation in the Early Modern Period," *Sixteenth Century Journal* 35/1 (2004): 65–78; A. Macfarlane, *The Family Life of Ralph Josselin, a Seventeenth-Century Clergyman* (Cambridge, 1970); H. N. Ouwerling, "De Meierijsche predikantenfamilie Hanewinkel," *Taxandria* 22 (1915): 52; L. Roper, *The Holy Household: Women and Morals in Reformation Augsburg* (Oxford, 1989); W. Frijhoff, *Wegen van Evert Willemz* (Nijmegen, 1995); H. Kuyper, *De opleiding tot den dienst des Woords bij de Gereformeerden, I, Inleiding, Geschiedenis* (The Hague, 1891). A helpful modern study of Reformed preachers' families was published by Trouw, and called *Land van domineeskinderen* (Amsterdam, 2002). On material culture in a preacher's household, H. L. M. Defoet, et al., *De Bijbel in huis: Bijbelse verhalen op huisraad in de 16de en 17de eeuw* (Zwolle, 1991). A tract about preachers' incomes, *Bewys Dat het een Predicant Met zyn Huysvrouw Alleen niet mogelijck en is op vijfhondert guld: Eerlijk te leven* (Delft, 1658), is an example of a supplementary primary source for preachers.

### Netherlandish Society and Religion

For the Dutch Republic there are more works than ever; this time I used K. Davids, J. Lucassen, eds., *A Miracle Mirrored: The Dutch Republic in European Perspective* (Cambridge, 1995); P. van der Coelen, et al., *Everyday Life in Holland's Golden Age: The Complete Etchings of Adriaen van Ostade* (Amsterdam, 1998); M. Prak, *Gouden Eeuw: Het raadsel van de Republiek* (Nijmegen, 2002); S. Schama, *The Embarrassment of Riches: An Interpretation of Dutch Culture in the Golden Age* (Berkeley, 1988); G. D. J. Schotel, *Het maatschappelijk leven onzer vaderen in de zeventiende eeuw*, 2nd ed. (Amsterdam, 1905); A. K. Wheelock, A. Seeff, eds., *The Public and Private in Dutch Culture of the Golden Age* (Newark, 2000); A. Schuurman, J. de Vries, A. van der Woude, eds., *Aards Geluk: De Nederlanders en hun spullen van 1550 tot 1850* (Amsterdam, 1997).

For Reformed life in the Republic, I started with P. Benedict's excellent *Christ's Churches Purely Reformed* (New Haven, 2004), and R. B. Evenhuis's specific study of Amsterdam, *Ook dat was Amsterdam*, 5 vols. (Amsterdam, 1965–67), which also includes good information about Jacob Rolandus the Older. Also P. H. A. M. Abels, *Nieuw en ongezien: Kerk en samenleving in de classis Delft en Delfland, 1572–1621* (Delft, 1994); W. Bergsma, *Tussen Gideonsbende en publieke kerk: Een studie over het gereformeerd protestantisme in Friesland, 1580–1650* (Hilversum, 1999); A. Th. van Deursen, *Bavianen en Slijkgeuzen* (Assen, 1974), "Dutch Reformed Parish Life in the Second Half of the Seventeenth Century," in *Bunyan in England and Abroad*, ed. M. van Os and G. J. Schutte (Amsterdam, 1990), and *Een dorp in de polder: Graft in de zeventiende eeuw* (Amsterdam, 1995); A. Th. van Deursen, G. J. Schutte, *Geleefd geloven: Geschiedenis van de protestantse vroomheid in Nederland* (Assen, 1996); J. P. Elliott, "Protestantization in the Netherlands: A Case Study" (Doctoral thesis, Columbia University, 1990); C. Kooi, *Liberty and Religion: Church and State in Leiden's Reformation, 1572–1620* (Leiden, 2000); H. Roodenburg, *Onder censuur: De kerkelijke tucht in de gereformeerde gemeente van Amsterdam, 1578–1700* (Hilversum, 1990); C. A. Van Swigchem, *Een huis voor het Woord: Het Protestantse kerkinterieur in Nederland tot 1900* (The Hague, 1984); W. Verboom, *De catechese van de Reformatie en de Nadere Reformatie* (Amsterdam, 1986). On the abhorrence of Reformed for idols, see C. Eire, *War Against the Idols* (Cambridge, 1989).

On Catholic life in the Dutch Republic, G. Vanden Bosch, "Jezuïetenpastoraat in Friesland: Gerard Carbonel als missiepater in Leeuwarden en omgeving, 1613–1627," in *Geloven in het verleden: Studies over het godsdienstig leven in de vroegmoderne tijd, aangeboden aan Michel Cloet*, ed. E. Put, M.-J. Marinus, H. Storme (Leuven, 1996); P. W. F. M. Hamans, *Geschiedenis van de Katholieke kerk in Nederland* (Brugge, 1992); F. Hoppenbrouwers, *Oefening in Volmaaktheid: De zeventiende-eeuwse Rooms-Katholieke Spiritualiteit in de Republiek* (The Hague, 1996); B. Kaplan, et al., *Catholic Communities in Protestant States: Britain and the Netherlands, c. 1570–1720* (Manchester, 2009); C. Kooi, "'A Serpent in the Bosom of Our Dear Fatherland': Reformed Reaction to the Holland Mission in the Seventeenth Century," in *The Low Countries as a Crossroads of Religious Beliefs*, ed. A. Gelderblom, M. Van Vaeck, J. de Jonghe (Leiden, 2004); in the same volume, C. Parker, "Obedience with an Attitude: Laity and Clergy in the Dutch Catholic Church of the Seventeenth Century"; W. A. J. Munier, "Een mislukte poging tot de inplanting van de Reformatie in de heerlijkheid Borgharen door Heer Philibert van Isendoorm à Blois," *Nederlands Archief voor Kerkgeschiedenis* 65 (1985): 160–89; H. Parker, *Faith on the Margins* (Cambridge, 2008); the classic L. J. Rogier, *Geschiedenis van het Katholicisme in Noord-Nederland in de zestiende en zeventiende eeuw*, 4 vols. (Amsterdam, 1947); M. Spiertz, "De katholieke geestelijke leiders en de wereldlijke overheid in de Republiek der Zeven Provincien," *Traiecta* 2 (1993): 3–20; M. Wingens, *Over de grens: De bedevaart van katholieke Nederlanders in de zeventiende en achttiende eeuw* (Nijmegen, 1994); J. Tracy, "With and Without the Counter-Reformation: The Catholic Church in the Spanish

Netherlands and the Dutch Republic, 1580–1650," *Catholic Historical Review* 71/4 (1985): 547–75; J. C. Van der Loos, *Vaderlandsche Kerkgeschiedenis*, 2 vols. (Kampen, 1937), a very passionate pro-Catholic sort of history with nice documents.

For life in Dutch Brabant, H. Roosenboom, *De dorpsschool in de Meierij van 's-Hertogenbosch van 1648 tot 1795* (Tilburg, 1997), was especially useful in the dispute between Timothy Rolandus and the schoolmaster of Boxtel. For the area more generally, I consulted V. A. M. Beerman, *Stad en Meierij van 's-Hertogenbosch van 1629 tot 1648* (Nijmegen, 1940), and *Stad en Meierij, 1648–1672: De eerste vijfentwintig jaren van het Staatsche regime* (Helmond, 1946); A. C. Brock, *De stad en Meijerij van 's-Hertogenbosch* ('s-Hertogenbosch, 2001); P. Th. A. Dorenbosch, *De Boxtelse St. Petrus*, 2 vols. (Boxtel, 1983); O. V. Henkel, *Drie eeuwen Protestanten ten zuiden van de Moerdijk* (Hague, 1948); J. C. A. Hezenmans, *'s-Hertogenbosch van 1629 tot 1795: Historische studien* ('s-Hertogenbosch, 1977); F. Hoppenbrouwers, "De politieke Reformatie in de kwartieren Maasland en Oisterwijk van de Meierij van 's-Hertogenbosch, 1677–1795," *Brabants Heem* 43 (1991): 8–19; G. Meindersma, *De gereformeerde gemeente s'Hertogenbosch* (Zaltbommel, 1909); W. Meindersma, "De Groote Kerkelijke Vergadering van Den Bosch in 1648," *Nederlands Archief voor Kerkgeschiedenis* 7 (1910), 125 ff.; J. Peijnenburg, *Zij maakten Brabant katholiek*, 2 vols. (Den Bosch, 1987–88); G. Rooijakkers, "Confrontatie of Accommodatie? Het Protestantse beschavingsoffensief in de Meierij van 's-Hertogenbosch, 1648–1800," in *Brabants Heem* 43 (1991): 1–7; G. Rooijakkers, *Rituele repertoires: Volkscultuur in oostelijk Noord-Brabant, 1559–1853* (Nijmegen, 1994); H. Roosenboom, "Tot voltreckinge der Reformatie: Onderwijs als Protestantiseringsinstrument in de Meierij van 's-Hertogenbosch, 1648–1795," in *De Dynamiek van Religie en Cultuur*, ed. M. Monteiro, G. Rooijakkers, J. Rosendaal (Kampen, 1993), 218–38; M. Roscam Abbing, E. Vink, "De dominee, de drossaard en de paapse stoutigheden: Over een richtingenstrijd in Oirschot en Best," in *Noordbrabants Historisch Jaarboek* 10 (1993): 99–121; H. van Velthoven, *Stad en meierij van 's-Hertogenbosch*, 2 vols. (Amsterdam, 1935–38); J. Biemans, "De paapse poppecraam:

Rituelen en gebruiken van katholieken in de classis 's-Hertogenbosch in gereformeerde ogen, 1677–1795," *Brabants Heem* 43 (1991): 20–31.

Works about religious life in the Spanish Netherlands and particularly Antwerp are legion, but I especially consulted M.-J. Marinus, *De contrareformatie te Antwerpen* (Brussels, 1995), and her "De financiering van de contrareformatie te Antwerpen, 1585–1700," in *Geloven in het verleden: Studies over het godsdienstig leven in de vroegmoderne tijd, aangeboden aan Michel Cloet*, ed. E. Put, M.-J. Marinus, H. Storme (Leuven, 1996); G. Marnef, *Antwerp in the Age of Reformation: Underground Protestantism in a Commercial Metropolis* (Baltimore, 1996); A. Thijs, *Van Geuzenstad tot katholiek bolwerk: Maatschappelijke betekenis van de Kerk in contrareformatorisch Antwerpen* (Turnhout, Belgium, 1990).

## Jesuits in the Low Countries and the Holland Mission

I started with E. Put, *De Jezuieten in der Nederlanden en het Prinsbisdom Luik, 1542–1773* (Brussels, 1991). Also G. Ackermans, "Propagandisten in de Missio Hollandica," *Trajecta* 6 (1997): 233–62; J. Andriessen, *De Jezuieten en het Samenhorigheidsbesef der Nederlanden, 1585–1648* (Antwerp, 1957); G. vanden Bosch, "Jezuietenpastoraat in Friesland: Gerard Carbonel als missiepater in Leeuwarden en omgeving, 1613–1627," in *Geloven in het verleden: Studies over het godsdienstig leven in de vroegmoderne tijd, aangeboden aan Michel Cloet*, ed. E. Put, M.-J. Marinus, H. Storme (Leuven, 1996), and "Over de doden niets dan goeds? Zeventiende eeuwse elogia en necrologia van jezuieten in de Hollandse Zending als bronnen voor religieuze mentaliteitsgeschiedenis," *Trajecta* 6 (1997): 334–45; J. de Brouwer, *De Jezuïeten te Aalst*, vol. 1: *Stichting en opheffing, 1620–1773* (Aalst, 1979), and *De Jezuïeten te Brussel, 1586–1773* (Mechelen, 1979); A. Deneef, *Les jésuites belges, 1542–1992* (Brussels, 1992); H. van Goethem, ed., *Antwerpen en de jezuïeten, 1562–2002* (Antwerp, 2002); R. Hardeman, *F. Costerus: Vlaamsche Apostel en Volksredenaar, 1532–1619* (Alken, 1933); W. G. Haverkamp, ed., *Jezuïeten in Nederland: Rijksmuseum Het Catharijneconvent* (Utrecht, 1991); F. van Hoeck, *Schets van de geschiedenis der Jezuieten in*

*Nederland* (Nijmegen, 1940); J. Kleijntjens, "De Jezuieten in de Hollandsche Missie," *Haarlemsche Bijdragen* 55 (1938): 23–67; L. Labbeke, "De recrutering van de Jezuïeten in het Hertogdom Brabant, 1584–1640" (Licentiate thesis, Catholic University Leuven, 1995); H. Meeus, ed., *Ad Maiorem Dei Gloriam: Jezuieten in de Nederlanden tijdens de Zeventiende Eeuw* (Antwerp, 1997); M. Moehlig, "Het jezuietencollege to Antwerpen in de zeventiende en achttiende eeuw" (Licentiate thesis, Catholic University Leuven, 1988); A. Poncelet, *Histoire de la Compagnie de Jésus dan les anciens Pay-Bas*, 2 vols. (Brussels, 1927–28); E. Steenackers, "Le Chanoine Jean de Froidmont: Bienfaiteur de Saint Jean Berchmans," *Handelingen van de Koninklijke Kring voor Oudheidkunde, Letteren en Kunst van Mechelen* 34 (1929): 19–63; H. Storme, *Preekboeken en Prediking in de Mechelse Kerkprovincie in de 17e en de 18e eeuw* (Brussels, 1991), which includes plenty on the Jesuit Franciscus Costerus.

Some helpful general works on the Jesuits include, above all, J. O'Malley, *The First Jesuits* (Cambridge, 1993), his "Attitudes of the Early Jesuits Towards Misbelievers," in *Religious Culture in the Sixteenth Century: Preaching, Rhetoric, Spirituality, and Reform* (Aldershot, 1993), and his edited volumes, *The Jesuits: Culture, Sciences, and the Arts, 1540–1773* (Toronto, 1999), *The Jesuits II: Culture, Sciences, and the Arts, 1540–1773* (Toronto, 2006). On education I read F. de Dainville, *L'éducation des jésuites, XVIe–XVIIIe siècles* (Paris, 1978), and V. Duminuco, ed., *The Jesuit Ratio Studiorum: 400th Anniversary Perspectives* (New York, 2000). An example of a helpful monograph on the order at work is J. Selwyn, *A Paradise Inhabited by Devils: The Jesuits' Civilizing Mission in Early Modern Naples* (Aldershot, 2004). See also J. N. Tylenda, *Jesuit Saints and Martyrs* (Chicago, 1998), 2d ed.

On missionaries abroad in general, J. S. Cummins, ed., *Christianity and Missions, 1450–1800* (Aldershot, 1997), plus R. Forster, *European and Non-European Societies, 1450–1800*, 2 vols. (Aldershot, 2007).

On Jesuits abroad, especially in Brazil, I read much more than I needed to for this version of the book (I plan another version, for a Dutch-language audience, which will go into more detail about Jacob's mission); but I used as an entry point into Jesuit missionary mentality the important seventeenth-century history by the prolific Netherlandish Jesuit polemicist of the time, Cornelius Hazart, *Kerkelijck historie van de gheheele werelt, namelijck van de voorgaende en de tegenwoordighe eeuwe, inde welcke verhaelt worden de gheleghentheden der landen, manieren, ceremonien ende religien der inwoonderen, maer namelijck de verbreydinghe des H. Gheloof, marterleren ende andere cloecke Roomsche Catholycke daeden, inde ghewesten des wereldts, met over de veertigh copere platen verciert*, vol. 1 (Antwerp, 1667); the basic work on Jesuits in Brazil in Portuguese, and containing many primary documents, is S. Leite, *Historia da Companhia de Jesus no Brasil*, 5 vols. (Rio de Janeiro, 1948). More recent are D. Alden, *The Making of an Enterprise: The Society of Jesus in Portugal, Its Empire, and Beyond, 1540–1750* (Stanford, 1996); A. G. Bailey, *Art on the Jesuit Missions in Asia and Latin America* (Toronto, 1999); D. Block, *Mission Culture on the Upper Amazon: Native Tradition, Jesuit Enterprise, and Secular Policy in Moxos, 1660–1800* (Lincoln, 1994); O.-E. Cabral de Mello, *Imagens do Brasil 1630–1654* (Sao Paulo, 1983), has excellent images; H. Clastres, *The Land Without Evil: Tupi-Guarani Prophetism* (Urbana, 1995); T. M. Cohen, *The Fire of Tongues: António Vieira and the Missionary Church in Brazil and Portugal* (Stanford, 1998); H. Lemmens, ed., *Padre António Vieira: Een natte hel: Brieven en Preken van een Portugese Jezuiet* (Amsterdam, 2001); M. Haubert, *L'Eglise et la défense des "Sauvages": Le Père Antoine Vieira a Brésil* (Brussels, 1964); T. Cohen, " 'Who Is My Neighbor?' The Missionary Ideals of Manuel da Nóbrega," in *Jesuit Encounters in the New World: Jesuit Chroniclers, Geographers, Educators, and Missionaries in the Americas, 1549–1767*, ed. J. Gagliano, C. Ronan (Rome, 1997), 211–28; D. W. Forsyth, "The Beginnings of Brazilian Anthropology: Jesuits and Tupinamba Cannibalism," *Journal of Anthropological Research* 39/2 (1983): 147–75; R. Garfield, *A History of São Tomé Island, 1470–1655: The Key to Guinea* (New York, 1992); also with interesting information on São Tomé is R. Harms, *The Diligent: A Voyage Through the Worlds of the Slave Trade* (New York, 2002); L. Palacin Gómez, "The Jesuits and the Struggle for the Freedom of the Indians in Brazil," in *Jesuit Encounters in the New World: Jesuit Chroniclers, Geographers, Educators, and*

*Missionaries in the Americas, 1549–1767*, ed. J. Gagliano, C. Ronan (Rome, 1997), 229–57; J. Hemming, *Red Gold: The Conquest of the Brazilian Indians* (Cambridge, Mass., 1978), and *Amazon Frontier: The Defeat of the Brasilian Indians* (London, 1995); J. Heyndrickx, ed., *Philippe Couplet, S.J., 1623–1693: The Man Who Brought China to Europe* (Leuven, 1990); Nic Perquin, *Gaspar Berse: de eerste Nederlandsche jezuietenmissionaris* (1929); S. Schwartz, *Implicit Understandings: Observing, Reporting, and Reflecting on the Encounters Between Europeans and Other Peoples in the Early Modern Era* (Cambridge, 1994).

## Michael Sunbloom

The primary sources about "Michael" and his family consist of my own notes and memories, my correspondence with Michael over the years, and interviews conducted with Michael and various of his friends in recent years. Records are in my possession.

### Modern Studies of Conversion

"Faith in Flux," *The Pew Forum on Religion and Public Life*, poll from April 27, 2009, http://pewforum.org/Faith-in-Flux.aspx; C. J. G. Griffin, "The Rhetoric of Form in Conversion Narratives," *The Quarterly Journal of Speech* 76 (1990): 152–63; M. Heirich, "Change of Hearth: A Test of Some Widely Held Theories About Religious Conversion," *American Journal of Sociology* 83 (1977): 653–80; A. M. Hoenkamps-Bisschops, "Bekeringsonderzoek: Geschiedenis en meth-odologische problemen," *Gedrag: Tijdschrift voor Psychologie* 10/1 (1982): 57–73; H. Bahr, S. Albrecht, "Strangers Once More: Patterns of Disaffiliation from Mormonism," *Journal for the Scientific Study of Religion* 28/2 (1989): 180–200; J. Beckford, "Accounting for Conversion," *British Journal of Sociology* 29 (1978): 249–62; L. Rambo, *Understanding Religious Conversion* (New Haven, 1993); P. Richter, "Church Leaving in the Late Twentieth Century: Eschewing the Double Life," *Sociology, Theology, and the Curriculum* (1999): 175–86; R. Stark, R. Finke, *Acts of Faith: Explaining the Human Side of Religion* (Berkeley, 2000); R. Stark, *The Rise of Christianity*

(Princeton, 1996), and W. James's classic *The Varieties of Religious Experience* (New York, 1902).

Also important on modern conversion were six large volumes containing dozens of helpful studies: D. Bromley, ed., *Falling from the Faith: Causes and Consequences of Religious Apostasy* (Newbury Park, 1988), A. Buckser, S. Glazier, eds., *The Anthropology of Religious Conversion* (Lanham, Md., 2003), R. Hefner, ed., *Conversion to Christianity: Historical and Anthropological Perspectives on a Great Transformation* (Berkeley, 1993), L. Francis, ed., *Joining and Leaving Religion: Research Perspectives* (Leominster, U.K., 2000), C. Lamb, M. D. Bryant, eds., *Religious Conversion: Contemporary Practices and Controversies* (London, 1999), and C. B. Kendall, et al., *Conversion to Christianity from Late Antiquity to the Modern Age: Considering the Process in Europe, Asia, and the Americas* (Minneapolis, 2009).

*Studies of Modern Tolerance and Tolerance in the Family*

Works on tolerance are too numerous to list, but most useful of all was M. Marty, *When Faiths Collide* (Oxford, 2005), plus L. Bretherton, *Hospitality as Holiness: Christian Witness amid Moral Diversity* (Aldershot, 2010); L. J. Hammann, H. M. Buck, eds., *Religious Traditions and the Limits of Tolerance* (Chambersburg, Pa., 1988); F. Schenk, *The Matrimonial Impediments of Mixed Religion and Disparity of Cult* (Washington, D.C., 1929); J. Naughton, *Catholics in Crisis: The Rift Between American Catholics and Their Church* (New York, 1996); J. Carroll, *An American Requiem: God, My Father, and the War that Came Between Us* (New York, 1996); J.-F. Revel, M. Ricard, *The Monk and the Philosopher: A Father and Son Discuss the Meaning of Life* (New York, 1998); Noah Feldman, "Orthodox Paradox," *New York Times*, July 22, 2007; R. Callister, "For Better or Worse, For Apostasy? How Faith Issues Affect Couple Relationships," *Sunstone* (November 2006): 21–33; and numerous studies of the family and faith cited under Jacob's story, such as G. A. Kooy, *Gezinsgeschiedenis: Vier eeuwen gezin in Nederland* (Assen, 1985). The sheik, rabbi, and minister in L. Goodstein, "Three Clergymen Tell How Differences of Faith Led to Friendship," *New York Times*, November 24, 2009. R. Putnam,

D. Campbell, *American Grace: How Religion Divides and Unites Us* (New York, 2010), appeared just as I finished this book.

### Some Mormon Studies

General historical and sociological works include L. Arrington, D. Bitton, *The Mormon Experience* (New York, 1979); C. Bushman, *Mormons in America* (Oxford, 1999), and *Contemporary Mormonism: Latter-Day Saints in Modern America* (Westport, Conn., 2006); M. Cornwall, T. Heaton, L. Young, *Contemporary Mormonism: Social-Science Perspectives* (Urbana, 1994); D. J. Davies, *An Introduction to Mormonism* (Cambridge, 2003); T. Givens, *People of Paradox: A History of Mormon Culture* (Oxford, 2007); J. Shipps, *Mormonism: The Story of a New Religious Tradition* (Urbana, 1985); J. Embry, *Black Saints in a White Church: Contemporary African American Mormons* (Salt Lake City, 1994); for more details on Mormon converts as mentally ill, see J. Spencer Fluhman, *A Peculiar People: Anti-Mormonism and the Making of Religion in Nineteenth-Century America* (forthcoming, University of North Carolina Press); criticisms of polygamy reviewed in L. Thatcher Ulrich, "Presidential Address: An American Album," *American Historical Review* 115/1 (February 2010): 1–25.

### Studies of Modern Homosexuality and Religion (Including Mormonism)

I consulted among others J. McNeill, *The Church and the Homosexual* (Kansas City, 1976); J. Naughton, *Catholics in Crisis* (New York, 1997); K. Mahaffy, "Cognitive Dissonance and Its Resolution: A Study of Lesbian Christians," *Journal for the Scientific Study of Religion* 35/4 (1996): 392–402; S. L. Jones, M. A. Yarhouse, *Ex-Gays? A Longitudinal Study of Religiously Mediated Change in Sexual Orientation* (Downers Grove, Ill., 2007); A. Sullivan, "Virtually Normal," in *Catholic Lives: Contemporary America*, ed. T. J. Ferraro (Durham, 1997), 171–86; and numerous studies by A. K. T. Yip, "Leaving the Church to Keep My Faith: The Lived Experiences of Non-Heterosexual Christians," in *Joining and Leaving Religion: Research Perspectives*, ed. L. Francis (Leominster, U.K., 2000), "Gay

Christians and Their Participation in the Gay Subculture," in *Deviant Behavior* 17 (1996): 297–318, "Attacking the Attacker: Gay Christians Talk Back," *British Journal of Sociology* 48/1 (March 1997): 113–27, "Gay Male Christians' Perceptions of the Christian Community in Relation to Their Sexuality," *Theology and Sexuality* 8 (1998): 40–51, "Gay and Lesbian Christians: The Lived Experiences," *Sociology, Theology, and the Curriculum* (1999): 187–96. Many of these ideas were summed up in more simplified form in a recent documentary film, *For the Bible Tells Me So* (2007). Other useful works included a newspaper article by the molecular biologist Dean Hamer and the scholar of circadian rhythms Michael Rosbash, "Sexual Orientation Has Deep Biological Roots," *Los Angeles Times*, February 23, 2010.

Pathbreaking in Mormon culture was Carol Lynn Pearson's *Goodbye I Love You: A True Story of a Wife, Her Homosexual Husband, and a Love that Transcended Tragedy* (New York, 1986), and her more recent *No More Goodbyes: Circling the Wagons Around Our Gay Loved Ones* (Walnut Creek, Calif., 2007). A special edition of *Reunion, the Family Fellowship Newsletter*, from 2006, sums up the current tensions in Mormon culture on the subject. The church ad campaign is mentioned at www.foxnews.com/politics/2010/09/04/mormons-new-ad-campaign-seeking-dispel-myths-pr-romney-run/; Mormons near the rear in attitudes toward homosexuals, at http://religions.pewforum.org/comparisons#; the poll on unfavorable impressions of homosexuals, at http://pewforum.org/PublicationPage.aspx?id=645; the poll on unfavorable impressions of Mormons noted in www.deseretnews.com/article/700054363/Mormons-need-to-work-to-increase-favor.html; the polls regarding voting for a Mormon president, www.freerepublic.com/focus/f-news/1741561/posts, and www.gallup.com/poll/26611/some-americans-reluctant-vote-mormon-72yearold-presidential-candidates.aspx. Changing Mormon views on homosexuality at www.religionnewsblog.com/18866/mormon-homosexuality. On affective memory and method acting, see www.theatrgroup.com/Method/affective_memory.html.

## Carl and Mathilda

Primary documents in Sweden, consisting mostly of separate registers recording baptisms, house visits by the pastor, first communions, moving, and marriages, in the parishes of Simtuna and Frösthult between 1850 and 1900, are located in the regional archive of Uppsala. The specific references for Carl and Mathilda's families are first of all in Simtuna, Husförhörsboken AI:20, 1856–60, AI:21, 1861–65; AI:22, 1866–70; AI:23, 1871–75; AI:24, 1876–80; AI:25, 1881–85; AI:27, 1886–90; Moving Book, B:2, 1876–92; Baptisms, C:5, 1829–61; C:8, 1872–82; First Communions, DI:2; Marriage, E1:2. Also in Frösthult, the Husförhörsboken in AI:9, 1851–60; AI:12, 1866–70; AI:13, 1871–75; AI:14, 1876–80; AI:15, 1881–85; AI:16, 1886–90; AI:17, 1891–95; Marriages, E:I, 1862–94; Baptisms, C:3, 1768–1862.

Other primary documents are in manuscript family histories in my possession, including transcribed interviews with Mathilda Petersson Harline and her children, plus some letters.

Secondary sources: The Swedish-Mormon immigrant experience is treated thoroughly in W. Mulder, *Homeward to Zion: The Mormon Migration from Scandinavia* (Minneapolis, 1957), while S. Easton Black, S. Anderson, R. Maness, eds., *Legacy of Sacrifice: Missionaries to Scandinavia, 1872–1894* (Provo, Utah, 2007), treats Mormon missionaries in Sweden; for general Swedish immigration, see H. Runblom, H. Norman, eds., *From Sweden to America: A History of the Migration* (Minneapolis, 1976), B. L. Lowell, *Scandinavian Exodus: Demography and Social Development of 19th-Century Rural Communities* (Boulder, 1987), and H. A. Barton, *Homeland Swedes and Swedish Americans, 1840–1940* (Carbondale, 1994).

# Acknowledgments

Thanks first of all to the various archives that cared for the Rolandus documents and whose staffs offered such willing assistance, including, in the Netherlands, the Algemene Rijksarchief in The Hague, the Rijksarchief Den Bosch, the Gemeente Archief Amsterdam, and the Stadsarchief Boxtel; in Belgium, the Algemene Rijksarchief in Brussels, and the Rijksarchief Antwerp; and in Rome the Jesuit Archive. The staffs of the libraries of the Katholieke Universiteit Leuven, the Ruusbroecgenootschap (in Antwerp, especially Erna Van Looveren), and Brigham Young University all provided wonderful service and expertise in locating and making accessible published books and articles.

In Belgium a number of other individuals and institutions also lent support and intelligence, including Guido Marnef of the Universiteit Antwerpen, who helped arrange a research fellowship with the affiliated University Centre Saint Ignatius, as well as ideal working conditions at the Ruusbroecgenootschap next door. My thanks to Thom Martens and Theo Clemens of the Ruusbroec for their hospitality and their generosity with working space, ideas, and materials. Thanks as well at the University of Antwerp to Luc Duerloo, Henk de Smalle, and other members of the History Department who helped me feel welcome during my months there. At the Katholieke Universiteit Leuven,

I am indebted as ever to Jan Roegiers, who helped organize a research fellowship there, not to mention assorted dinners and social occasions with the other residents of the Quint, who showed more warmth and hospitality to a foreigner than any foreigner usually expects. Other current and emeritus faculty at Leuven who have done the same include Herman and Monique Van der Wee, through so many memorable walks and conversations and meals; Michel Cloet, through years of support and kindness; Eddy Put, through his usual pointed and wise advice on the manuscript as well as help with this piece of information or that; and Johan Verberckmoes, through being so welcoming and pointing out sources of information about Jacob Rolandus that I didn't know. Thanks as well to Wilfried Decoo and Carine Decoo-Vanwelkenhuysen in Antwerp for their helpful reading of the manuscript.

Others who read the manuscript and offered encouragement and suggestions were Kendall Brown, Karen Carter, Randy Christiansen, Karen Cope, Carlos Eire, Rachael Givens, Linda Gibbs, McKay Harline, Chris Hodson, Kevin Kenner, Bill Larson, Diarmaid MacCulloch, Louis Perraud, Janette Plunkett, Kathryn Richey, Henk van Nierop, and Timothy Wright. My thanks to them all. Special thanks to John Demos and Aaron Sachs, editors of the Narrative History series, who offered unusually detailed suggestions. All of them helped to make the book better than it would have been without their help.

Jeff Hardy and Bekki Richards were excellent research assistants. Ben Kaplan kindly shared material from his own research on religious tolerance. Christine Kooi, John O'Malley, Brad Gregory, Erika Rummel, Tom Brady, Geoffrey Parker, and Ed Muir supported the project as well, through their examples of scholarship and imagination and their willingness to engage in the thankless task of writing letters of support for research grants.

A most grateful thanks to the institutions who provided those grants and made the research possible, including a fellowship from the American Council of Learned Societies, a Franklin Research Grant from the American Philosophical Society, and grants from the Kennedy Center, and College of Family, Home, and Social Sciences at Brigham Young University. Thanks as well at BYU to office support from Julie

Radle, Sara Moore, Dan Kirkpatrick, Michelle Flammer, and Brett Myers, and various other staff members through the years that this book was being written.

In Sweden thanks to my new friends Annika Hedermo and Bengt Svensson, Staffan Larson and Ibba Andersson, and my newly discovered family Annica and Göran Dahlgren and Inga and Calle Ekblom, among a vast array of cousins, all of whom have helped make my stays in Sweden unforgettable. I thank as well the staffs of the local library in Enköping, and the State Archive in Uppsala.

At Yale University Press I thank Chris Rogers, Laura Davulis, Phillip King, and Christina Tucker for their enthusiasm, helpfulness, and willingness to listen to what I am sure were sometimes silly ideas. Thanks to Bill Nelson for his patience and skill in making the map. And thanks to my agent, John Ware, for his usual good advice, hard work, and know-how.

At home I thank my wife Paula for not only reading the manuscript and offering ideas and encouragement but for putting up with the years of inconvenience occasioned by historical research; I hope that some of the advantages help to compensate. Thanks as well to our children, Andrew, Jonathan, and Kate, who have endured inconveniences as well, including my sometimes severely flawed parenting, and from whom I've learned more than they might imagine. Thanks as well to my own parents, Lloyd and Kay, for their long support, encouragement, and example of hospitality toward others.

CPSIA information can be obtained
at www.ICGtesting.com
Printed in the USA
JSHW040438260822
29687JS00002B/161